MYTHS AND TEXTS

JOHN B. VICKERY

❧ MYTHS AND TEXTS

Strategies of Incorporation and Displacement

Louisiana State University Press

Baton Rouge and London

Copyright © 1983 by Louisiana State University Press
ALL RIGHTS RESERVED
Manufactured in the United States of America
Designer: Barbara Werden
Typeface: Linotron Sabon
Typesetter: G&S Typesetters, Inc.
Printer: Thomson-Shore, Inc.
Binder: John H. Dekker & Sons

LIBRARY OF CONGRESS CATALOGING IN PUBLICATION DATA

Vickery, John B.
    Myths and texts.

    Bibliography: p.
    Includes index.
    1. Mythology in literature.   I. Title.
PN56.M95V5   1983   809'.9337   83-9337
ISBN 0-8071-1123-6

FOR JOY

'Ωκεῖαι χάριτες γλυκερώτεραι· ἢν δὲ βραδύνῃ,
πᾶσα χάρις κενεή, μηδὲ λέγοιτο χάρις.

ANONYMOUS, *Anthologia Graeca*, X, 30

CONTENTS

ACKNOWLEDGMENTS

For assistance of various sorts, I am grateful to several sources. First, I have benefitted from a fellowship awarded by the John Simon Guggenheim Memorial Foundation which generously permitted me to work simultaneously on this and another project during the tenure of its award. Second, I am indebted to the Committee on Research of the Academic Senate of the University of California, Riverside, which over the years has consistently provided timely support. One of my research assistants, Patrick Whiteley, has been as scrupulous as he has prompt in checking my sources, proofreading the manuscript, and alerting me to the more manifest absurdities of its content even when it entailed interruptions of his own writing. Audiences as near as California and as distant as Hungary have afforded interest and assistance of a different but no less important sort. Still closer to home is she of the dedication whose wry disclaimer that but for her my readers would have had to face much more of this stuff should be applauded for its wit though not for its veracity.

For permission to incorporate materials from periodical and other publications, I am indebted to the following: in Chapter I to a revised version of "D. H. Lawrence's Poetry: Myth and Matter," *D. H. Lawrence Review*, VII (1974); in Chapter II to "Three Modes and a Myth," *Western Humanities Review*, XII (1958) and part of "Myth and Ritual in the Shorter Fiction of D. H. Lawrence," *Modern Fiction Studies*, V (1959); in Chapter III to revised versions of "*The Plumed Serpent* and the Eternal Paradox," *Criticism*, V (1963) and "*Finnegans Wake* and Sexual Metamorphosis," *Contemporary Literature*, XII (1972); in Chapter IV to revised versions of "*The Plumed Serpent* and the Reviving God," *Journal of Modern Literature*, II (1972) and "The Scapegoat in Literature," T. Orbison *et al.* (eds.), *The Binding of Proteus* (Bucknell University Press, 1980); in Chapter V to revised versions of "*The Centaur*: Myth, History, and Narrative," *Modern Fiction Studies*, XX (1974) and "Myths and Fictions in the Contemporary American Novel:

The Case of John Barth," *Hungarian Studies in English*, XII (1979); in Chapter VI to a revised version of "Orpheus and Persephone: Uses and Meanings," *Classical Mythology in 20th Century Thought and Literature*, Proceedings of the Comparative Literature Symposium, XI (Texas Tech University Press, 1980).

For permission to quote material held in copyright, I am indebted to the following:

Excerpts from *The Sense of an Ending* by Frank Kermode. (Copyright © 1966, 1967 by Oxford University Press.) Reprinted by permission of Oxford University Press.

Excerpts from *The Variorum Edition of the Poems of William Butler Yeats*, eds. Peter Allt and Russell K. Alspach. (Copyright © 1940 by Georgie Yeats and 1957 by Macmillan Company.) Reprinted by permission of Macmillan Company and A. P. Watt Ltd.

Excerpts from *The Collected Poetry of Aldous Huxley*, ed. Donald Watt. (Copyright © 1971 by Laura Huxley.) Reprinted by permission of Harper & Row, Publishers, Inc., Chatto & Windus Ltd., and Mrs. Laura Huxley.

Excerpts from *The Collected Poetry 1959* by Robert Graves. (Copyright © 1958 by Robert Graves.) Reprinted by permission of Robert Graves and Cassell and Co., and A. P. Watt Ltd.

Excerpts from *The Rites of Passage* by Arnold Van Gennep, trans. by Monika B. Vizedom and Gabrielle L. Caffee. (Copyright © 1960 by Monika B. Vizedom and Gabrielle L. Caffee.) Reprinted by permission of Routledge & Kegan Paul Ltd. and Humanities Press, Inc.

Excerpts from *The Complete Poems of D. H. Lawrence*, ed. Vivian de Sola Pinto and F. Warren Roberts. (Copyright © 1964, 1971 by Angelo Ravagli and C. M. Weekley, Executors of the Estate of Frieda Lawrence Ravagli.) Reprinted by permission of Viking-Penguin, Inc., Laurence Pollinger Ltd., and the estate of Frieda Lawrence Ravagli.

Excerpts from *The Letters of D. H. Lawrence*, ed. Aldous Huxley. (Copyright © 1932 by the Estate of D. H. Lawrence; renewed by Angelo Ravagli and C. M. Weekley, Executors of the Estate of Frieda Lawrence Ravagli.) Reprinted by permission of Viking-Penguin, Inc., Laurence Pollinger Ltd., and the estate of Frieda Lawrence Ravagli.

Excerpts from *Collected Poems* by David Gascoyne. (Copyright © 1965 by Oxford University Press.) Reprinted by permission of Oxford University Press.

Excerpts from *Collected Poems*, 2nd ed., by Edwin Muir. (Copyright © 1960 by Willa Muir.) Reprinted by permission of Oxford University Press.

Excerpts from *The Collected Works of Paul Valéry*, ed. Jackson Matthews, Bollingen Series XLV, Vol. 1: *Poems*, trans. David Paul; *On Poets and Poetry*, selected and trans. James R. Lawler. (Copyright © 1971 by Princeton University Press.) Reprinted by permission of Princeton University Press.

Excerpts from *Going to Meet the Man* by James Baldwin. (Copyright © 1948, 1951, 1957, 1958, 1960, 1965 by James Baldwin.) Reprinted by permission of Dial Press.

Excerpts from *Selected Works*, Vol. II, by Rainer Maria Rilke, trans. J. B. Leishman. (Copyright © 1960 by the Hogarth Press Ltd.) Reprinted by permission of the author's literary estate, the translator, and the Hogarth Press Ltd.

MYTHS AND TEXTS

INTRODUCTION

MYTHS, fictions, structures, even literature and writing itself are concepts presently at the heart of numerous controversies. To engage them as part of linguistic, philosophic, and cultural explorations devoted variously to construction, deconstruction, or reconstruction is doubtless instructive and, in some instances, even valuable. And if some master builder could but develop a superbonding agent applicable to all materials, no matter how diverse, the welter of competing and contradictory theories of contemporary criticism might conceivably, just conceivably, come to cohere into an actual vantage point, a real ivory tower rather than one of Babel set in ambergris. In the meantime, there are ample opportunities for humbler craftsmen to clear the ground, set the shorings, and even to essay a pouring of the lesser foundations for some of the outbuildings. Amid the heady speculations of the innumerable town mice drafting cosmic urban renewal projects of critical theory, there is still, though just barely, room for a country mouse to hoard a few nuts of an immediately practical order against the long winter when survival depends more on sound nutrition and a natural protective coat and less on wind, however Aeolian, agitating motley woven of fustian.

In what follows, therefore, no attempt will be made to offer an inclusive definition of myth, a detailed description or analysis of the human imagination, much less of the relations obtaining between them and literature itself. This emphatically does not mean that such efforts would necessarily be fruitless, only that they demand a different focus from the one at hand. The present concern centers on a series of modern literary texts possessing mainly classical and classically related mythic and ritualistic patterns. The chief interest, however, is not in identifying the presence of specific patterns but in exploring the uses to which they are put by the individual authors. At the same time, in a world of reader response and the postautonomy of the text, even the country mouse knows that such uses are also, perhaps preeminently, a function of the critical activity, of consciousness as constitutive, of the reader as "formularizing" agent. Hence the subtitle of the study. But true to his cautious, conserving instincts, the country mouse also recalls the long history of writers generating, and readers responding to, texts in relation to key concepts—structure, theme, character, narrative, and point of view—which predicate a range of functions and elements. The time for their dismantling or radical transformation may indeed be imminent, but premature jettisoning in wholesale fashion seems ill advised. More to the point is a careful exploration of such concepts as they operate in actual textual instances. To bring them into collocation with the concept of myth tests their powers of accommodation and continuing viability. It also suggests ramifications in the forms and functions of literature perhaps scarcely entertained hitherto. Myth has been seen by some as a substance, an identity, a model or paradigm; to others it is more a matter of mystery, protean process, incalculability, even absence. In many ways, it is a locus or matrix for the rival claims of determinacy and indeterminacy. As such, it may serve to exert a median pressure both on them and the critic struggling with them. How, then, mythic patterns, figures, actions, and images specifically inform and condition actual critical statements about such features of particular texts is a dominant concern of the present study.

The rationale for such an approach is partly empirical and partly pragmatic. It starts if not from "givens" then at least from things conventionally acceptable, on which ready agreement is possible, no matter how provisionally, and involving a minimum of special pleading. Thus, whatever the ultimate definition of myth in general may be, it would be a curious one indeed that could not or would not include classical myths such as those of Andromeda, Leda, Orpheus, Persephone, and the like. Limiting our attention to such myths may be defended by analogy with the commonsense philosophy of G. E. Moore. Holding up his hand before him and his audience was, for Moore, indubitable proof of the existence of a material object. Pointing to the story of Orpheus is similarly indubitable as to what one means by a myth. Nor is this simplistic reductionism. Just as all material objects are not of the same order or kind as human hands, so all myths need not be, for all one knows, of the same kind or order as the Orpheus tale. Even those of us with only elementary logic and class theory can perceive that much. What some may see as the inhibiting limitations of such an allusionist approach may afford others the opportunity for controlled investigations of a restricted order. The conscious limiting of a subject, as the history of thought since at least Aristotle's time indicates, is the means of clarification and knowledge. Our perpetual fond longing for an increase in critical significance might well become an achieved reality were we to increase our piecemeal critical engineering (to adapt Karl Popper's famous phrase) and decrease, if not suspend, random and reckless rocket trips to some hermeneutic moon. The former will not soon attain the ultimate goal, admittedly, but neither are they as prone to abort.

Something of the same attitude underlies the concept of the imagination, which seems to have at least a formal or conventionalist relation to both myth and literature. One could find ample evidence and illustrations in literature as well as myth on which to frame not only a theory but a phenomenology of imagination. The central focus here, however, is precisely the uses of mythic elements in specific works of literature. It is in and through this relationship, complex and varied as it is, that the workings of the imagination are exhibited. But what actually is revealed are all the authorial strategies of form, point of view, and verbal figures employed in rendering the mythic elements, which in turn reveal a historically and logically prior sequence of imaginings. Psychology and epistemology view one another warily across a gulf whose historical dimension renders phenomenology moot as arbiter. It may be that the faintly Kantian notion of the imagination as something apprehended through perceivable differences in language may have to suffer the same fate Gilbert Ryle meted out to the concept of mind. Prejudgment of that issue aside, it seems wiser, more commonsensical if you will, to treat the imagination as all those strategies and figures alluded to earlier together with the protean, variable, and metamorphic relations obtaining between them. In short, by talking about identifiable techniques and strategies, about perceptibly differing uses or forms of language, person, scene, and object, one is at the very least talking about operational or instrumental evidence of the imagination. Moreover, one may be talking about the imagination itself in the only fashion in which it is meaningful to do so, that is, in the way which avoids committing a category mistake.

A similar caution is exercised on the complex and problematic question of the relation between myth and literature. Ideally, this calls for a working out of the nature and kinds of relationship obtaining between the class or classes of specific myths, the concept of myth as a structural principle, literature as a class of verbal constructs, and specific literary works. The magnitude of this task is apparent from the fact that no one has done it, though there are enough scattered generalizations rattling around to sink the proverbial battleship. And indeed, not too long ago, G. S. Kirk suggested that a unitary theory of myth, much less of myth and literature, may not be viable, given the diversity of materials, contexts, and cultures. What can be probed more readily are the relationships between particular myths and specific literary texts. Beyond this, one can also explore how metamythical concepts such as that of the dying and reviving god or the scapegoat are incorporated in particular works and how such concepts are displaced in response to the formal and cultural demands of the work in its process of formation. And finally, it is possible to attend to the creative artist's own ideas about the nature and function of myth and how these condition his work. What inflections certain poets place on a mythic narrative like the Leda or Orpheus story, how novelists like D. H. Lawrence or James Joyce adapt a critical or scholarly construct such as that of the dying god, and how a writer is drawn to mythic materials and perspectives not simply by his inclination to esotericism but by his intense awareness of the sensory and physical qualia of his environment, all these are directly accessible to the critic even though not all of the above conceptual relationships between myth and literature may have been worked out. Indeed, such a critical venture as the present one contributes directly to a preliminary charting of the relationships between specific myths as narrative units and equally specific literary works.

From this, it is clear that the major concentration in what follows is on literature rather than anthropology, psychology, philosophy, or any of the current way stations and halfway houses appearing in the intellectual Yellow Pages under the headings of hermeneutics, semiotics, narratology, and the like. This, however, means no more than that a language choice has been exercised; the election of certain acts of semantic and syntactic exclusion in no way should be, or can be logically, construed as ontological or epistemological denial. All too often it is assumed that one's making a certain set of statements entails a denial of the value or ontological significance of other conceivable but unuttered statements. Such an assumption occurs with a mindless regularity conducive to despair. In other words, to use a particular critical language is not to deny the possibility of using some other language. For one to speak English does not mean the impossibility of one's speaking French, a fact doubtless of great solace to many groups, particularly bilingual education programs and comparative literature departments. Since such critical languages are generally subject to the same laws of linguistics and logic, it is also perfectly possible for one to hook up with another as part of a single intellectual articulation. Thus, it is hoped, what is said here has some linkage, if only implicitly, with other disciplines and interdisciplines such as those mentioned above.

At the same time, we should bear in mind that the actualities of language use are not so simple as R. S. Crane seemed to imply some years ago. He was at pains to demonstrate that criticism possessed a variety of languages in which to couch its perceptions. As a result, he urged that as critics we be aware of which language it is that we are electing and of the implications of that choice. However salutary the observation and recommendation, an equally undeniable fact is ignored. Critics, like other human beings, speak out of passions and perceptions and attitudes rather than out of a rigorous concern for the demands of a theory and the sorts of statements logically possible in the chosen kind of discourse. As a consequence, their—our—utterances most nearly resemble a composite of several languages, a kind of conceptual cross between pidgin English and the verbal resources of *Finnegans Wake*. Pursued sedulously, even deliberately, they become a critical speaking in tongues as it were. Thus, to suggest that the controlling assumptions and method in the following essays are structural and even, dare one say it, formal does not mean that the actual language employed will always be wholly congruent with the method those terms imply.

In places, the issue of myth almost totally submerges in the texts under consideration and the focus becomes preeminently matters of thematics, narrative, or point of view. This is intuitively deliberate, for one of the underlying convictions of this study is that the examination of the role of mythic materials in literature does not involve a distinctive or unique method. Even less does it demand an indifference to traditional matters of form, structure, and theme. Precisely how such matters utilize while at the same time shaping mythic materials as discernible elements in literary expression is, as we have said, the underlying concern of this study. To that end, the essays are organized around the aforementioned critical categories. They proceed from the logic of the creative process to works instancing the interplay of mythic elements with structure, theme, and character, and finally to the emergence of questions of narrative, author, and point of view. These, in turn, reach out beyond the linguistic and artifactual bounds of the text to engage issues of voice and self that implicitly raise in passing the time-honored and currently debated question of the nature of literature as well as the reality of the personal self and the function of human speech.

This study begins its exploration of the interpenetration of myth and literature by considering the poetry of D. H. Lawrence from a special, perhaps even limited, perspective. It is at pains to show how Lawrence carves out for himself a poetic and a poetry grounded in both myth and matter, in the archetypal as well as in the immediate reality of the experientially given. The one grows out of at the same time as it animates the other. It is in the achieved balance between the two that his work—and much of modern literature deploying myth—attains its peculiar and distinctive power. Because his texts afford such fertile opportunities for critical exploration of this general subject, they command what to some may seem a disproportionate measure of attention in several other places as well.

The next three essays address themselves—with a variety of illustrations as well as differing techniques or emphases—to some of the major strategies for involving mythic images, figures, and narratives in the structures, themes, and characters of modern literary works. Authors range from early moderns such as Henrik Ibsen, Fyodor Dostoyevsky, and August Strindberg to contemporaries such as James Baldwin, Jean Genet, and Bernard Malamud. The last two essays balance the emphasis on what might be thought of as the largely internal aspects of works. They do so by considering those issues of narrative and point of view whose nature becomes problematic and whose implications reach beyond the work itself to involve problems of author, self, and voice and the identity of each. In doing so, they attend particularly to the ways in which myth's anonymity, fictionality, and story nature impinge on these problems as revealed both in the novel and in poetry. Particular questions and solutions or responses are examined with reference to authors as heterogeneous in type and time as Rainer Maria Rilke, Hart Crane, Robert Lowell, John Updike, and John Barth.

In the course of this study, some authors—notably Lawrence and Joyce—are examined in greater detail than others. Nevertheless, all are seen, and shown, to be striking and illuminating instances of literature's resourcefulness in incorporating mythic elements into the individual imaginative vision. To underscore this limitless adaptability, the critical emphasis modulates between close scrutiny of individual texts and more general explorations of typological and functional structures and motifs. Throughout, however, the main effort has been to delineate the diversity of responses and to register at least some provisional general classifications. It is hoped that these may contribute to the formulation of a poetic capable of more fully assessing not only the linguistic but the psychological range of literature's possibilities.

There was a myth before the myth began,
Venerable and articulate and complete.

From this the poem springs: that we live in a place
That is not our own and, much more, not ourselves.

WALLACE STEVENS

ONE · Myth and Poetics: The Creation of a Cosmos

SOMETIME around the late 1940s and 1950s the centrality of myth to literature burgeoned as a modern critical notion. As a result, many bathed in burning fountains while pursuing the quest for myth wherein they might find themselves with an older, more unified, mythic consciousness. Heroes bore a thousand faces while gods peered from behind myriad masks, and both were found to populate more literary works and more unexpected ones than had hitherto been dreamt of. Now, however, criticism, chastened by its earlier Little Jack Horner performances, pursues avenues at once more theoretical and more functional. Whatever the ultimate role of the former for the reading and interpretation of literature, it clearly cannot help but deal with the latter. The roles and uses of myth in particular genres and literary periods form the inescapable ground and basis for any informed theory concerning the nature and relationship of myth and literature. Such a concern with functions implicitly discloses possibilities unrealized as well as realized and in so doing opens up a recognition that for literature myth's roots are in the experiential fully as much as in the archetypal. The artist's actual creative practice is notoriously pragmatic in its method and empirically minded about its materials. Immediate experiential realities and perceptions as much as overarching visions dictate the form of a work of art. Garlic as well as sapphires clot the bedded axletree and indeed commingle so finely that one merges with and into the other. So it is, in at least a significant number of instances, with myth's presence in literature. It grows out of the artist's sensitivity to and reaction concerning the world that is ground, container, and other for the self which in apprehending the metonymic character of experience responds by articulating its metaphoric role, which results in myth.

How myth not only informs but gestates and comes into being for a body of creative work can best be traced in the poetry of D. H. Lawrence, which reflects his own conviction of the continuously emergent self and its organic rhythms of systole and diastole. Glancing backward from what we can egotistically and ironically call our vantage point in the last quarter of the twentieth century, we can readily see that modern poetry, like many other manifestations of the contemporary scene, has long oscillated in a dialectic of truly Hegelian magnitude and finality. In the now distant days of the century's beginning Georgian pastoralism and softness were countered by T. S. Eliot's cunningly adapted (and adopted) Unreal City and Ezra Pound's verbal calisthenics designed to firm up the image of the Muse. And when William Butler Yeats, Eliot, and Pound seemed to threaten a poetic *putsch* compounded of esoteric mythologies, arcane lore, and symbolistic hierophantics, they in turn were polarized by the phenomenological concreteness, astringent directness, and functionalism of William Carlos Williams, the Black Mountain school, and concretists like Eugen Gomringer. Yet through all this, both the reading public and the various poetic factions have sustained a certain puzzled admiration and respect for Lawrence's poetry. Obviously his poetry was flawed and not all of a piece. Some of it seemed hopelessly mired in outmoded manners and language, while other portions appeared to have leapt in a single bound beyond current or past notions of form. But the best, of which there is more than generally acknowledged, was of a high and virtually unique order. And it was this uniqueness which resulted in Lawrence's mediating happily between, say, the mythopoesis of *The Waste Land* and the physicalist givens of *Paterson*. For what motivated his best poetry, and indeed his whole imaginative vision, was a delicately balanced sense of the realities of matter and the potentialities of myth.

Obviously one cannot expect to explore this subject definitively here. Consequently, what follows is more in the nature of a sketch of the chief structures of matter and myth in the Lawrentian cosmos. From them, we will acquire an enlarged sense of the genesis of myth in literature, of how that genesis is compounded of the poet's immediate perceptions of the external world, of his reading and its accompanying memories faulty as well as precise, and of his creative, imaginative, and linguistic freedom which enables him to generate new inflections and variants of the mythic structure informing his work. The genesis of this world lies in the fact that Lawrence's basic human responses consist of a reverence for life (though not always of people) and a desire to reveal its true nature. Given these impulses, he was bound, on looking around the society available to him, to be struck by the extent to which it appeared a demoniac parody of civilization and man's imaginative and mythopoeic capacities. Though not so sustained as, say, Charles Baudelaire or Eliot in his poetic evocations of metropolitan horror, he is, nevertheless, powerful and direct. In "City Life," for instance, he sees the residents with iron hooks embedded in their faces drawn back and forth to work by invisible wires of steel "like fearful and corpse-like fishes."[1] This damnation of the city, however, entails much more than simply economic exploitation. It also is allied with a hideous kind of ethnocentricity scathingly caught in "The English Are So Nice." There the reiterated use of *nice* pounds relentlessly on the brain until the full remorseless weight of cultural snobbery is felt as something almost tangible and certainly omnipresent.

When this ethnocentric impulse is turned inward, it becomes class and moral corruption compounded of two aspects. One is the unconscious estheticizing of art and the resultant inability to correlate tragedy and existence. In "After the Opera" the speaker sees the theater audience's "looks of shocked and momentous emotion" and feels pleasure that "they take tragedy so becomingly" until the scene is juxtaposed against another which reveals genuine suffering:

> But when I meet the weary eyes
> The reddened, aching eyes of the bar-man with thin arms,
> I am glad to go back where I came from.

The other aspect of corruption is the smug cultivation of the *frisson* as the mark of ultimate sophistication but with no sense of existence's real capacities for terror. Purveyors of this attitude are ironically

1. *The Complete Poems of D. H. Lawrence*, ed. Vivian de Sola Pinto and Warren Roberts (New York, 1971). Subsequent quotations are identified in the text by the appropriate poem title and are all from this edition.

dubbed and drubbed as latter-day sinners in the poem having this phrase for a title:

> they calmly assert: We only thrill to perversity, murder,
>   suicide, rape—
> bragging a little, really,
> and at the same time expect to go on calmly eating good
>   dinners for the next fifty years.

For Lawrence, this corruption centers in the bourgeois whom he rightly sees as the defining class of the culture. Contemplating its members impels him to the jeremiad, whose generic traits he was to utilize resourcefully over the years. This and a just combination of abstract and concrete epithets make up "How Beastly the Bourgeois Is." The burden of his loathing stems from the disparity between the social appearance and the moral, human reality. On the surface the bourgeois male is "eminently presentable" and "god's own image," but beneath it he is no more than a hollow, parasitic fungus:

> Touch him, and you'll find he's all gone inside
> just like an old mushroom, all wormy inside, and hollow
> under a smooth skin and an upright appearance.
>
> Full of seething, wormy hollow feelings
> rather nasty.

The revelation of the disparity occurs when his sensibility faces any demands he is not prepared for or accustomed to. Any "new life-demand" on his emotions, understanding, or intelligence decomposes him, turning him into "a mess, either a fool or a bully."

Endemic to such people and to the culture as a whole is a covert but relentless concentration on emasculation and erotic perversion. This point Lawrence makes sharply in poems like "Thomas Earp," "Puss-Puss," and "London Mercury." Taken together, they form a kind of encapsulated animal fable to be set against the bestiary properties of *Birds, Beasts and Flowers*. Ultimately, however, what is most stultifying, because apparently inescapable, within the confines of the civilization and its perspective is the sense of ego omnipresence, a theme that Lawrence returns to time and again in his letters as well as his novels. In the poetry it is graphically rendered in "Death Is Not Evil, Evil Is Mechanical," where man is confined to a Dantesque inferno by the inescapable "I," "the obscene ego" that controls his emotions:

> a grey void thing that goes without wandering
> a machine that in itself is nothing
> a centre of the evil world-soul.

Ultimately the individual is overcome by this parody of human existence and becomes a function of solipsistic egotism rather than of unmediated experiential totality. At this point he is ready for another world and so can—if he is fortunate—renounce the old, as Lawrence himself did in "New Heaven and Earth" when he declared:

> I was so weary of the world,
> I was so sick of it,
> everything was tainted with myself,
> skies, trees, flowers, birds, water.

Such, in sum, is the world of his own time and place that Lawrence found threatening himself and man in general with inanition and atrophy. Yet even in his rendering of it, we are struck by the vividness of his perceptions which capture unerringly the delusory reality of the scene. These provide him both the impetus to "cross into another world," "a new world," and the essential elements with which to constitute and populate that universe. On a personal level, this transition is rendered in *Look! We Have Come Through!* as a psychological achievement in terms of interpersonal relations. But it is also a preludium to poetry's version of the onset of myth creation as is signaled by its being immediately preceded by a functioning ritual of passage. His disengagement from the old and transition to the new self-creation accords precisely with Arnold van Gennep's classic account of such rituals' structure. Basically, what Lawrence renders, apart from the shriveling life of parody, is an almost neurasthenically keen awareness of bodies in motion. Consequently, it is scarcely too much to say that his "new world" was really grounded in an epistemological physics, a knowing, felt group of boundaries or circumferences defining the dimensional entities among whom man moves and has his being. Thinking of this "new world" of Lawrence's as a form of physics helps both to organize its rich diversity and also to comprehend the interaction of its elements. The controlling concepts of mass, motion, and energy adapt themselves effortlessly to Lawrence's universe. In the process, they reveal the pattern of his mind which could meld the physical, the emotional, and the imaginative into a seamless perceptual unity and their expression into ontological metaphors of myth.

The poet's precision in delineating the structures of the given and their relationships as functions of the perceiving subject do suggest the epistemologist's and the physicist's reality. Yet since these concepts and relations are implicit and mediated by the self-reflexivity of his language, they become, too, mythic signs encoding metaphors for rather than discursive statements about existence. In short, the poet's imagination functions as did that of the early Greeks, who so fascinated him, when they enunciated a descriptively dynamic account of the basic nature of the world in terms of generally received notions such as *physis*. In terms of accuracy of measurement, predictive power, and the rest, we now know they were really producing not so much a science as a conceptual myth, or fiction if you will. Though Lawrence's terms are contemporary, his process similarly issues in a myth though one grounded in physics rather than religion. It was not for nothing that he read F. M. Cornford with care.

At virtually every stage of his career Lawrence was profoundly responsive to the myriad forms of physical mass in the universe. For him, unlike physicists generally, mass in its ultimate reality was construed as the entity's or phenomenon's *living* substance. To this he always reacted with the keenest pleasure, which in the poetry translated itself into knowledge as momentous as that of Einsteinian physics. This quality is clear in the opening of "The Wild Common," which is alive with movement, color, and shape:

> The quick sparks on the gorse-bushes are leaping
> Little jets of sunlight texture imitating flame;
> Above them, exultant, the peewits are sweeping:
> They have triumphed again o'er the ages, their
> screamings proclaim.
>
> Rabbits, handfuls of brown earth, lie
> Low-rounded on the mournful turf they have bitten
> down to the quick.

The awareness of all these bodies engaged in their characteristic motions prompts Lawrence to exclaim "how splendid it is to be substance, here." He then exalts the awareness of his own consubstantiality with the physical world until in the end he declares "all that is God takes substance." With this final assertion there is a significant indication that Lawrence's physics is not of the nineteenth-century materialistic variety, though admittedly it has some surface flavor of a Spinozistic metaphysic. Instead it attends, like that of Einstein, to the role of the observer and, moreover, to his phenomenological character as an imaginative being. This attitude is emphatically rendered in "Demiurge," where Lawrence also disclaims a purely spiritual reality:

> Even the mind of God can only imagine
> those things that have become themselves:
> bodies and presences, here and now, creatures with a
>   foothold in creation
> even if it is only a lobster on tip-toe.

The central and perhaps most striking thing about Lawrence's concern with physical mass is this desire and verbal capacity to render the reality in felt, receptive terms. Thus, the essential nature both of the creatures in "Little Fish" and of the observer-poet's response to them is caught in lines as precise as an equation:

> Quick little splinters of life,
> their little lives are fun to them
> in the sea.

Such studies are not, moreover, confined to mass in motion but are directed to the nature of the bodies in relation to context. For instance, "Trees in the Garden" precisely differentiates by a process which might be described as a kind of contextual magnification. In its way it is one of Lawrence's most brilliantly sustained contributions to what his onetime friend Bertrand Russell called our knowledge of the external world. As such, it is its own best commentary:

> Ah in the thunder air
> how still the trees are!
>
> And the lime-tree, lovely and tall, every leaf silent
> hardly looses even a last breath of perfume.

And the ghostly, creamy coloured little trees of leaves
white, ivory white among the rambling greens
how evanescent, variegated elder, she hesitates on the green
    grass
as if, in another moment, she would disappear
with all her grace of foam!

And the larch that is only a column, it goes up too tall to
    see:
and the balsam-pines that are blue with the grey-blue
    blueness of things from the sea
and the young copper beech, its leaves red-rosy at the ends
how still they are together, they stand so still
in the thunder air, all strangers to one another
as the green grass glows upwards, strangers in the silent
    garden.

Here the whole weight of the poem and the trees is directed exactly to the latter's absence of motion. As a result they have to be defined or recorded relationally rather than in terms of their characteristic motions as occurred in "The Wild Common." Differences of height, color, and conformation are precisely rendered yet structured in a comparative perspective that enhances while respecting the reality of each object. Description, diction, alliteration, and sound recurrence, syntax balanced between the exclamatory and declarative, and rhythm, all work toward a common goal. The ultimate epistemological recognition of the physical reality is achieved in the final phrase "strangers in the silent garden." What "garden" contextually relates, "strangers" alienates into epistemological isolation and self-identity. Between them they provide the terms that encompass the reality of the trees conceived of not as objective but as intersubjective because contingent upon the observer and his relative point of view.

The poems discussed above in connection with Lawrence's interest in bodies and physical mass are striking but representative only. Scarcely a poem of his does not in some casual or fleeting image seize the palpable world with a kind of clairvoyant joy. Poems like "Baby Running Barefoot," "A White Blossom," "Green," and "Andraitx-Pomegranate Flowers" are vibrant with their felt knowledge of human and vegetable bodies and their several motions. Yet in this "new world" Lawrence is concerned with the nature of motion and of mass. It does not consist simply of a quality or attribute inhering in animate or inanimate objects. Essentially, for Lawrence, motion as a fundamental concept in our knowledge of physical bodies is a function of attraction or repulsion. Causality, as a result, is less a mechanistic than a teleological principle and nowhere does this reveal itself more clearly than in human relationships and the interaction of individuals. In short, love is the knowing motion by which bodies converge or diverge so that to understand their nature and behavior involves studying the forms and principles of love. The logic of his own desire to understand and to communicate the intricate mysteries of moving bodies dictated that Lawrence return again and again—as he did in his novels, short stories, poems, and essays—to expressions and manifestations of love.

In the Lawrentian cosmos, mass in motion is personalized and individualized with the result that it appears as living substance actuated by love. But as any reader of Lawrence knows, love is not equatable with a motion of attraction solely. We have seen how he shows a keen sense of the minutiae of objects, which allows him to discriminate finely among their several natures. So also he notes, by both introspection and observation, the complex and oscillatory rhythms of advance and recoil that constitute love. One of Lawrence's best-known poems, "Love on the Farm," marvelously conveys the duality of direction in this quintessential human motion. The "golden light" that is the "heart's delight" of the woman is threatened by the "large, dark hands" of the leaves at the window, thereby at the outset presaging the recoil from the husband's return. Subsequent stanzas develop this pattern of recoil, flight, and terror in the face of inexorable advance and deploy it through vegetative, bird, and animal images which naturally enough culminate in the human scene between husband and wife. At this juncture, however, Lawrence brilliantly reverses and balances the motion in such a way as to render the full complexity of love. The woman imaginatively identifies herself with the trapped rabbit and its terror before death, but the terror and resistance are dramatically transformed:

> his lips meet mine, and a flood
> Of sweet fire sweeps across me, so I drown
> Against him, die, and find death good.

Here there is no merging of advance and recoil, merely the joining of recoil with the stasis of submission. Yet it is sufficient to counter powerfully and economically the motif of sexual and emotional fear that dominates the bulk of the poem and that otherwise could be taken for the total absence of love. Instead it is Lawrence's final graph of the motion of love, which moves the mass of mankind in all the strange and unpredictable directions it takes.

The converse motion of that traced in "Love on the Farm" is rendered in the narrative parabola of "Lightning." There the man is conscious of the girl's love-motion toward him by "the lurch and halt of her heart," "her breath . . . warm against my neck," and "the sense of her clinging flesh." Hence he continues his own emotional and physical advance and seeks to "claim her utterly in a kiss." But here the finality and directional simplicity of "utterly"—already prefatorily suggested as doubtful by her heart's not only lurching but also halting—is devastatingly thwarted. The kiss, which was to seal the mutuality of the attraction, of the simultaneous forward movement of two human bodies, becomes the repudiation of that motion in favor of one that more accurately reflects the differences in the nature of the two bodies:

> the lightning flew across her face,
> And I saw her for the flaring space
> Of a second, afraid of the clips
> Of my arms, inert with dread, wilted in fear of my kiss.

Sexual apprehension and moral timidity are undoubtedly part of this reaction and occasion the same anger and disappointment as they do in *Sons and Lovers*. However, when Lawrence carries his studies in human movement further and to a deeper level, dialectic rather than acceleration appears as the fundamental principle operative in the motion of love. The advance and recoil, the convictions and their denial, of lovers in Lawrence are a familiar drama. Scarcely a novel is not replete with them, and much of *Look! We Have Come Through!* is given over to charting love's motion as one of struggle and violent oscillation. One of the most succinct yet inclusive renderings of this pattern occurs in the final stanza of "History." Its title indicates both the generic nature of the motion and also the connection between human records of the past and the epistemological physics of man's being. It is perhaps less accident than symptom that his one sustained discursive commentary on the subject should have been entitled *Movements in European History*. History, Lawrence suggests implicitly, is a function of human beings and their actions and these in turn are characterized by contrary motions of their emotional molecular structure. As a result, the poem renders the pattern of movement of two individuals while at the same time it reflects the emotional movement endemic to the species as a whole. Thus, in the course of the poem "miseries" and "scars" and "battle" are set over against ecstasy and beauty and serenity issuing in the final recognition:

> Your life, and mine, my love
> Passing on and on, the hate
> Fusing closer and closer with love
> Till at length they mate.

The merging of advance and recoil as the essential motion between interacting human bodies is realized as a paradox accepted, though barely, in "A Young Wife." This is announced in the opening and closing lines: "The pain of loving you / Is almost more than I can bear." Despite the tremulous uncertainty here, the wife goes on in the poem to define precisely and unequivocally the dialectical relation of love. She, in a sense, is a step beyond the mating of love and hate found in "History," at a point where the fusion has already occurred. Hence she describes the relation not in terms of motion but of light, not in terms of teleological advancement but of perceptual polarities inherent in the physical laws governing bodies. The impetus to recoil is still present, but now it is recognized as a concomitant of the different structure of the bodies and the relation in which they stand to one another:

> I walk in fear of you.
> The darkness starts up where
> You stand, and the night comes through
> Your eyes when you look at me.
>
> Ah never before did I see
> The shadows that live in the sun!
>
> Now every tall glad tree
> Turns round its back to the sun
> And looks down on the ground, to see
> The shadow it used to shun.

> At the foot of each glowing thing
> A night lies looking up.

Bodies which stand in proximity to one another create shadows, and when human bodies are drawn together, the shadows they cast are the impulse to recoil into separate identity and the comforting light of selfhood. But both shadows and bodies are part of the relation and cannot be defined or described without the other. And no more can love, the teleological motion of human bodies, be characterized save as a dialectic of attraction and recoil.

Thus far, our treatment has stressed matter rather more than myth in Lawrence's poetry. This is inevitable not only since it is man's world which gives rise to myth rather than the other way around but also since the surface of the verse in the main echoes this progression. The verse seizes on objects and their movements in the same manner as did the observant and passionate eye of the author in life. Yet Lawrence was no simple hedonistic materialist dedicated solely to imagistic capturings of the physical scene. His poetic physics has its animating force or impulse just as does the mathematical physics of Einstein, and in both cases it resides in the concept of energy. For Lawrence, it is precisely here that myth enters and assumes a crucial role in his poetic cosmology. Myth, man's original narrative pictographs of an ordered universe and the ways in which its order came about, is the energy force that impels human bodies to advance or retreat, accelerate or decelerate because ultimately it is the human imagination's direct action on itself. This daring conjunction of myth and atomic energy is clearly spelled out in "Swan," which opens:

> Far-off
> at the core of space
> at the quick
> of time
> beats
> and goes still
> the great swan upon the waters of all endings
> the swan within vast chaos, within the electron.

The bird brooding upon the watery chaos summons up ancient creation myths even as its presence in the electron confirms its role as the proton, the positive energy charge at the center which issues in the visible matter of physical bodies and their motions. This last is underscored in "When the Ripe Fruit Falls," where Lawrence declares "space is alive/ and it stirs like a swan." For Lawrence, then, at the heart of reality is something alive, active and utterly natural, from which creation issues.

"Swan," however, carries this implication a crucial step further. It is as if Lawrence sensed that the image of the "swan upon the waters" is too passive a figure, too easily allied to creation myths like the Greek and the Christian in which the act is an isolated achievement demanding no further participation on the part of the initiating forces. Consequently, after a section ruling out ordinary or natural actions for the swan—neither "happy energy" nor "passive upon the atoms"— Lawrence introduces his version of the Leda myth:

> But he stoops, now
> in the dark
> upon us;
> he is treading our women
> and we men are put out
> as the vast white bird
> furrows our featherless women
> with unknown shocks
> and stamps his black marsh-feet on their white and marshy
>   flesh.

Here the mythic quality of the swan is established unequivocally even as the creative energy impelling human bodies is shown to be natural or immanent rather than transcendent. The swan is not Zeus but the natural force of fecundation seen naturally rather than humanly and what is incarnated is the myth or story, the imagination's own initial positive energy charge.

Lawrence finds that myth is both central to the natural physical world and also the record of man's apprehending that world numinously. It follows that he also accepts the meaningful pleasure of tangibility and the principle of what might be called explanatory limitation. To place myth or divine story at the nuclear core of the universe is to call attention to the autonomy of experiential response; for myth is preeminently story or narrative, that is, a verbal form of the experience described and not an explanation of the experience. Thus, to ask about the meaning or nature of myth is the same as to inquire into the constitution of the proton. It is something of which one cannot speak so that, as Wittgenstein reminds us, "thereof one must remain silent." It is this realization that lies behind poems like "Terra Incognita." There Lawrence insists:

> There are vast realms of consciousness still undreamed of
> vast ranges of experience, like the humming of unseen harps,
> we know nothing of, within us.

Simultaneously he urges also that man must escape the limitations of the epistemological trap for the sake of his ultimate ontological goal:

> knowing we can never know,
> we can but touch, and wonder, and ponder, and make our
>   effort
> and dangle in a last fastidious fine delight.

The realms of consciousness and the ranges of experience are those of myth, of the imagination creating the numinous reality of the physical world. As such, it is palpable being rather than discursive knowledge and an occasion of "fine delight" rather than information. In short, myth—to borrow the image of "History"—is the sun of consciousness and experience set over against the inevitable shadows and night of unconsciousness and ignorance. This ontological polarity to myth is vividly conveyed by Lawrence in "The End, the Beginning" both in the title and in the text:

> If there were not an utter and absolute dark
> of silence and sheer oblivion
> at the core of everything,
> how terrible the sun would be,
>
> . . . .
>
> But the very sun himself is pivoted
> upon a core of pure oblivion.

Against the creative speech of myth stand the silence and oblivion of eternal mystery grounded in world and mind alike.

What the foregoing suggests is that myth, for Lawrence, is the verbal or narrative form of matter, the living substance which "we can but touch, and wonder, and ponder, and make our effort." While both myth and matter are "pivoted/ upon a core of pure oblivion," they are neither static nor passive entities quietly awaiting their inevitable annihilation. The interaction of mass and motion, of human bodies and love has already been examined. It is important, however, to note too that myth—the energy concept of Lawrence's epistemological physics—also is dynamic, possessing its own particle and wave patterns of movement. Just as love involves the two motions of advance and recoil so myth in Lawrence's "new world" possesses two basic forms of motion. These are sex and death and together they comprise, in his view, the fundamental rituals of mankind. It is because of the centrality of myth to the human universe and because ritual in Lawrence is essentially myth in motion that he attends so exhaustively to the forms and actions of sex and death in his work and life. Yet he does not regard them as being motions of advance and retreat or progression and retrogression. Both are motions natural to and observable in human bodies so that their dialectical relation is not moral so much as ontological. They are the ritual actions by which life is inaugurated and terminated and it is in that motion of opening and closing that the universal or cosmic parallel to the dialectic of individual love occurs.

To explore the major forms of myth's motion in Lawrence's poetry is beyond the scope of the present essay, which is concerned only to establish the necessary interactions of myth and experiential matter in Lawrence's creative imagination. Some indication, however, of the variety and originality of his treatment may perhaps be useful in that it will enable us better to perceive literature's almost inexhaustible resourcefulness in effecting strategies for the incorporation and displacement of myth. As in his response to the world of objects and mass, so he finds the ritual of sex viable and real primarily in the animal sphere. Matching the exuberance of awareness in "The Wild Common" and "Little Fish" is the declarative calm of "The Elephant Is Slow to Mate." Perception and play are rightfully flashing moments involving "Quick little splinters of life," but the sexual ritual is cumulative and weightier in its solemnity. That is what the elephants instinctively recognize and demonstrate, for "oldest they are and the wisest of beasts."

Consequently, their pattern of movement becomes an implicit paradigm of that which is appropriate to human rituals as well:

> They do not snatch, they do not tear;
> their massive blood
> moves as the moon-tides, near, more near,
> till they touch in flood.

Over against this steady serenity of movement progressing inevitably to full realization there is the astringent complaint of human unfulfillment in "You," where the depth of the response is reflected in the brevity of the utterance:

> You, you don't know me.
> When have your knees ever nipped me
> like fire-tongs a live coal
> for a minute?

The difference between animal and human rituals of sexuality is, for Lawrence, not only a matter of motion but also a quality of concentration or attention. Neither elephant nor tortoise (see "Tortoise Gallantry") dilutes or contaminates the mythic motion of sex with extraneous concerns. Man, Lawrence complains in "I Wish I Knew a Woman," cannot approach the sexual goal naturally as "a red fire on the hearth" in which he can "really take delight." The sexual motion in man is not allowed in and of itself:

> without having to make the polite effort of loving her
> or the mental effort of making her acquaintance.
> Without having to take a chill, talking to her.

To bring about this state of serene concentration in human sexuality Lawrence invokes the figures and actions of myth directly. One such instance occurs in "Whales Weep Not!," which is both clinically graphic and mythically invocatory in its rendering of the mating of whales. The emphasis is on the hugeness of the creatures and the mammoth happiness of their passionate existence. At the end of the poem Lawrence suddenly observes:

> and Aphrodite is the wife of whales
> most happy, happy she!

and Venus among the fishes skips and is a she-dolphin
she is the gay, delighted porpoise sporting with love and the
    sea
she is the female tunny-fish, round and happy among the
    males
and dense with happy blood, dark rainbow bliss in the sea.

Though not terribly effective, the poem nevertheless clearly indicates that Lawrence sees the mythic love goddesses as the meeting ground of animal and human sexuality. By a metamorphic process of immanent incarnation the goddesses are transformed and absorbed into the wholly natural world of the whales. The effect, of course, is to obliterate the distance between myth and matter, between anthropomorphic deities and wholly instinctual creatures. As a result, myth is seen to be the energy function of all moving bodies and not simply of human beings capable of imaginative creation.

Nor is this strategy restricted to the ritual movement of sex. It also functions, and even more strikingly, in connection with the mythic motion of death. There are, of course, a great many of Lawrence's poems that deal with death in a consciously ritualistic but only implicitly mythic mode. Poems like "New Heaven and Earth," "November by the Sea," "Under the Oak," and, of course, the superb "The Ship of Death" focus on the preparation for and the experience of death as a ritual by which rebirth may be achieved. In a sense, they and Lawrence, in the main, are concerned with the verbal enactment of the experience rather than its narration. Yet there are poems which explicitly make myth the core of both feeling and meaning. One of the very best of these is the celebrated "Bavarian Gentians," which also brilliantly shows how Lawrence mates the polar motions of sex and death and ultimately the twin realities of myth and mystery.

The poem opens with Lawrence musing on the gentians present in his house during the deathly seasons of autumn and winter. Their color and shape, "tall and dark," in contrast to the "yellow-pale day" cause him to identify them with the chthonic forces of the underworld. They become "torch-flowers of the blue-smoking darkness, Pluto's dark-blue blaze." Then at almost the precise middle of the poem the gentians become a talismanic guide for the poet's own descent into the underworld of death:

Reach me a gentian, give me a torch!
let me guide myself with the blue, forked torch of a flower
down the darker and darker stairs, where blue is darkened
    on blueness
down the way Persephone goes, just now, in first-frosted
    September.
to the sightless realm where darkness is married to dark
and Persephone herself is but a voice, as a bride,
a gloom invisible enfolded in the deeper dark
of the arms of Pluto as he ravishes her once again
and pierces her once more with his passion of the utter
    dark.[2]

The myth of the rape of Persephone by the god of darkness and
death becomes the poet's opportunity to "touch, and wonder, and
ponder" the seizing of the individual by another through the action of
an irresistible power or force or energy. Convinced as he is that man's
fundamental rituals are sex and death, Lawrence invokes the myth as
narrative guide and psychological reinforcement for his own imaginative submission to or participation in the ultimate motions of human
bodies. In so doing, he articulates his understanding of what links and
encompasses sex and death:

Give me a flower on a tall stem, and three dark flames,
for I will go to the wedding, and be wedding-guest
at the marriage of the living dark.

It is the sacred marriage, the *hieros gamos*, of opposites memorial-
ized in myths such as that of Persephone and rituals such as those of
the Eleusinian mysteries wherein man's naturally fearful recoil from
the unknown other is merged with his equally natural attraction to the
fascinatingly new. Together they constitute the "vast realms of consciousness" and the "vast ranges of experience" accessible to man beyond the limitation of material knowledge. The "living dark" is both
vibrant with sexuality and redolent of death so that what Lawrence
carefully calls "the marriage of [not in] the living dark" is clearly the
mating or merging of sex and death, the two ritual motions of man-

2. I deliberately use this version of the poem, which is from MS "A," since it more
sharply points up the sex-death relation.

kind. The sacred marriage, in short, is to myth what love is to matter in Lawrence's epistemological physics: the concept which functionally coordinates the polar motions of human bodies and living substance in general. But because "Bavarian Gentians" embraces both the sacred marriage and the Persephone legend it does more than integrally relate sex and death. As "The Ship of Death" tells us, man "must take/ the longest journey, to oblivion," which, it has been suggested, is the ontological other to myth. Yet the poet as "wedding-guest" celebrates the juxtaposition and union of myth and oblivion by following the figure of Persephone into "the living dark" of absolute and unpredictable mystery. In this way, "Bavarian Gentians" demonstrates how myth reaches out to and merges with mystery, matter with nothingness, and speech with silence in the ultimate and moving body of the poem. And in that achievement lies the persistence of Lawrence as a poet, embracing but not absorbed into either Eliot's myths or Williams' matter. In narrating the nature of the world as he perceives and senses it, the poet articulates his myth of incorporation which simultaneously reveals its structural displacement of other myths into if not unique then distinctive and characteristic forms and figures. At the same time, the myth calls attention to its irreducibly linguistic nature and hence to the presence of silence and the unknowable which infuses the act of imaginative speech with the limitations of the human condition by which alone those limitations are rendered irrelevant.

1. The world is everything that is the case.

LUDWIG WITTGENSTEIN

⌘ TWO · Myth and Structure: Figures and Forms

LAWRENCE'S locating of myth at the core of the physical world and at the center of the self's focal acts of construction illuminates both the problematics of ontology and the limits of epistemology. More important, it illuminates the structural nature of literature since that act of location occurs as an integral feature of the creative autonomy of experiential response, which is the poem. Literature, Lawrence affirms, consists of myth and matter, both immemorial archetypes and experiential perceptions and intuitions grounded in personal immediacy. The knowing awareness intrinsic in the employment of language is dialectically conditioned by the intractable mystery of the brute presence which simply is. Myths, fictions, and symbolic constructions generally are both forms of knowledge and admissions of ignorance, even as the entities, bodies, and objects in literature are both manifestly given with an undeniable weight and density and merely invented as airy chimeras compounded out of nothingness. The poetic text, Lawrence's example appears to suggest, is a growing edge between the known and the unknown, which places myth and matter under both rubrics in a transitively symmetrical relationship that endlessly issues in the profoundest ignorance as well as the most certain knowledge. Experience or matter and myth are not so much nations with clearly demarcated borders replete with official checkpoints as they are differing currents which merge and diverge in accordance with local conditions that may in certain circumstances and on given occasions make it impossible to declare univocally the specific identity of the area or entity under examination. Thus, what is so fascinating about Lawrence's poetry, as we have seen, is not simply the presence of mythic features but the subtle and far-reaching manner in which these arise from and reach out to the immediate physicalities of bodies, movement, color, and shape.

This congruence of the mythic and the existential in the artistic imagination suggests, on the simplest level, that one reason poets employ myths is that they are profoundly and perennially interesting. The myth is familiar through its reiteration by many writers and so gives a sense of the continuity of human life, of tradition, of the perennial character of human interests. At the same time, it challenges the poet, for it dares him to tell the same story differently, conveying his own attitude toward it and exemplifying his own solution to the problems of technique inherent in the tale. In addition, poets find myths interesting for much the same reasons as everyone else: their curiosity is aroused as to the meaning of these tales and why they should have been articulated, and they are puzzled by the motives and behavior of their human and divine characters. Importantly, then, myths enter poetry because individual men and women see to it unconsciously as well as consciously. To suggest what happens in the process, how a poem's theme, genre, rhetorical devices, and symbolic action reveal even as they are shaped by the poet's intellectual beliefs about and emotional attitudes toward the myth is surely a vital aspect of the critical activity. For in doing so, one engages many of the issues of structure and form that lie at the heart of the individuality of the literary work.

Two principal ways of approaching the problem of myth and literary structure immediately suggest themselves. One is to take a single myth or mythic figure and examine the ways in which different writers develop its basic pattern in their own idiom. The other is to select a single author with a view to studying both the varieties and continuities of mythic elements and patterns developed in his work. Though there are a number of possibilities with regard to the first, a conveniently representative one presents itself in the case of the handling of the Leda myth by modern poets as diverse as William Butler Yeats, Aldous Huxley, and Robert Graves. The second approach will be taken later in the essay, where the concentration is on the short fiction of D. H. Lawrence. It should be stressed that the concern here is with the simplest and most obvious comparative features of mythic structure in these poems. Yeats's Leda poem, for instance, has a rich and detailed critical history that testifies to its complexity. Similarly, the multiplication of the instances of Leda's textual incorporation, as in, say,

T. Sturge Moore and others, would increase the strategies of her displacement without materially increasing the demonstrability of the central argument. In short, to engage Yeats's "Leda and the Swan" and other similar poems would turn this study exclusively into an examination of literary structure at the expense of other equally important concepts.

When we turn to the myth of Leda, we find that the form of the classical story employed by the three poets is the best-known one, that in which, as Apollodorus tersely remarks, "Zeus in the form of a swan consorted with Leda."[1] But this simple enough formulation is where exact congruence among all three poets ends, a fact which implicitly suggests the degree to which strategies of displacement dominate and condition the interrelation of myth and literature. Thus, Yeats and Graves focus exclusively on the mating aspect of the myth; both are fascinated by the beauty-and-the-beast (or bird) motif, by the idea of and implications in sexual relations between a human being and an animal. Huxley, on the other hand, deals with the entire story, expanding it in many places to include Leda's views of marriage and Jove's agony at his unfulfilled libidinal passions. The result is that Huxley's is a rather long narrative poem, while the other two are brief and compressed. Graves has written what is essentially a lyric, a controlled expression of a complex emotion generated by his perceiving a relation between lust and fear. Yeats's poem, however, though as brief as that of Graves, is not really a lyric at all but a fragment of an epic. Other obvious parts of this unwritten epic which come to mind are "The Second Coming," the Byzantium pieces, and the material of *A Vision*.

For Yeats the story of Leda and the swan is not only a myth, it is also a part of man's history. When seen in relation to his cyclical theory of history the story emerges as the imaginative record of the genesis of the classical period. Thus, it is important both in itself and in terms of what it portends for humanity. Yeats's view of the incident is, then, to borrow Cornford's phrase, a mythistorical one.[2] A literally incredible tale of great antiquity is viewed as recording an event that is part of a historical continuum. The importance of the event depends

1. Apollodorus, *The Library*, ed. and trans. Sir James G. Frazer (2 vols.; London, 1921), II, 23.
2. See F. M. Cornford, *Thucydides Mythistoricus* (London, 1907), viii, 131–32.

upon its reality, upon its having happened, for once it is part of the cycle it must necessarily lead to or cause other events. Thus Yeats's own age is indissolubly linked to the past of classical myth by the ordered stream of occurrences that we call history. Indirectly this same impulse to fuse myth and history, fact and fiction, may explain Yeats's particular interest in Irish legends of heroic exploits. For in such stories Yeats was feeding his imagination not upon the wildly implausible speculations of creation myths or even upon the dying god figures that intrigued the authors of *The Waste Land* and *Finnegans Wake* but upon the deeds and characters of men who, the tales assured him, had actually lived. In these legends Yeats could see the fascinating improbabilities of myth made actual, a part of human history. And since these heroes, these superhuman figures, had lived once, the cycles of history would bring them back, as James Joyce says, "by a commodius vicus of recirculation."

In the case of Huxley and Graves the connection between genre and the poet's attitude toward the myth is even more clear-cut. Huxley's narrative mode is appropriate to his concern with the entire story of Leda. At the same time, it reflects what may be called his "sociological" attitude toward the myth. Thus, the poem opens with a description of the natural setting, a statement of Leda's social status and appearance, and a direct transcript of her conversation which reveals her character and the tensions under which she is laboring. All of these clearly approximate the sociologist's concern (albeit of a Malinowskian order) with contextual analysis. And when it becomes apparent that the institution of marriage is responsible for Leda's unhappiness, then it is obvious that Huxley, like the sociologist, is interested in the problems of people living together:

> Yet these few days since I was made a wife
> Have held more bitterness than all my life,
> While I was yet a child.[3]

Tensions of a related kind are found when the focus shifts to Jove, who "upon his silk-pavilioned bed/ Tossed wrathful and awake," beset by erotic memories and fantasies. Here again, the poet's phrasing signifi-

---

3. Aldous Huxley, *Collected Poetry* (New York, 1971), 85. All quotations from this poem are from this edition.

cantly reveals the stance of the social scientist, for Jove's trouble is diagnosed not simply as lust but rather "Libido like a nemesis/ Scourged him with itching memories of bliss."

The same clinical interest in human behavior appears in the detailed accounts of Jove's discontent and later in Leda's encounter with the swan. In the former, the god's "focused passion" is so intense that all of human life "seems/ An alien world, peopled by insane dreams" and filled with "monstrous shapes" and "unthinkable flowers." Distorted vision, however, is not the only consequence of this erotic frenzy. Like a Victorian confronted with cruelty and injustice in nature and society, Jove begins to express religious doubts and questionings:

> This world so vast, so variously foul—
> Who can have made its ugliness? In what
> Revolting fancy were the Forms begot
> Of all these monsters? What strange deity—
> So barbarously not a Greek!—was he
> Who could mismake such beings in his own
> Distorted image.

Finally, when Jove's pains are allayed by the sight of Leda, the poet suggests that this is due as much to provincialism of the Greek god, for whom "in Greece alone were bodies fair," as it is to Leda's beauty.

Equally detached and analytically descriptive is the poet's account of Leda's meeting with the swan. Unlike Yeats, Huxley does not have the encounter open with "a sudden blow" and a helpless girl but instead presents a scene of drowsy sensuality overlaying a flickering sense of fear and loathing:

> Couched on the flowery ground
> Young Leda lay, and to her side did press
> The swan's proud-arching opulent loveliness,
> Stroking the snow-soft plumage of his breast
> With fingers slowly drawn, themselves caressed
> By the warm softness where they lingered, loth
> To break away. Sometimes against their growth
> Ruffling the feathers inlaid like little scales
> On his sleek neck, the pointed finger-nails
> Rasped on the warm, dry, puckered skin beneath;

> And feeling it she shuddered, and her teeth
> Grated on edge; for there was something strange
> And snake-like in the touch.

It is on this same note of ambivalence that the poem culminates:

> Hushed lay the earth and the wide, careless sky.
> Then one sharp sound, that might have been a cry
> Of utmost pleasure or of utmost pain,
> Broke sobbing forth, and all was still again.

Here, as in a number of his novels, the sociologist-author finds that underlying the tensions and conflicts of human behavior and the shifting character of such social institutions as marriage and the family is the issue of sex. Thus, from Huxley's standpoint the myth of Leda and the swan involves the theme of what might be called the erotic puzzle, the question of to what degree, if any, the act of intercourse is pleasurable to the woman, an issue that has been debated in one form or another at least since the legend of Tiresias' blinding.

While Huxley's narrative concluded with a puzzle that challenges the sociologist with perplexity, Graves's lyric is certain and assured in its observations and conclusion. It is, moreover, a dramatic lyric in which the poet speaks directly to the heart, which he accuses of "bawdry, murder and deceit" and relates to Leda.[4] By focusing primarily on the heart rather than Leda, the author reveals the psychological character of his attitude toward the myth. He is concerned to examine the emotions generated by a contemplation of Leda's mating and so to characterize the nature of their source. Thus, the first two stanzas deal with the primary and secondary reactions of the heart or imagination to "That horror with which Leda quaked/ Under the spread wings of the swan," while the final stanza diagnoses the cause of their appearance. This psychological exploration takes on a more analytic character when we notice that the poet addresses not *the* heart, not the organ common to all mankind, but rather, simply, "Heart," which suggests that it is his own with which he is concerned. The more familiar, intimate form of address indicates that what follows is analogous to the

---

4. Robert Graves, *Collected Poems, 1959* (London, 1959), 115. All quotations from this poem are from this edition.

psychoanalytic discovery and exposure of one's own most intimate secrets, secrets hitherto hidden even from oneself.

In the same way that the poet's attitude toward the myth determines the poem's genre, his attitude influences the controlling rhetorical devices he employs. Yeats, as has been noted, sees the historical dimension of the myth and so, naturally enough, presents it as a scene from an epic. But because the epic deals with more than history, because it enshrines the whole sweep of human traditions, beliefs, and values, its events and characters are not simply past records—they are symbols of man's fate and destiny, images which look to the future as well as the past. And in doing so, the symbol reflects the cyclical character of the epic, which ends where it began but with a difference. It is small wonder, then, that Yeats's principal rhetorical device here is the symbol of Leda: her relationship with the godlike swan explains human history for him. Like all truly significant and moving symbols, Yeats's Leda is rooted in the concrete image with its guarantee of empirical reality, and it is out of this that she develops into a symbol, a condensed paradigm of the human situation. Thus, she first appears as "the staggering girl, her thighs caressed/ By the dark webs, her nape caught in his bill" and then with her divine conception she becomes the symbolic source of man's fate, of "The broken wall, the burning roof and tower/ And Agamemnon dead." [5]

In sharp contrast to the symbolic devices and language of Yeats is the rhetoric of Huxley. Just as the epic mode has been exchanged for the narrative form in Huxley's version of the Leda legend, so the symbol is replaced by statement. The sociological attitude is borne out by the use of statements whose emphatically descriptive character underscores the importance attached to detailed and exact observation. The natural scene is presented with all the orderliness and care of a nineteenth-century or Georgian poet:

> Brown and bright as an agate, mountain-cool,
> Eurotas singing slips from pool to pool;
> Down rocky gullies; through the cavernous pines
> And chestnut groves; down where the terraced vines

5. William Butler Yeats, *The Variorum Edition of the Poems*, ed. Peter Allt (New York, 1957), 441. All quotations from this poem are from this edition.

And gardens overhang; through valleys grey
With olive trees, into a soundless bay
Of the Aegean.

Even more detail is lavished on the core of the legend—Leda's seduction. In contrast to Yeats's compression of the scene into the single phrase "a sudden blow" and to Graves's focusing upon mankind's erotic imagination, Huxley dwells on the objective, physical aspects of the scene with all the eagerness of an impassioned behaviorist:

He, in exchange,
Gave back to her, stretching his eager neck,
For every kiss a little amorous peck;
Rubbing his silver head on her golden tresses,
And with the nip of horny dry caresses
Leaving upon her young white breast and cheek
And arms the red print of his playful beak.

Such statement language is perfectly adapted to sociological narrative in which the entire story is told. The brief lyric which focuses on a single action in order to find parallels to other facets of human life must, however, employ a language that is both highly figured and also condensed. Consequently, Graves's basic rhetorical devices in his Leda poem are simile and metaphor, the former providing the parallels, the latter the condensation. Significantly enough, however, he begins the poem with statements of a reflective and contemplative character:

Heart, with what lonely fears you ached,
How lecherously mused upon
That horror with which Leda quaked
Under the spread wings of the swan.

From this scene, in which the heart is a spectator to Leda's fate, Graves then moves, by the use of metaphor, into a more immediate and dramatic image that identifies the heart or erotic imagination with Leda:

Then soon your mad religious smile
Made taut the belly, arched the breast,
And there beneath your god awhile
You strained and gulped your beastliest.

Thus the legend and Leda appear as psychological surrogates, as projections of private desire and impulses which are perpetuated because they have been objectified in the legend. This is made explicit in the last stanza by the simile that identifies Leda and the heart through the qualities and behavior they have in common:

> Pregnant you are, as Leda was,
> Of bawdry, murder and deceit;
> Perpetuating night because
> The after-languors hang so sweet.

By these different rhetorical devices Graves gives us what are quite literally three different perspectives: first, the heart viewing Leda's experience from a distance; then, a close-up of the heart and Leda in which the one is superimposed on the other; and finally, the poet viewing both from the middle distance and pointing out their relationship. Through this technique Graves preserves the lyric's emphasis on both immediacy and insight or revelation.

While the poet's attitude toward his subject or myth largely determines the genre and rhetorical devices he will employ, the symbolic action of the poem is the product of both attitude and technique. Yeats, we have suggested, regarded the myth of Leda and the swan from the standpoint of history and so is interested for the light thrown on its effects. Leda's seduction inaugurates a series of events—the birth of Helen, her flight from Paris, the sacking of Troy, and the murder of Agamemnon, the hero, by his adulterous wife and her lover—with the profoundest repercussions for Greek thought and Western culture as a whole. Yet despite this historical focus Yeats's poem does not treat the Leda incident as something occurring in the past. In the first three sections verbs and participles combine to emphasize the presentness of the action:

> A sudden blow: the great wings *beating* still
> Above the *staggering* girl, her thighs *caressed*
> By the dark webs, her nape *caught* in his bill,
> He *holds* her helpless breast upon his breast.
>
> How *can* those terrified vague fingers *push*
> The feathered glory from her *loosening* thighs?

> And how *can* body, laid in that white rush,
> But *feel* the strange heart *beating* where it lies?
>
> A shudder in the loins *engenders* there
> The broken wall, the burning roof and tower
> And Agamemnon dead. (my italics)

The action is still going on in Yeats's mind and in the poem even though its original occurrence is buried in remotest antiquity. The mental faculty embodied in the poem is that of imagination, the power of reenacting an event or scene with such power and immediacy that one feels that it is occurring for the first time. That is to say, Yeats's poetic method here functions in a ritualistic manner, for one of the prime factors in ritual is that its participants feel they are performing some original act rather than merely commemorating a deed performed in the distant past.

On the other hand, the symbolic action of Huxley's Leda, while also suggesting the presentness of the past, is not that of ritualistic re-enactment. Instead it reflects the influence of the narrative mode and the sociological attitude by regarding the scene as an occurrence rather than a reenactment. Its point of view is that of a witness who exercises his faculty of observation and records what he has seen. Unlike Yeats, Huxley is not interested in the long-term results of Leda's experience; rather he is fascinated by the immediate motives and reactions of Leda and Jove. These complex forms of behavior culminate at the end of the poem with the erotic puzzle—whether Leda's sexual experience is one of delight or anguish—expressed in the "one sharp sound, that might have been a cry/ Of utmost pleasure or of utmost pain."

Ambiguity is also central to the theme of Graves's poem, though it is the ambivalence of the human heart, its ability both to lust for and to fear the same experience, rather than the erotic puzzle that dominates. At the outset the poet is struck by the heart's being beset by "lonely fears" at the same time as it "lecherously mused" upon Leda's fate. Its terrible secrets of "bawdry, murder and deceit" are kept because of the sensual pleasure provided by their recollection. Indeed, it is just this faculty of memory that dominates the entire poem and distinguishes it from the others. Where Yeats invokes the imaginative faculty to fuse past and present, and Huxley uses observation to give the past a sense of present immediacy or at least of recentness, Graves relies on various forms of memory to create a present understanding of the heart's past actions.

These differences in techniques and symbolic action are, it has been suggested, the products of the poets' emotional attitudes toward the myth. But at the same time they, in turn, are responsible for the expression of the attitude in public form. For Yeats, the epic mode, the historical attitude, and the rhetoric of symbolism all reflect his awe at the mingling of power and beauty in creation. Similarly, Huxley's sociological, narrative statements bear out his mood of objective detachment and philosophical curiosity about human behavior, particularly when exercised on the verge of the unbearable. And finally, Graves, by his psychological lyric with its rhetorical figures, mirrors his ironic view of human nature, including his own, its ambivalence, deceptions, and inconsistencies. In short, from these different attitudes and interests, there have emerged three distinct structural uses of the original myth: Yeats's poem employs myth as symbol; Huxley's narrative uses myth as story or report, almost as case study; and Graves's lyric treats myth as explanation or mirror.

*

When the creative artist engages a myth consciously and explicitly, as the foregoing poets do, the critical emphasis naturally falls, as we have seen, on the structural, rhetorical, and attitudinal adaptations, the strategies of displacement, of the individual writer. Here the myth proper, the narrative matrix as it were, is nearly constant; the literary form in which it is embodied is a compound of authorial choice or predilection conditioned at each point by prior decisions or inclinations and the necessities occasioned by those determinations. The myth is given, so that critical concentration falls on its literary functions or uses. At the same time, other alternatives and issues suggest themselves. What if the myth is not "given" explicitly? What if the author draws on different myths in different works? To what extent can the critic identify the presence of myth? And what critical consequences follow from the presence of various myths in various works? Such questions as these issue in the second critical approach mentioned earlier in this essay. Like the first, it is essentially comparative in character, but it differs in that the comparisons lack a common ground—the myth—so that the focus falls not upon the similarities and differences in the works themselves but rather upon the distinctive ways in which a myth or metamyth informs the specific literary text before us and what it contributes to the structure, texture, and cultural resonance of the work.

A particularly fruitful context in which to explore this second approach is the short fiction of D. H. Lawrence. Elsewhere I have pointed out the extent to which his fiction is rife with the subject matter—beliefs, habits of thought, and behavior—of anthropology and comparative religion.[6] And if one looks at the corpus as a whole, it organizes itself structurally into a half-dozen segments each of which embodies a particular pattern of myth and ritual. Taken together, they provide a clear index of those myths which especially fascinated and spoke most powerfully to Lawrence and of how he saw the interpenetration of ancient and modern, of myth and immediate experience occurring in life and art. Thus, to see Lawrence's mythopoeic imagination grappling with and exfoliating upon figures and actions such as the scapegoat, the sacrificial virgin, the sacred marriage, the animal totem, and the supernatural world is to perceive those central leitmotifs that serve as structural coordinates in his fiction. By restricting our attention to three representative tales—"England, My England," "The Virgin and the Gipsy," and "The Fox"—it will be possible to consider in some detail the interpenetration of mythic pattern and contemporary verisimilitude and to gauge the degree to which strategies of incorporation and displacement cohere in framing Lawrence's implicit assertion of the historical and formal meaningfulness of myth for literature.

In "England, My England" the gradual transformation of the passionate idyll of Egbert's and Winifred's marriage into a savage combat that culminates with World War I and Egbert's death is Lawrence's version of the metamyth of the dying god and the rites of expulsion that accompany the scapegoat. He takes great pains at the beginning of the story to stress the ancient, primitive character both of the scene and of the protagonists. Crockham, where the newlyweds settled, "belonged to the old England of hamlets and yeomen" and "it lay there

6. John B. Vickery, *The Literary Impact of The Golden Bough* (Princeton, 1973), Chap. IX.

secret, primitive, savage as when the Saxons first came."[7] It is one of those places where "the savage England lingers in patches" (*T*, 203). Into this bygone world come Winifred and Egbert to reflect its sense of the past: "She, too, seemed to come out of the old England, ruddy, strong, with a certain crude, passionate quiescence and hawthorn robustness. And he, he was tall and slim and agile, like an English archer with his long supple legs and fine movements" (*T*, 204). Egbert enhances this affinity by having "a passion for old folk-music, collecting folk-songs and folk-dances, studying the Morris-dance and the old customs" (*T*, 205).

The connection with the past demonstrated in the setting, in the appearance and the interests of the characters culminates in their marital behavior. Though the desire is their own, it is intensified by and derives from their immediate physical setting: "The flame of their two bodies burnt again into that old cottage, that was haunted already by so much bygone, physical desire. You could not be in the dark room for an hour without the influences coming over you. The hot blood-desire of bygone yeomen, there in this old den where they had lusted and bred for so many generations" (*T*, 206). In celebrating so triumphantly what Arnold van Gennep calls the fecundation rites of marriage, the couple not only fuse modern individuals with the medieval world of the yeoman but also suggest the truly primitive character of that world. One of the central rites of ancient times that persisted into more recent ages among the European peasantry is the mimetic observance by human beings of the sacred marriage of the god and goddess. It is just such an imitative rite that Egbert and Winifred are unconsciously involved in, as Lawrence intimates by juxtaposing the images of their union and the flourishing vegetation and garden which Egbert is said to have "recreated." Further support for this is found in Winifred's being regarded as "a ruddy fire into which he could cast himself for rejuvenation" (*T*, 206), since the procreative and purificatory powers of fire were frequently invoked in conjunction with the sacred marriage ritual.

Lawrence, however, is writing a story of savage irony and despairing anguish, and hence he focuses not on the joyous celebration of re-

7. D. H. Lawrence, *The Tales* (London, 1934), 204, 206. Subsequent references to this edition are hereafter cited parenthetically in the text as *T*.

newed life that normally follows the ritual marriage but on the expulsion and death of the protagonist. This is ironically prepared for in the midst of the ritual of erotic ecstasy by the intrusion of the author's mock invocation "Ah, that it might never end, this passion, this marriage!" (*T*, 206). That it will end is certain not only because Egbert and Winifred prove to be incompatible personalities but also because they are unconsciously miming the ritual existence of the fertility deity who suffers a cyclic rejection and demise. And in the same scene an image of the impersonal yet necessary cruelty inherent in the mythic world is revealed in the snake's endeavor to swallow a frog which is uttering "the strangest scream, like the very soul of the dark past crying aloud" (*T*, 206). Nor is it accident that this ritual of self-preservation should have been witnessed by Winifred, who is to take the lead in Egbert's expulsion from the marriage, the family, and life itself. In connection with the growing alienation that develops between Egbert and Winifred it is important to notice that the strain between them is not derived from the contrast of Egbert's indolent dilettantism to her passion for responsibility and duty or even from his habit of sponging off her father. These are, at the most, contributory factors. The genuine source of their estrangement lies in a virtually inevitable change in the structure of their world. Instructive here is van Gennep's point, made in *The Rites of Passage*, that the life of the individual passes through certain successive stages and that this is achieved through the intermediary of ceremonies calculated to make the transition a safe one. These rites of passage are threefold, consisting of what van Gennep calls "separation . . . transition . . . and incorporation."[8] The crucial change in the world of the two characters comes when they enter the state of parenthood. Here is the beginning of the ritual of separation, of detachment from the old world and the old life. Winifred finds in her child "a new centre of interest" so that "without anything happening, he [Egbert] was gradually, unconsciously excluded from the circle" (*T*, 209). Then, following their second child, she begins to resent and then despise that physical love which has already become of secondary importance to her in the role of dutiful and responsible mother. To provide a conscious justification for this

8. Arnold van Gennep, *The Rites of Passage*, trans. M. B. Vizadom and G. L. Caffee (London, 1960), 11.

attitude, she turns to the issue of money and his failure to earn a living. Having thus articulated her sense of critical detachment from her husband, she at length formulates what it is that really separates them: "It was that he stood for nothing" (*T*, 210).

With this we come to the central antithesis in the story, that between her husband and her father. The basic desire of the former is "to hold aloof. It was not his season" (*T*, 212). The latter, on the other hand, plunges into the struggle of existence with "an acrid faith like the sap of some not-to-be-exterminated tree. Just a blind acrid faith as sap is blind and acrid, and yet pushes on in growth and in faith" (*T*, 212). The "stoic and epicurean" husband confronts the hardy vegetative father and succumbs, in the last analysis, because he lacks the father's "will-to-power . . . the single power of his own blind self" (*T*, 213). Their struggle, however, is not direct but operates through and in the person of Winifred. For her, the basic familial unit is comprised of her parents, herself, and her child; in it she finds the core of life, "the human trinity for her" (*T*, 209). She does so because her father has maintained "a certain primitive dominion over the souls of his children, the old, almost magic prestige of paternity. There it was, still burning in him, the old smoky torch of parental godhead. . . . Fatherhood that had life-and-death authority over the children" (*T*, 213–14). The only thing that could have supplanted her father would have been Winifred's finding in her husband a greater male power and authority. But since Egbert does not possess this power, Lawrence ironically inverts the mythic formula which calls for the young ruler or deity to supplant the old one. Egbert rejects the possibility of his own divinity as a human being replete with power and becomes in contrast to the father a taboo-figure, "the living negative of power" (*T*, 214). And what he taboos by his very presence is Winifred's attempt to exercise "her dark, silent, passionate authority," "the old blood-power," "the old dark magic of parental authority" (*T*, 214–15). To this end he uses his own form of magic and witchcraft not only to transform her parental authority into "a sort of tyranny" (*T*, 215) but also to steal the children (the image is Lawrence's) from her. His magic is that which most completely captures children, namely, the exercise of complete license in behavior: "They could do as they liked with him" (*T*, 215).

Out of the two men's indirect struggle for the role of father has

come the ritual of separation celebrated by Winifred in her increasing
sexual reticence and by Egbert in his denial of her parental authority
coupled with his own rejection of responsibility. This, however, is but
the first stage in the rites of passage, that of detachment from the old
life. It is followed by what van Gennep calls the rite of transition, the
behavior that marks the interim stage between the old and the new
modes of life.[9] In "England, My England" this is reflected in the incident of the firstborn child's being lamed as a result of falling on a
sickle left in the grass by Egbert. With this the antithesis between
Winifred's passion for duty and authority (a worship of the hierarchy)
and Egbert's rejection of responsibility and power (a belief in liberty
and self-determination) is projected into the visible and external world
so forcefully that husband and wife are seen to be completely separated, to be living in different worlds. In the weeks that follow the accident, both are moving toward their new and distinct modes of existence. As a period of physical, emotional, and spiritual transition, it is
"a dark and bitter time" (*T*, 220) for all.

Yet this incident and its repercussions are not significant solely as a
rite of transition from marriage to legal separation. For in the early
part of the story Egbert has been identified as a representative and
worshipper of phallic potency, who, like the primitive divine king,
rules only so long as he can demonstrate his power as a fertility figure.
When Winifred denies him this, she makes him "lock up his own vivid
life inside himself" (*T*, 211) and thereby reduces him to virtual impotence. Both Egbert and the divine king react in the same way: through
a sacrifice of the firstborn, man may continue to live as he has, to re-
tain a wife as well as a throne, to prolong a marriage as well as a reign.
Clearly, such a rite could not be deliberately embarked upon by a
member of the civilized world of Lawrence's or our day, for whom it
would be a monstrously evil and immoral act. But as Lawrence seems
to indicate, it would be quite possible to desire this in the subcon-
scious, where the primitive and savage impulses of man linger even
yet. Thus, the contemporary consciousness registers this longing for
sacrifice literally as "a wicked look" and metaphorically as Egbert's
having "seven devils inside his long, slim, white body" (*T*, 211). In the
same fashion the ritual act itself is displaced into versimilitude and

9. Van Gennep, *The Rites of Passage*, 11, 21 ff.

motivational consistency by being transmuted into an accident occasioned by Egbert's habitual carelessness and thoughtlessness.

Egbert himself, immediately after the accident, seeks to assuage his deep sense of guilt by insisting on the unforeseen character of the event. What is at the core of this guilt, however, is not his own superficial carelessness but rather his profound and abiding responsibility. In times of great calamity, it was customary to sacrifice the firstborn. And for Egbert there could be no greater calamity than losing Winifred, for, as has been suggested, it is through her that his spirit of fertility is released and his rejuvenation effected. By indirectly attempting to sacrifice the child, Egbert is seeking to gain a new lease on life, to atone for his sins (especially the denial of parental authority's divinity), and to demonstrate that he, like Winifred's father, "had kept alive the old red flame of fatherhood, fatherhood that had even the right to sacrifice the child to God, like Isaac" (*T*, 214). That Egbert is using the child as a substitute for himself is further suggested by the weapon's being a sickle, the instrument employed in harvest rituals to sacrifice the fertility deity. Even more striking is the fact that, according to one authority, "the corn-spirit is conceived as a child who is separated from its mother by the stroke of the sickle." [10]

It is part, however, of Lawrence's ironic intention that this effort at prolonging a state of existence regarded as fruitful and idyllic should be thwarted. He is concerned not with the revival but with the death of human society and its protagonists. This is borne out by the sacrifice of the child, which as a ritual of transition proves to be "an agony and a long crucifixion" (*T*, 220). The irony appears in that the sacrifice is not complete, the child does not die, and so the father cannot restore the marriage to its sacred status. A further irony follows from the fact that the ultimate ritual sacrifice is made by Egbert as a result of his being the scapegoat in the accident. It is with his assumption of this role that the final stage of the rites of passage is reached. Following the marginal, transitional observance there is the absorption into a new world and a new mode of life. For Winifred the child's injury completely ends her passionate attachment to Egbert. The existence into which she is drawn is that of institutional religion, the Roman

10. Sir James G. Frazer, *The Golden Bough* (3rd ed.; 12 vols.; London, 1907–1911), VIII, 150.

Catholic church. Here she finds an alternative to the life of passion, sensuality, and distraction she has known with Egbert.

It is from this that Egbert's own ritual of absorption or assimilation follows. When Winifred becomes "purely the *Mater Dolorata*," he finds that for him "she was closed as a tomb . . . the tomb of his manhood and his fatherhood" (*T*, 221). Like the primitive scapegoat, he finds that he is shut out forever from the community he has known, compelled "to turn aside," to wander "hither and thither, desultory," possessed of "no real home" (*T*, 221). Even clearer evidence of his assumption of the role of ritual outcast from society is the hatchetlike cleft in his brow developed since the accident which he bears as his Cain-like "stigma" (*T*, 221). It is this together with his relation to her and her family that gives him for Winifred "the Ishmael quality" (*T*, 223). But the scapegoat is not simply the creature who wanders in lonely isolation until overtaken by death. It is also representative of the divinity whose death is preordained as an elaborate ritual of sacrifice. Egbert's divinity is revealed by his appearing to Winifred's now nunlike soul as "an erect, supple symbol of life, the living body" and to her Christianized eyes as "Baal and Ashtaroth," "a supple living idol" that "if she watched him she was damned" (*T*, 224, 223).

To her he appears godlike, but to himself he is the object of sacrifice. Thus, in the landscape bits of vegetation seem to him "like a sprinkling of sacrificial blood" (*T*, 222). And from this his imagination comes to be dominated by "the savage old spirit of the place: the desire for old gods, old, lost passions, the passion of the cold-blooded, darting snakes that hissed and shot away from him, the mystery of blood-sacrifices, all the lost, intense sensations of the primeval people of the place, whose passions seethed in the air still, from those long days before the Romans came" (*T*, 222).

The opportunity for the blood sacrifice of the scapegoat is provided by World War I, into which he is projected by his wife and father-in-law. With his enlistment the various rites associated with the scapegoat are performed. The customary inversion of the social hierarchy is reflected in Egbert's awareness that joining the army meant "he was going to put himself into the power of his inferiors. . . . He was going to subjugate himself" (*T*, 225). Similarly, Winifred's being "so ready to serve the *soldier*, when she repudiated the man" (*T*, 227) mirrors the scapegoat's being permitted sexual intercourse with a woman usually forbidden him.[11] And finally, Egbert's being wounded twice before his death approximates the custom of beating and wounding the scapegoat before putting him to death. By these rites he is confirmed in his role; now he is not simply expelled from his family, he has "gone out of life, beyond the pale of life" (T, 227). Nor is it without significance that Lawrence should present Egbert under the image of "a man who is going to take a jump from a height" (T, 227), for the scapegoat commonly met his fate by being hurled from a cliff. Out of these rites comes a feeling of participation in an inescapable experience that sustains him through even his death agonies and permits him to will the completion of the scapegoat ritual by which the ritual of the dying god is enacted.

A mythic pattern of a quite different order structures the next tale to be considered. Instead of a separation from a fulfilling life and a submission to death, there is a crisis situation threatening death from which the protagonist is rescued and brought to a fuller awareness of and participation in life than she has hitherto known. "The Virgin and the Gipsy" elaborates the myth of the virgin whose salvation follows from her exposure to a sacrificial death, in short, the Andromeda story. Central to this salvation is her meeting the stranger, the gypsy who focuses her resistance to her narrow, hypocritical family and its "rectory morality" (T, 1050). When instead of concealing or ignoring "the dark, tremulous potent secret of her virginity" (T, 1059) she accepts its power to arouse desire, she is capable of accepting the challenge of the outcast which is none other than to become an outcast oneself, to dare to go one's own way.

The steps by which Yvette comes to this awareness are all designed to underscore the mythical and ritualistic character of the narrative. Thus, the first meeting between the young people and the gypsies is described in only partly ironical fashion as occurring between Christians and pagans. Emerging from her private palm-reading session with the gypsy woman, Yvette maintains a "witch-like silence," a manner that is intensified later at a dance when she suggests a "young virgin *witch*" (T, 1045) who "might metamorphose into something uncanny" (T, 1062). This quality appears only after her meeting with the stranger, a figure traditionally thought to cast spells and perform

11. See Frazer, *The Golden Bough*, IX, 355.

other magical feats. And significantly enough, Lawrence twice repeats that the gypsy-stranger's desire exercises a spell-like power over her. As a result of this, too, she finds her soul stolen from her body and drawn to the world of the gypsies.

Nor is the gypsy simply the stranger as magician; he is also the stranger as representative of the fertility spirit. This is borne out not only by the sexual power Yvette perceives in him and by his being linked with a kindling fire but also by Yvette's being likened in his presence to a flower about to blossom, an act for which he is responsible. His absorption with "the mysterious fruit of her virginity" (*T*, 1067), Mrs. Fawcett's insistence that for Yvette to have a love affair with him would be prostitution, and Mr. Eastwood's declaration that "'he's a resurrected man'" (*T*, 1078), all combine to identify him as the fertility figure who appears as a stranger to assist in the ritual defloration of unmarried girls.

Strikingly enough, this ritual itself does not seem to take place in the story, though some readers may feel that the ending of Section IX is discreetly ambiguous on this score. Instead, Yvette participates first in a watery sacrifice of her life and then in a divestiture in the presence of a fertility figure which restores her to a full sense of life's significance. Her encounter with the water is a ritual both of purgation or purification and of protection. The first of these is borne out not only by the usual purificatory qualities attached to water but also by the presence of the larch and laurel trees, both of which are sacred and one of which forms a part of traditional ceremonies of purification. Yet from its being a raging torrent to which Yvette is exposed, it is clear that this rite is more than baptismal in character. It is also the ritual sacrifice that precedes the baptismal introduction into a new existence. The Andromeda aspect of the story is subtly brought out by the image of the water as "a *devouring* flood" (*T*, 1089; my italics). This image together with the attendant descriptions suggests that the threat to which Yvette is exposed is that of both the folklore monster—it is described as "a shaggy, tawny wave-front of water advancing like a wall of lions" (*T*, 1089)—and the universal flood that represents a return of chaos.

As stories like "Daughters of the Vicar" make clear, however, chaos in itself is not an unrewarding prospect for Lawrence. It represents that dissolution of the old existence without which no new life can come into being and acquire form. Thus, when Yvette feels "as if the flood was in her soul" (*T*, 1090), we see that it is a psychological dissolution of universal proportions as well as a terrifying natural event. As a ritual of protection, the torrential stream is linked to flood sagas such as in the Bible. The central point here is that the flood functions as a judgment and punishment whereby only the righteous are preserved from destruction. The death by water of the Mater signifies the final assessment of her evil nature. In effect, then, the scene recapitulates Wilhelm Wundt's point that the universal flood (*Sintflut*) develops into a sin flood (*Sündflut*).[12]

With the removal of Yvette's dress, a "death-gripping thing" (*T*, 1092), her purgation of the old, deathlike existence of the family is complete, and as prophesied by the gypsy woman, she comes into contact with the dark man who stirs the flame warming her heart. Her understanding of what he has done for her is seen in her acquiescence to his subsequent departure. Like the fertility figure of myth, he lives the cyclic existence of nomad so that his disappearance is as inevitable as his appearance. Enhancing this parallel is the comment on the letter from "some unknown place": "And only then she realized that he had a name" (*T*, 1097). By her belated discovery of the gypsy's name, Lawrence emphasizes the archetypal nature of the entire story. Essentially, then, the two leading characters participate in what T. H. Gaster regards as the true function of myth, namely, "the translation of the punctual into terms of the durative, the real into those of the ideal."[13] As Yvette Saywell and Joe Boswell, they are characters, human beings; as the virgin and the gypsy, they are archetypes with associations that extend far beyond the rectory and village of Papplewick.

A still different kind of mythic structure informs "The Fox" and "St. Mawr," namely, the animal or totemic myth. In totemism an intimate relation is assumed between certain human beings and certain natural or artificial objects, the latter being called the totems of the former.[14] The outlines of the totemic myth are most apparent in "The Fox" partly because it is shorter and partly because it is a much less complex story than "St. Mawr." "The Fox" deals with the develop-

12. Wilhelm Wundt, *Elements of Folk Psychology*, trans. E. L. Schaub (New York, 1916), 391.

13. T. H. Gaster, *Thespis* (New York, 1950), 5.

14. Frazer, *The Golden Bough*, VIII, 35.

ment and resolution of a romantic triangle involving two women and a man. Through the use of psychological associations and prophetic dreams, the story gradually reveals its totemic form. At the outset Nellie March and Jill Banford are gentlemen farmers who are rather consistently unsuccessful because of a combination of their disinclination for hard work and of unfortunate circumstances, the most notable of which is a marauding fox that carries off their hens. The first stage in the development of the totemic myth occurs when Nellie encounters the fox one evening, for as a result "she was spellbound—she knew he knew her. So he looked into her eyes, and her soul failed her" (*T*, 421). The depth of the impression made on her by this meeting is indicated in part by Lawrence's repetition of the image of the spell and possession five times in the two pages following. Ultimately "it was the fox which somehow dominated her unconsciousness, possessed the blank half of her musing" (*T*, 423), a state that continues from August to November.

The second stage of the myth is reached with the arrival of Henry Grenfel in search of his grandfather, the former owner of the farm and now dead. The stage of confrontation is succeeded by one of identification. Nellie first finds herself "spellbound" by Henry just as by the fox; then she sees the man as quite literally the animal. This identification is due first to his physical appearance and later to his basic form of behavior, that of a foxlike secret watcher. With this stage the totem moves into her consciousness from her unconscious; with the animal-man "in full presence" she accepts the spell that hitherto has been imposed on her and abandons the attempt "to keep up two planes of consciousness" (*T*, 429). Now "she could at last lapse into the odour of the fox" (*T*, 429), for the strangeness of her attraction has been modified by the appearance of the man. The implausibility deliberately courted in David Garnett's fable *Lady Into Fox* is avoided by Lawrence through the "desacralizing" of the totemic myth into a psychological abreaction which though unusual nevertheless possesses the verisimilitude necessary to the realistic ground of the tale.

The story then enters on the third or prophetic phase of the myth. For the very night of Henry's arrival Nellie dreams of herself and the fox:

> It was the fox singing. He was very yellow and bright, like corn. She went nearer to him, but he ran away and ceased singing. He

seemed near, and she wanted to touch him. She stretched out her hand, but suddenly he bit her wrist, and at the same instant, as she drew back, the fox, turning round to bound away, whisked his brush across her face, and it seemed his brush was on fire, for it seared and burned her mouth with a great pain. (*T*, 430)

The prophecy immediately begins to work itself out next morning when Nellie notices that "something about the glint of his khaki reminded her of the brilliance of her dream-fox" (*T*, 431). It is fulfilled a fortnight later when Henry declares his love to Nellie and asks her to marry him, for as she is about to join Jill upstairs, "quick as lightning he kissed her on the mouth, with a quick brushing kiss" (*T*, 443).

While prophetic concerning their ultimate relationship, the dream is also revelatory about the nature of the fox and, by extension, Henry. To anyone familiar, as Lawrence was, with anthropological studies of myth such as *The Golden Bough*, the above description of the fox suggests that he is to be identified with the primitive fertility deity or, more specifically, with Dionysus as the corn spirit. Significantly enough, during harvest season the man who hits the last corn with his sickle is called the Fox and during the evening dances with all the women. Thus, in Frazer as well as Lawrence, fertility figure, man, and animal are all connected. Nor is it irrelevant that at the beginning of the story, before confronting either the fox or Henry, the two women regard the fox as "a demon" (*T*, 420). He moves from devil to god as Nellie becomes increasingly aware of what he represents and of what she desires. At the same time, with Nellie's feeling that "his brush was on fire" (*T*, 430), the dream hints too at the fate of the fox. This image recalls the custom of fastening burning torches to foxes' tails as punishment for having destroyed the crops in the past. In this there is perhaps an oblique foreshadowing of the fox's death at the hands of Henry and his gun.

The prophetic phase adumbrates the phallic relation of Nellie and Henry, the death of the fox, and, in a second dream of Nellie's, the death of Jill. In the last stage of the myth, that of the sacrificial action, these events are made real. The story's problem, of course, centers on the human triangle; though Nellie is drawn to Henry, Jill, impelled by her own sexual drives, stands resolutely between them, threatening the success of his pursuit. The only resolution can be the removal of Jill herself in some swift, irreversible fashion. Preparatory to this, however, Henry slays the fox, an action that is too heavily emphasized to be merely gratuitous plot embroidery. In point of fact, this reflects that part of the totemic myth in which the divine animal is solemnly sacrificed as part of an annual ritual.

A clue to the most important reason for Henry's slaying of the fox is Frazer's remark that totemism "appears to be mainly a crude, almost childlike attempt to satisfy the primary wants of man," an attempt that operates through the magical creation of that which is sought.[15] For what Henry clearly wants is Nellie, and to this end he eventually attempts the removal of Jill. What he creates is, in short, the absence of Jill, an event that is magical in the sense that it is apparently uncaused and yet follows from the concentrated will of Henry. The slaying of the fox is both a rehearsal and a primitive adumbration of the human death insofar as it demonstrates Henry's resolve in the face of the sacrificial slaying of the creature most sacred to the society. To observe the totemic sacrifice of the fox is to be able to perform it in connection with the totem of modern society, namely, another human being.

In carrying out this twin sacrifice, Henry employs what van Gennep calls "positive rites" in which the individual's wish is translated into an act.[16] Central here is the ability to focus one's spiritual and emotional energies on a single end: "In his heart he had decided her death. A terrible still force seemed in him, and a power that was just his. If he turned even a hair's breadth in the wrong direction, he would lose the power" (T, 473). This rite of separation by sacrifice is identical with that of assimilation by which Henry draws Nellie to him. In both cases the act is first mimed in the imagination as a magical guarantee of its physical success. Like Frazer's savages, Henry believes that the central feature of the hunt resides in the conquest of the soul:

> First of all, even before you come in sight of your quarry, there is a strange battle, like mesmerism. Your own soul, as a hunter, has gone out to fasten on the soul of the deer, even before you see any deer. And the soul of the deer fights to escape. Even before the deer has any wind of you, it is so. It is a subtle, profound battle of wills which takes place in the invisible. (T, 434)

And it is in this spirit that Henry stalks, in turn, Nellie, the fox, and, finally, Jill.

15. Frazer, The Golden Bough, I, 108.
16. Van Gennep, The Rites of Passage, 8.

These rites, however, are not simply isolated events performed for immediate practical ends; they are also the behavioral concomitant of Henry's character and the culmination of his prototypical social function. Just prior to Jill's death Henry is likened to "a huntsman who is watching a flying bird" (*T*, 473). That this is more than a casual simile is suggested by Jill's having been described as a bird on more than one occasion. Even more important is the scene that inaugurated the hunt motif, the scene in which Henry first thinks of marrying Nellie. Lawrence here emphasizes Henry's basic nature: "He was a huntsman in spirit, not a farmer, and not a soldier stuck in a regiment. And it was as a young hunter that he wanted to bring down March as his quarry, to make her his wife" (*T*, 434). With this, we find a broader perspective on the totemic myth and ritual, one which links them to a way of life characteristic of the society itself. Frazer formulates this pattern clearly when he observes that although totemism "probably always originated in the hunting stage of society, it has by no means been confined to that primitive phase of human development but has often survived not only into the pastoral but into the agricultural stage."[17] And as we have seen, in "The Fox" the survival of totemism and the mingling of the two stages of society are both present: in the midst of the agricultural life of the two women appear both the totemic respectful awe felt by Nellie for the fox and the "stranger-youth" who is a hunter.

Just as the totemic myth and ritual underlie the narrative development, so they also define the relationships of the characters. For Nellie, Henry is the totem animal to be revered and respected; for Jill, whose own totem is the bird, he is the sinister antagonist, a natural enemy to be feared. For Henry, Nellie March is the game he seeks and Jill is a bothersome creature whose intrusive demands and influence on Nellie ultimately overcome the taboo on the slaying of a human being. Thus, in a sense, both women are objects of the hunt, the one because she is desired, the other because she is not. Mediating between them is the fox, which is also overcome by the hunter. In the case of Jill, as already noted, the fox slaying is a rehearsal for the human death. Nellie, on the other hand, is won over or at least subdued following the death of the fox. What is contingent and fortuitous in the realism of the narrative pattern becomes necessary and inevitable in terms of the totemic myth. Indeed, it is precisely this tension between the un-

17. Frazer, *The Golden Bough*, VIII, 37.

predictability of the modern world's depiction and the sequential certitude of the displaced ritual that confers on the narrative its peculiar suspenseful power. For Nellie, the fox, which is her totem, contains what Frazer calls the external soul, that projection of one's life drives into the objective world which keeps one in contact with reality and so alive as an individual. With the slaying of the fox Henry has, in effect, acquired her soul and so can sway her to his will, an achievement symbolized by her changing from breeches, "strong as armour," to a dress in which she is "accessible" (T, 458). From all of this it is apparent that if, as Bronislaw Malinowski says, totemism is "a mode of social grouping and a religious system of beliefs and practices," then it is central to the meaning of "The Fox." The various attitudes toward the fox obviously produce conflicting groups within the society as a whole. At the same time, Henry's drive to marry Nellie qualifies as religious in Malinowski's sense, that is, as expressing the desire "to control the most important objects" in man's surroundings.[18]

---

18. Bronislaw Malinowski, *Magic, Science and Religion* (New York, 1948), 20.

Openness, too, is a form of architecture.

GEORGE SANTAYANA

 THREE · Myth and Theme: From Paradox to Metamorphosis

ONE way of critically organizing literary structures is, as we have just seen, in a progression from the obvious, apparent, and explicit to the subtle, hidden, and implicit presence of mythicoritualistic elements and patterns. In many ways the same can be said of the thematic dimension of literary works. As one scholar remarked some time ago, the "'line of myth' extends from, and marks the gradations from one extreme, at which we find absolute, inclusive myth, to the other extreme, at which we find many myths, of lesser or no intensity, and either with a grasp upon only a small segment of reality or else with no such grasp at all." This rather than the presence or absence of mythic elements accounts for the difference of mythic tonality felt between, say, *King Lear* and *Irene* or between *Joseph and His Brothers* and *Studs Lonigan*. Two factors are most directly relevant to this range of primacy. One is the awareness of myth as a viable activity endemic to the human mind and spirit. The other is the process of infiguration's being directed by habits of thought which produce myths that are hypostatized or "dogmatized" and so lack the resonance necessary to sound imaginative depths.[1] The author's awareness or acceptance of the mythopoeic propensities of the human mind may be limited or his perceptions may be shaped by restrictive or simplistically held myths. If so, his works will tend to reflect the socioliterary conventions of his day that stress verisimilitude and realism, or propriety and rules. But to pursue this range of thematic possibility would take us too far afield at the present, involving as it would a consideration of the kinds of myth—religious, sociological, political, historical, scientific—oper-

1. Robert Heilman, "The Lear World," in *English Institute Essays 1948*, ed. D. A. Robertson, Jr. (New York, 1949), 30, 33.

ative in different times and cultures as well as of their relevancy to criticism proper.

A more manageable as well as productive issue is the writer's reaction to the idea of myth itself and his treatment of it as a thematic component in his work. In the modern period—since at least Goethe—the artistic mind, regardless of in what literary mode it expresses itself, has been seriously engaged by the concept of myth. With the emergence of the great modernists such as Yeats, Joyce, Eliot, and Lawrence an even more self-conscious and ultimately ironic attitude was generated concerning myth. Two illuminating instances appear in the fictive attitudes of Lawrence and Joyce, which taken together encompass the modern temper with regard to mythopoeic thought and its literary import. In many ways Lawrence's attitude toward myth as object and theme reminds us of the nineteenth century's response to Darwin and human origins. On the one hand, there is the empiricist's inevitable acceptance of fact or reality and the exciting, breathtaking consequences it holds out. On the other hand, there is the somewhat culture-bound traditionalist's recoil from the prospective dislocations following from the emergence of new perspectives. By contrast, Joyce looks resolutely forward, at least by implication, to contemporary postures toward myth. His ironic and ultimately comic stance concerning myth, as well as everything else subject to language and the vision of the artist, divests him of the need to choose between two extremes. Instead, his comic spirit envelops myth as well as reality and points toward that sense of the infinitude of conceptual possibilities which writers such as Jorge Luis Borges, Samuel Beckett, and John Barth have developed as the quintessential artistic perspective of the late twentieth century. Lawrence, in effect, seeks a decision procedure for discriminating between radically opposed alternatives—between myth as constitutive human truth and myth as cultural and epistemological regression. Joyce transcends the issue by rooting reality for the artist in language which is subject to the ceaseless metamorphosing activity of the mind as generator and receptor. Nowhere are these two attitudes better developed and the theme of myth as cultural fact demanding a response no matter how ambivalent more clearly formulated in the cases of Lawrence and Joyce than in *The Plumed Serpent* and *Finnegans Wake*.

*

Critics have alternately called *The Plumed Serpent* Lawrence's best work and dismissed it as forced rhetoric and unconvincing make-believe. Such a range suggests at the least a stubborn, independent vitality which resists easy categorizing. And yet the novel's plot is far from obscure or complicated. Kate Leslie, the widow of an Irish patriot, has come to Mexico because she is convinced her marriage, Europe, and the first half of her life—she is forty—are all at an end. There she meets Don Ramón Carrasco and General Viedma, better known as Don Cipriano, both of whom exercise a powerful attraction on her by the impression of concentrated purpose and integrated personality they convey. Don Ramón interests her through his efforts to regenerate the mythicoreligious impulse in men, particularly his own people, while Don Cipriano holds out a strange, personal, sexual appeal to her. Kate's alternating approach to and withdrawal from both the men and the new religious life constitute the major part of the book. Contributory and conflicting influences in her debate over the viability of life amid these circumstances are provided by Ramón's first wife, Doña Carlota, and her death; the myths and rituals of Quetzalcoatl celebrated by Ramón and the peasants; the Church-instigated attacks on Ramón culminating in his attempted murder, which only Kate's intervention forestalls; her own acceptance of Cipriano as lover and husband; and the relationship between Ramón and Teresa, his second wife.

Most critics are indeed prepared to admire Lawrence's masterly descriptions, his evocation of sense of place and his handling of individual scenes, but many are also distressed by what they believe to be his humorless obsession with his plan, naïve at best and insane at worst, for saving Mexico and the world. Drawing conviction from Lawrence's own remark that "I do mean what Ramón means—for all of us," the latter regard *The Plumed Serpent* as preeminently a program novel.[2] But such a reduction of the novel to a program does an injustice to Lawrence by slighting and simplifying the degree to which myth and theme interpenetrate and condition one another. Granted his undoubted fascination with the ancient culture and religion of Mexico, granted also his obsession with the image of the savior—outlined in *Kangaroo* and amplified in *The Plumed Serpent*—and his

2. D. H. Lawrence, *The Letters*, ed. Aldous Huxley (New York, 1932), 640.

conviction of his own wisdom and rightness, still Lawrence was sensitive and sensible enough to recognize that none of these could be effectively embodied in any five- or ten-year plan. He indeed "mean[s] what Ramón means—for all of us." But what Ramón means, in terms of the novel, is a matter of image and symbol rather than ideology and program. Ramón signifies not a revived pantheon worshipped by adult children festooned with feathers and daubed with paint who indulge their playful exuberance through simpleminded foot stomping and unreflective throat cutting. Instead, he signifies the recognition of a cultural and personal dead end, of a crisis that spells the nullity of human life, and with this the individual's quest for a new and truly human mode of existence. While Ramón does attempt to proselytize among his own people, he also often falters, often doubts himself, and so recognizes that his role includes the exploratory and the tentative. For him, "the world had gone as far as it could go in the good, gentle, and loving direction, and anything further in that line meant perversity. So the time had come for the slow, great change to something else—what, he didn't know."[3]

Lawrence's central postulate for the novel is just this: for the world and man to proceed in their present courses will lead further and further away from the realization of their own essential natures. In *The Plumed Serpent* this leads inevitably to the question Ramón implicitly asks, "What should men do?" His answer, as we have seen, is, "Change to something else." To many this vague "something" has been taken to mean a refurbished "pre-Columbian religion." A meaning more in keeping with the main drift of Lawrence's mind appears in *Mornings in Mexico*: "One man can belong to one great way of consciousness only. He may even change from one way to another. But he cannot go both ways at once."[4] Man should change his "way of consciousness" if he would escape the perversity of his present existence. It is precisely this change that is charted dramatically in the course of the novel.

This, however, does not exhaust the relevance for *The Plumed Ser-*

3. D. H. Lawrence, *The Plumed Serpent* (London, 1950), 221. Subsequent references to this edition are hereafter cited parenthetically in the text as *PS*.

4. Eliseo Vivas, *D. H. Lawrence: The Failure and Triumph of Art* (Bloomington, 1964), 65; D. H. Lawrence, *Mornings in Mexico and Etruscan Places* (London, 1956), 46. Subsequent references to this edition are hereafter cited parenthetically in the text as *MM* or *EP* as appropriate.

pent of what Lawrence calls "the eternal paradox of human consciousness" (*MM*, 46). In the same essay he shows his awareness of the kind of problem a novel like *The Plumed Serpent* confronted him with. Pointing out the white man's sense of the difference between his and the Indian's consciousness and ways, he says: "There's only two things you can do. You can detest the insidious devil for having an utterly different way from our own great way. Or you can perform the mental trick, and fool yourself and others into believing that the befeathered and bedaubed darling is nearer to the true ideal gods than we are" (*MM*, 45). The second of these he calls "just bunk, and a lie"; the first is "quite natural" (*MM*, 45). In effect, he agrees with those critics and readers who regard the content of Ramón's Mexican New Deal as abhorrent lunacy. The inference to be drawn is that what Lawrence is doing in *The Plumed Serpent* is not what a great many of his critics have thought he was doing. But if he rejects the view that "the befeathered and bedaubed darling is nearer to the true ideal gods than we are," then what is he doing?

The answer is found in his response to "the eternal paradox of human consciousness." He insists that "the only thing you can do is to have a little Ghost inside you which sees both ways, or even many ways" (*MM*, 46). *The Plumed Serpent* is shaped by the perspective of "the little Ghost . . . which sees both ways," one version of which is myth's view of itself from the perspective of the modern world which is the only context in which it continues as an existent reality. It looks toward (but does not reproduce) the consciousness of the Indian with Cipriano and toward that of the white race with Kate Leslie. Out of this we get the alternating annihilation of forms of consciousness as first one then the other mode is uppermost. Kate's attraction to Cipriano signals both the death of her white rational consciousness and the extent of her understanding the Indian mythic consciousness. The mediate knowledge of the latter is achieved through the immediate experience of the former. And the exact reverse situation occurs when her repugnance toward the whole Mexican interlude floods her mind. At such moments she expresses as much scepticism, resistance, and outrage concerning Ramón's ideas and methods as do any of Lawrence's severer critics.

At the same time the pattern of oscillation is not the only thing perceived by the Ghost, who is both Lawrence and the attentive reader, both the mythic imagination and its sceptical other. The Ghost can see many ways and in *The Plumed Serpent* it also sees the evidence of Ramón's change from one way of consciousness to another—here not from white to Indian or from modern to ancient but from anthropocentric to theocentric. In the process, Lawrence has him demonstrate a point made in *Mornings in Mexico*, namely, that "man, little man, with his consciousness and his will, must both submit to the great origin-powers of his life, and conquer them" (*MM*, 77). Unlike Kate, Ramón is not pictured in the novel as undergoing his change of consciousness; it has already happened before the book begins. What this change, with its twin processes of submission and conquest, consists of is indicated obliquely and symbolically through his actions in the novel. Here the dances, hymns, rituals, and myths which bulk so large in his life frequently obscure their own real significance. Actually they delineate the form, not the content, of the human quest for a way of facing the crisis of history. As Ramón says to Kate, "'Quetzalcoatl is to me only the symbol of the best a man may be, in the next days'" (*PS*, 292). This form is one of movement through trials, tests, and mortal combats to ultimate exaltation, which suggests that it is a complex image of a psychic journey of adventure, exploration, and attainment. What Ramón is portrayed as doing publicly is a narrative emblematic of what he has already done in the privacy of his own consciousness. It is so projected to provide a proximate model for others, like Kate, to follow in their own interior worlds: "'Quetzalcoatl is just a living word, for these people, no more. All I want them to do is to find the beginnings of the way to their own manhood, their own womanhood'" (*PS*, 224–25). That Lawrence saw his own use of primitive myth and ritual in this functional light is suggested by a remark in *Etruscan Places* only a few years later: "Try as you may, you can never make the mass of men throb with full awakenedness. They cannot be more than a little aware. So you must give them symbols, ritual and gesture, which will fill their bodies with life up to their own full measure" (*EP*, 51). It is substantially this observation which *The Plumed Serpent* dramatizes with its eclectic freight of mythic symbolism. Indeed, the heavy stress upon "ritual and gesture" underlines the extent of modern man's inability to "throb with full awakenedness."

In other words, Ramón "means" not so much a revival of pre-Columbian religion as the attainment of an integrated personality through exposure to a serious interest in the cultural implications of myth and ritual. Such a personality recognizes a power greater than the self but rooted in the individual. Only with such a personality is man able to explore successfully the boundaries of the acceptable, of the civilized, and perhaps even of the right itself. For Lawrence—as Kate Leslie testifies—Ramón's achievement is not the creation of a cult but the scrupulous fulfilling of a rite of self-knowledge in which doubt, hesitation, and despair play as significant a part as personal conviction or doctrinal certitude.

Ramón's goal, as well as Lawrence's, is in the purest sense a religious humanism in which ancient myth and ritual form the means rather than the end. As Carlota, his pious wife, complains, he has rejected traditional modes of worship: "He says he wants to make a new connection between the people and God. He says himself, God is always God. But man loses his connection with God" (*PS*, 177). There are, of course, as Ramón repeatedly asserts, various ways, racial as well as personal, of reestablishing the connection, but whatever the way the end is the recovery of meaning and wholeness for the individual and his fragmented society. And because he himself seems to have succeeded in doing so, his presence evokes a desire in others " 'to find the beginnings of the way to their own manhood, their own womanhood. Men are not yet men in full, and women are not yet women' " (*PS*, 225). Recovering a sense of one's own deepest nature is the initial step in breaking out of the querulous echo chamber of human isolation and in answering Kate's prayer: "Let me still believe in some human contact" (*PS*, 112). Because the way of reestablishing these contacts, personal, sexual, and religious, is largely exploratory, the thematic pattern of *The Plumed Serpent* is organized around a quest motif which, surprisingly enough, recalls that elaborated for contemporary culture by *The Waste Land*.

Like Eliot's seminally archetypal poem, Lawrence's novel juxtaposes past and present, moves from the satiric to the mythic mode of expression, progresses from despair and frustration to a tremulous hope, and attempts to recover the religious sense of the past in order to ensure its revival in the present. And though Lawrence introduces certain additional symbols of his own, he begins with the modern wasteland, Mexico, a place of rocks, heat, drought, and above all death, a death made "ragged, squalid, vulgar, without even the passion of its own mystery" (*PS*, 53). Eliot's crowd flowing over London Bridge is re-created in Kate Leslie's vision of the streets, busy with the frantic activity of automobiles and omnibuses, "where the natives in white cotton clothes and sandals and big hats linger like heavy ghosts in the street" (*PS*, 54). Mexico is, as Kate keeps repeating with monotonous regularity, the "heavy continent of dark-souled death" (*PS*, 54) at once oppressive, sinister, and threatening. That this is not to be taken as simply an expression of Kate's personal animus is indicated by Ramón's awareness of the same ghostly crowds: "I see a skeleton walking ahead of a great number of people, waving a black banner with *Viva la Muerte!* written in large white letters. *Long live Death!*" (*PS*, 43).

Yet it is to Mexico that Kate, Owen, and Villiers—literally going south in the winter—are driven by their own restlessness. Significantly, all three reject the shaded section of the stadium in order to sit in "our 'Sun,' which isn't going to shine a great deal after all" (*PS*, 9). And it is because of a sudden shower of rain that Kate meets Cipriano and through him Ramón. Leaving Owen and Villiers at the bullfight, "picking over the garbage of sensations, and gobbling it up like carrion birds" (*PS*, 29) and later refusing to speak to the polyglot Pole with his easy assumption of familiarity, she demonstrates that she has consciously rejected that frenetic search for novel sensations which galvanizes the dead into a spasmodic illusion of life.

In Mrs. Norris' garden Ramón reinforces her conviction that "she had heard the *consummatum est* of her own spirit, [that] it was finished in a kind of death agony" (*PS*, 53–54). Like Eliot's protagonist in the hyacinth garden, she is neither living nor dead, and she knows nothing. But she is prepared to follow Ramón. The nature of their quest is again rendered in terms reminiscent of Eliot. The latter's roots and branches growing out of stony rubbish are matched by Ramón's assertion: "'All that matters to me are the roots that reach down beyond all destruction. The roots and the life are there. What else it needs is the word, for the forest to begin to rise again'" (*PS*, 86).

This vision with its promise of new life is instrumental in Kate's decision to separate herself from Owen and Villiers, to remain in Mexico, and to take the first step of her journey, that from Guadalajara to Sayula. At this point, she and Ramón become complementary figures, illuminating the dual sex of Tiresias and the dual role of Eliot's protagonist, since as Kate painfully discovers, "We are all fragments. And at the best, halves" (*PS*, 416). Ramón's is essentially the way of action; Kate's is the way of comprehension, of the critical intelligence that follows upon the act and attempts to understand it. In this respect she is totally dependent on Ramón; but insofar as she is also, at least potentially, Malintzi, the earth goddess, the bearer of the sacred mystery of sex, she has her own active part to play in the quest. Both then simultaneously indicate the way and suggest its goals. Between them they establish the magnetic needle of *The Plumed Serpent* oscillating between the creative and the critical, the mythic and the satiric.

In his role as protagonist Ramón is equally concerned with the destruction of the old and the creation of the new which, however, finds its source in the prehistorical, primeval condition of man. On the one hand, such a procedure is vulnerable to the charge made by Joachim, Kate's second husband: "'evil was the lapsing back to old life-modes that have been surpassed in us'" (*PS*, 147). On the other hand, there is Kate's admission: "'We must go back to pick up old threads. We must take up the old, broken impulse that will connect us with the mystery of the cosmos again, now we are at the end of our own tether'" (*PS*, 147). Taken literally and historically, Ramón is indeed engaged in an absurd attempt to regain a paradise lost. But regarded mythically and symbolically, the paradise he conceives is eternally present though overlaid with the impedimenta of a mechanical, rationalistic culture. These two views connect when it is recognized that this paradise is present but unattainable save as an image held in the minds of author and public alike. And in the last analysis Ramón is concerned not with a lost culture but with a lost manhood.

As his initial step Ramón divests himself of his immediate social identity. The Spanish *hacendado* defined through his old loyalties to custom, class, tradition, Church, and family is painfully transformed into the god-man figure of Quetzalcoatl. His wife and two sons either unable or unwilling to follow, Ramón leaves behind. Impassively he watches Carlota call upon the Christian God to punish his blasphemy and, incidentally, vindicate her own righteousness. Equally impassively he accepts the news of her death as well as his own complete estrangement from his sons. Thus it is clearly his own experience that gives meaning to the ancient ritual participated in by Cipriano and Kate as they don the robes of the initiate: "Leave no thread nor thing that can touch you from the past. The past is finished. It is the new twilight" (*PS*, 351). Similarly, Teresa, Ramón's second wife, literally abandons her own past to become a new woman.

More sweeping since it transcends his personal life is Ramón's destruction of the images of the dead gods. In it is symbolized the divestiture of his spiritual identity. Once more the ritual itself is preceded by his personal experience. In his interview with the bishop he attempts to explain that "God is One God, but the peoples speak varying languages, and each needs its own prophet to speak with its own tongue" (*PS*, 283). Failing to do so, he dares to reject the ancient authority of the Church and to put Christ with the worn-out foreign saviors. In a curiously impressive chapter entitled "Auto Da Fé," amid the lamentations of the people, "exclaiming, half in dismay, half in joyful lust of destruction," the sacred images are carried out of the church, transported across the lake, and committed to fire until "all that was left was a fierce glow of red coals of wood, with a medley of half-fused iron" (*PS*, 307). Thus Ramón's own break with the Church is followed by the ritual celebration of it as the personal becomes the group experience.

Since Ramón's own quest for the integrated personality is completed before the novel opens, not all of its stages are presented either dramatically or through narrative. Some are inferred from other events of a similar order. Thus, it seems probable that in addition to his social and spiritual divestiture, Ramón underwent a spiritual transformation of a far-reaching order that made him something quite other than he had been. The essentials of this experience can be inferred from the ritual prayer he engages in at the beginning of Chapter XI. The prayer's aim apparently is to achieve that state which was responsible for his original spiritual transformation. Basically this is an elemental contact with "the other strength" (*PS*, 181) resident in the deepest reaches of his own psyche.

It is because of this contact, renewed through prayer, that Ramón is capable of leading the spiritual divestiture of his people. His role in the destruction of the old gods shows clearly that his quest is intimately connected with the fate of his people. Like Eliot's protagonist, he is simultaneously the Fisher King and the Grail Knight, father and son, savior and saved, a duality resolved in the god-man figure of Quetzalcoatl. His acceptance of this name and role marks his assumption of a new spiritual identity, that of the divine leader, which implies a new social identity as well. Yet he is no messiah with a mystique of his own perfection slickly programming the next move and imperturbably grinding up the opposition. Aware of the primacy of the individual's saving transformation, he is constantly tempted to deny his people: "I had better go into the desert and take my way all alone, to the Star where at last I have my wholeness, holiness. The way of the anchorites and the men who went into the wilderness to pray. For surely my soul is craving for her consummation, and I am weary of the thing men call life" (PS, 271). Preoccupied with his own quest and indifferent to their happiness or material well-being, he confesses at times to detesting and despising the masses.

Yet as savior and spiritual leader it is his function to restore life to the dead, who depend on a close personal contact. To save them is part of saving himself. His submission to contact with them is an index of the control and integration he has achieved in his own being. In one sense, Kate, Cipriano, Teresa, and the anonymous natives who participate in or simply observe the rituals of Quetzalcoatl are held by Ramón's personal magnetism. Kate makes sporadic attempts to leave Mexico despite her growing involvement with Cipriano only to admit that "perhaps Ramón is the only one I couldn't quite escape from, because he really touches me somewhere inside" (PS, 219). Even Cipriano, as he explains to Kate, has certain reservations: "'I believe in him, too. Not in your way, but in mine. I tell you why. Because he has the power to compel me. If he hadn't the power to *compel* me, how should I believe?'" (PS, 219). The possibility of Cipriano's betrayal noted by Kate is matched by her fear for Ramón's safety since she recognizes that the Mexicans take more satisfaction in destroying heroes than in temporarily raising them high. Ramón, then, must serve as the vulnerable bridge at once connecting and separating God and man. Evidence of weakness in him would mean collapse of the others. Indeed his success consists in preserving his own inviolate manhood even as he leads the others to recover their own. Only if they become his equals and therefore independent of him can they meet in the meaningful communion of the Morning Star.

Just as the other stages in Ramón's integrative quest have had both private and public expressions, so does the final one. His personal ambivalence and ultimate acquiescence to the people's revival is matched by the dominant mood permeating the community as the novel ends.

Again as in Eliot, the mood is one not of achievement and fulfillment but of partial vision and uncertain hope. The ruins of civilization are admitted, the wasteland is behind Ramón, Cipriano, and Kate, but the promised land, "the peace that passeth understanding," has not yet been realized in society at large. In the ceremonial robes, the dances and rituals of Quetzalcoatl, Ramón has provided a ritual of worship; in the hymns he has offered the symbols of belief; in his own person he has revived the dying god. But the last line of the Fourth Hymn to Quetzalcoatl speaks only of hope not triumph: "Wait! Only wait! Little by little it all shall come upon you" (PS, 278). And Kate's last words, which are also the last words of the novel, are simultaneously a plea and a confession of weakness: "'You won't let me go!'" (PS, 476). Clearly for Kate as for the others, only the beginnings of the way have been explored.

Complementing Ramón, and in one sense dominating the novel, is Kate Leslie. Through her, Lawrence reveals the fragmented personality, the neuroses-haunted ego seeking to become an integrated human being. In Ramón we see the goal as achieved; in Kate, the struggle toward that achievement. In her frustration and intense nervous irritability she is reminiscent of Eliot's Belladonna, the Lady of the Rocks, the lady of situations. A widow, she has remarried; her two children no longer need her and her past has given her much experience but little fulfillment. Closely associated with her is the figure of the temptress, whom Lawrence calls "the Aphrodite of the foam: the seething, frictional, ecstatic Aphrodite" (PS, 451). Vaguely contemptuous of her husband and his ideas, she has yet used him to achieve her own sexual gratification. And though she frequently thinks of Cipriano as an absurd little Mexican general, she is also physically aware of him and excited by his desire. Finally, there is no question of her undoubted attraction to Ramón, intensified by his masculine elusiveness, or of her tendency to see Teresa as an unworthy though successful rival. All of these are significant factors in her complementing Ramón by playing the sceptical, questioning, satiric role to his mythic one. Her resistance to Ramón and what he seems to stand for is due in large part to his "religion's" forcing her to restructure her sexual drives. Thus in the end she sees the full horror of her role—the conqueress, the powerful love-woman, the insatiable grimalkin playing "with love and intimacy as a cat with a mouse. In the end, they quickly ate up the love mouse, then trotted off with a full belly and a voluptuous sense of power" (*PS*, 469).

Kate's ambivalence with respect to Ramón, Cipriano, and Mexico itself can thus be charted in terms of a sexual dichotomy in her own nature. She is enough of a woman to recognize her own incompleteness, to acknowledge Ramón's and Cipriano's force and power over her; yet she is also honest enough to admit that "even when she had [a man], in her heart of hearts she despised him, as she despised the dog and the cat" (*PS*, 268). In brief, she wants both to conquer and to yield. Instinctively, she responds to the religion of Quetzalcoatl and the Morning Star where opposites promise to be reconciled; rationally, however, she repudiates both as a signal instance of masculine perverseness and primitive claptrap. It is indeed "as if she had two selves: one, a new one, which belonged to Cipriano and to Ramón, and which was her sensitive, desirous self; the other hard and finished, accomplished, belonging to her mother, her children, England, her whole past" (*PS*, 459).

The emergence of that self which belongs to Ramón and Cipriano has been persuasively traced by others who note in Kate's progression from Guadalajara to Sayula to Ramón's hacienda the familiar pattern of initiation. Not without considerable danger to herself she passes through the stages of separation, transition, and incorporation, leaving her old life as Kate Leslie behind and beginning a new one as Malintzi, consort of Huitzilopochtli. Equally important is the fact that these three stages are presented in sexual terms. Initially Kate rejects that perverted form of sex described by Villiers: " 'But you *should* have seen all those men rehearsing in the bedroom, throwing their arms about, and the toreador lying on the bed like Venus with a fat cigar, listening to her lovers' " (*PS*, 28). To this she adds her own observation of the flappers, slim and charming but with "their dark faces curiously macabre in the heavy make-up; approximating to white, but the white of a clown or a corpse" (*PS*, 123). The equation of death and perversion is completed by the fifís, who are far more ladylike than the flappers and far more nervous. Nor, in retrospect, does her own marriage to Joachim or Ramón's to Carlota offer any more promise of fulfillment or meaning.

The period of transition is indicated in Kate's uneasy relationship with Cipriano. To guide her are the omens of Ramón's unsuccessful marriage to Carlota, destroyed by Carlota's insistent will and possessiveness, and his marriage to Teresa, apparently dependent on her willingness to yield and serve. For a time she sees Cipriano as both her savior and her executioner. The peace he brings her is accompanied by "this darkness on her breast, the heaviness of this strange gloom. Die before dying, and pass away whilst still beneath the sun" (PS, 263). Hence she wavers, accepting Cipriano as a lover but rejecting him as a husband, marrying him under the aegis of Quetzalcoatl but refusing a civil ceremony. It is with considerable difficulty that she emerges as Malintzi, herself possessing the mystery of sex, recognizing herself to be reciprocal, as dependent on Cipriano as he is on her. But like the music of Quetzalcoatl, what she learns plunges "straight through to the soul, the most ancient and everlasting soul of all men, where alone can the human family assemble in immediate contact" (PS, 135). Thus, groping and uncertain, she attains the knowledge that Teresa has apparently intuited without effort, that "men and women had incomplete selves, made up of bits assembled together loosely and somewhat haphazard" (PS, 114). In recognizing Cipriano, Kate finds her sexual nature just as in recognizing Ramón she finds her spiritual self.

But clearly, as Lawrence himself admits, Kate's emergent self as Malintzi is frequently subjected to the nagging of the past and of reason. As the product of her age and her society, Kate is not only the lady of situations but the representative of the European critical intelligence. However flawed by the demands of her own ego, her will, her sense of her own unique individuality, she is still capable of watching people "as one reads the pages of a novel, with a certain disinterested amusement. She was never *in* any society: too Irish, too wise" (PS, 44). The resultant dichotomy between involvement and detachment is the cultural counterpart to her sexual ambivalence. On the one hand, she is aware that "the almost deathly mysticism of the aboriginal Celtic or Iberian people lay at the bottom of her soul. It was a residue of memory, something that lives on from the pre-Flood world, and cannot be killed" (PS, 444). On the other hand, she knows herself to belong "too much to the old world of Europe, she could not, could not make herself over so quickly" (PS, 450).

Exercising her highly developed sense of taste and discrimination, Kate fancies herself the unerring judge of America, Mexico, and, most significantly, of Ramón himself. For though she recognizes her attraction to Ramón both as a man and a possible savior, she yet resists every step of the way, criticizing, at times joining forces with the pious Carlota, at times openly sceptical and contemptuous of what he is trying to do. Thus, her reactions serve as an ironic critical counterpoint to Ramón's actions, juxtaposing the fragmentation of the satiric against the timeless and mythic quest for wholeness. Without Kate's critical faculty and her resistance, her transformation into Malintzi would be singularly lacking in interest. For, in effect, it is dependent on the compelling power of Ramón and Cipriano. It is not of her own choice and will that she becomes Malintzi. On the other hand, her desperate efforts to achieve integration, to reconcile body and mind and to achieve a viable mode of human existence elicit a sympathetic response from the reader, who finds mankind's frustration mirrored in her vacillation.

In brief, the three stages of Kate's sexual initiation are counterpointed by a shift in her consciousness from the rational to the intuitive and in Lawrence's style from the satiric to the mythopoeic. In both cases, the transitional period is the one most emphasized. Initially, *The Plumed Serpent* is dominated by Kate's European point of view. Her Irish self, the part that is soon to be attracted by and sympathetic to Ramón is quiescent except for infrequent flashes when she recognizes the latent power in individual Indians. The prevailing mood is bitingly satiric and Kate herself is in a state of intense irritability rising into uncontrollable fury though she thinks of herself as essentially a good-tempered, tolerant person. Savagely she lashes out at the expatriate Americans who are "coldly and unscrupulously sensational" (*PS*, 17) as well as smugly superior and self-righteous. With equal savagery, she finds repellent all things Mexican, their politics, their culture, their art, because they make her feel irritable and because, in some indefinable sense, they seem to threaten her. The natives are a lot of noisy, dirty, vulgar, debased, untrustworthy Mexicans and whatever flashes of strength and poetry they reveal are immediately discounted by Kate as she gathers fresh material for her original estimate.

Her distaste and Lawrence's satire are concentrated in the fiasco of the bullfight. Ostensibly a symbol of honor, courage, and integrity, the bullfight is reduced through Lawrence's acid description to the sickening and prolonged torture of bull and horses, the mock-heroics of the picadors, and the debauchery of the toreador languidly receiving the adoration of his fans. The essentials in this contrast are: "She had come for a gallant show. This she had paid to see. Human cowardice and beastliness, a smell of blood, a nauseous whiff of bursten bowels!" (*PS*, 16). The bullfight stands as the symbol of Mexico's degeneracy and Kate's repudiation of it. Other details serve merely to support and reinforce this impression. Together they result in Kate's rejection of all things human until she can claim: "'The longer I live the more loathsome the human species becomes to me'" (*PS*, 26). Clearly in all of this we have her version of Ramón's earlier divestiture of his social identity.

In the second stage, that of transition, Kate's rational and intuitive faculties come into conflict. Extending from her taking a house in Sayula to her marriage to Cipriano, this stage, in effect, dominates the novel. While she herself increasingly attempts to make those changes in her sexual life which will transform Mrs. Leslie into Malintzi, her attitude continually vacillates. At one moment she remembers the love she has for England, home, and the old familiar rituals of Christmas; at another she finds herself admitting the power and beauty of Mexico. Her memories of Joachim conflict with her growing attraction to Cipriano and indeed to Ramón. The same attraction-repulsion can be endlessly documented in her response to Carlota and Teresa, to her servants, to the natives, indeed to everything with which she is confronted.

Corresponding to the bullfight in the first stage, the attack on Ramón focuses and illuminates her attitude. Lawrence makes no effort to mitigate the realistic horror of death. Stabbed by Ramón, one of the bandits dies, "while blood shot out like a red projectile; there was a strange sound like a soda-syphon, a ghastly bubbling, one final terrible convulsion from the loins of the stricken man" (*PS*, 316). Seven men are dead and Kate finds their death sickening as well as horrifying. Yet their death through her intervention has meant Ramón's continued life. For the first time death is not gratuitous and without significance. Though the violence is no less repulsive than at the bullfight, Kate herself is no longer merely a spectator. Compelled perhaps only by her attraction to Ramón, she nevertheless accepts violence and death as an integral part of life.

Kate's shuttling between attraction and repulsion finds its counterpart in the interplay of the satiric and mythopoeic. Rationally Kate is still the irritable spectator, claiming that she "would die rather than be mixed up in it any more. Horrible, really, both Ramón and Cipriano" (PS, 397). Persistently she mocks the identification of Cipriano with Huitzilopochtli and herself with Malintzi. Cynically she views Ramón's and Teresa's contentment as that of the complacent self-satisfied male and the complacent, slavish harem girl. Nothing is sacred, nothing immune to the attacks of Kate's self-lacerating intelligence.

But beneath conscious awareness and conscious criticism "away inside her a little light was burning, the light of her innermost soul. Sometimes it sank and seemed extinct. Then it was there again. Ramón had lighted it. And once it was lighted the world went hollow and dead, all the world-activities were empty weariness to her" (PS, 328). To fan the flickering light, the full weight of Lawrence's rhetoric is used, rising from the measured beat of the ceremonial dances and the hypnotic rhythms of Quetzalcoatl's Hymns to the mythopoeic descriptions of the initiation ceremonies of Cipriano, the execution of Ramón's attackers, and the marriage of Kate and Cipriano.

Yet even so Kate's resistance is not wholly overcome, nor is her critical faculty extinguished. The third stage in her quest for integration is emergent rather than achieved. At times the conflict within her is transcended and she finds what she herself refers to as "the peace which passeth understanding." Thus in brief moments of intuition she does comprehend and accept what Ramón means. For instance, she becomes one with humanity, her individuality, race, and background submerged as she participates in the dance of Quetzalcoatl or listens to his hymns. More important, by finding her own womanhood she is able to overcome her dislike of people, especially men, and to accept Cipriano "finally and forever as the stranger in whose presence she lived" (PS, 453). For her this is dramatically imaged in the sight of him bathing in the lake at sunrise. This vision of what is composed, luminous, and unconscious is a projection of that communion experience of integration which is taking place within her. Significantly she achieves this experience only after Cipriano has led her to subdue her desire to conquer and so to submit herself to the mystery of sex, a "mystery greater than the individual. The individual hardly counted" (PS, 162). Together they become Huitzilopochtli and Malintzi, the ever-virginal. But time and again Kate relapses in greater or lesser measure into her old, critical, irritable self. The ghost of European rationalism and scepticism dies hard and apparently Kate never fully achieves the integration of self that she wishes for and for which Ramón is the model.

The Plumed Serpent, then, seems to end on a note of irresolution. It is as if Lawrence himself recognizes both the rational and the intuitive, the realistic and mythic modes of consciousness, and gives each its due, but their fusion lies beyond his vision. Yet Kate's final scene with Ramón, read closely, suggests the reverse. Always Kate has suffered herself to be led and compelled while reserving the right to judge and criticize. Her final plea, quite consistently, is to have Ramón and Cipriano relieve her of the burden of choice—in short, to make her stay. It is Ramón who penetrates the subterfuge: "'It is you who don't want. . . . You needn't commit yourself to *us*. Listen to your own best desire'" (PS, 475). This she interprets as a total rejection, qualified only by Cipriano's desire to keep her in Mexico at any cost. What Kate is looking for is a savior who will save her in spite of herself, who will accept all responsibility. Ramón is to become not the guide but the master; in this way the authoritarian icon, whether secular or sacred, would indeed be reincarnated. But Ramón quite rightly refuses the final temptation to his role, that of winning converts by fiat. Kate, as Malintzi, is herself her own way, the bearer of the mystery, but she is also ultimately responsible for making the choice and finding the way. As Ramón told her very early in their acquaintance, "'The miracle is always there . . . for the man who can pass his hand through to it, to take it'" (PS, 72). In sum, the existence of the miracle and the necessity of the individual's reaching for it are together "what Ramón means—for all of us."

*

Where Lawrence and Joyce, The Plumed Serpent and Finnegans Wake, converge is in their conviction of the centrality of human freedom and of the necessity of self-determination in its attainment. Where they diverge is in their treatment of myth as theme. The former's authorial attitude is protagonistic in that it is through the redaction of a displaced quest myth that the freedom to rely on the individual self is established. To tell the story of Kate and Quetzalcoatl is to experience both the validity and the temptations of myth. Joyce's authorial attitude, on the other hand, is more nearly spectatorial in that both he and his reader pull free from the ceaseless round of existence in which the characters of the metamyth of the dying god subsist. Joyce achieves a vantage point of imaginative emancipation from the linearity of human existence and the cyclic course of mythic narrative alike through a rapt encyclopedic concentration on the fact of change and the theme of metamorphosis. For him, myth becomes less a metaphor embracing psychic integration than a metaphor for metaphor itself. In the process the solemn magic of metaphor's symbolizing activity is matched by the comic absurdity with which it invests its own infinitude of relational capacities. Out of this methodological conjunction there emerges the poignant hilarity of *Finnegans Wake* that results from the adaptation of the dying god myth, with all its tragic associations, to the sphere of comic immortality.

One cannot read very far in *Finnegans Wake* without realizing that its allusions embrace the spectrum of human interests in a way exceeding even the encyclopedism of *Ulysses*. What this expansion of allusion reveals in part is Joyce's adaptation of primitive views of language, an adaptation that is designed to render both the mystery and magic of the artist's sense of reality. As Joyce came to see with increasing clarity, the artist's reality resides in language; for the literary imagination, the phenomenological is the verbal. And as early man's notion of language stresses, the act of naming is integrally connected with identification and hence with identity. Throughout the *Wake* Joyce indefatigably names the elements of his universe but in his own, not the world's, language, which admits of no principle of exclusion in the act of classifying. Consequently, the "naming" becomes a way of affirming the vegetative, natural world as human and vice versa. HCE, for instance, is told that "your hair grows wheater."[5] And later his demise is set in a ritual context of cycles of sorrow and resurrection that makes him vegetative as well as human: "on the bunk of our breadwinning lies the corpse of our seedfather" (*FW*, 55 : 7—8). Moments later touristlike watchers of the cyclical contest of life find it equated with a symbol of the deity as fertility figure: "their convoy wheeled encirculingly abound the gigantig's lifetree, our fireleaved loverlucky blomsterbohm" (*FW*, 55 : 26—28).

Such instances obviously testify to Joyce's use of the dying and re-

5. James Joyce, *Finnegans Wake* (New York, 1947), 26 : 8. For convenience, line references are included following the colon. Subsequent references to this edition are hereafter cited parenthetically in the text as *FW*.

viving god as a symbol of vegetative fertility. But they do more. Such linguistic matters as the fusion of "white hair" and "wheat" or of "corpse" and "crops" indicate that in the verbal realm of the artist, the act of allusion is from word to word rather than from word to thing. This means that language wholly encompasses the reality of the *Wake* so that the character of the one is the character of the other. And in Joyce's *Wake* language, the dominant feature is metamorphosis whereby the words, persons, and objects of one reality level distinguishably merge with all others. Thus, the metaphors of Joyce's last book are essentially total rather than partial and its allusions dynamic patterns of interlocking narratives. In short, the evolution of this theme from *Stephen Hero* to *Finnegans Wake* marks Joyce's lifelong search for artistic freedom. The imaginative strictures imposed by Irish Catholicism and its verbal codification of reality yield first to *A Portrait*'s heightened awareness of the human relevance of the phenomenological, then to its crystallization in the language of comparative folklore with *Ulysses*, and finally to the active, achieved awareness of language itself as the artist's total freedom wherein he is both creature and creator. The parabola is from a language of limits and fixity to a language of limitlessness and metamorphic fluidity.

This attitude to language is important in the *Wake* not only as establishing the final stage in the development of one of Joyce's lifelong themes. It also is the methodological or technical basis of his ritualizing narrative into contemporary myths that provide archetypal actions appropriate to the archetypal characters originally created in *Ulysses*. With this the ordinary demarcation between principal narratives that lead to allegory is broken. Tristan does not remain a figure of pathos immured in a *Liebestod* of surpassing beauty, nor do Tammuz and the other dying and reviving gods continue to arouse ritual grief, religious awe, and historical curiosity. The former is spied on by salacious old voyeurs and the latter are continually urged to lie down, go away, and cease disturbing the social peace. The profound becomes trivial, the refined and tender are transformed into the vulgar and coarse, and the religious tragedy segues into a continually expanding human comedy. Motivating this dynamic interfusion of narrative levels is the principle of thematic and verbal metamorphosis. This principle is, however, more than just a means of relation and transition between narrative forms. So sustained is its deployment and so conscious its manipulation that ultimately it emerges as the ground or sustaining narrative form of all the others. That is, the chief way of telling a story (or *the* story if you wish) in *Finnegans Wake* proves to be the metamorphic manner in which identity of narrator or characters is unspecifiable by exclusion because the sustaining metaphor of the work as a whole is metamorphosis dynamically actualizing itself. As a result, this principle generates its own kind of hero who embodies Joyce's tireless quest for human freedom and the true nature of the artist.

When metamorphosis ruthlessly dictates the entire action—as it does in dream (though not in nightmare)—the manner is inevitably comic in its essential nature. The absurdities of transformations and sudden, unexpected collocations in this form testify not to the meaninglessness of the existentialist universe but to the joyous delight of uncontrollable creative proliferation of scenes, images, characters at once new and familiar. Since the metamorphic impetus is toward comedy, laughter, and the incredible and since the other narrative heroes (whether cultural, romantic, resurrectionary, or sacrificial) are victims imprisoned in their particular natures and solemnities, it follows that the fundamental Joycean hero is the mock or comic hero. As such, he is not, however, separate from other types of hero. That would polarize the narrative levels into hypostatized extremes of the somber and frivolous, which is, of course, precisely what Joyce is seeking to avoid in *Finnegans Wake*. Hence the mock hero as an archetype is less a distinct figure than an informing spirit and function of the other heroes. He is what makes Tristan more than the mournfully suffering figure of Wagner or the nobly romantic creature of Bédier. Invested as he is with the mock hero's metamorphic properties, in *Finnegans Wake* he becomes:

> the spry young spark
> That'll tread her and wed her and bed her and red her
> Without ever winking the tail of a feather
> And that's how that chap's going to make his money and
> mark! (*FW*, 383:23–26)

In fusing death and mortality with the countervailing powers of life and fertility, Joyce closely imitates those dying gods who always experience revival or resurrection. At the same time he does add one distinctive and major facet to the pattern. The revival of HCE, as with primitive man's dying gods, is heralded by and indeed equated with signs of vegetative growth and flourishing, with the movements of the sun in its course and the actions of the moon, with the seasonal movement out of winter and into spring and summer, and with the exercise of vigorous, protracted, and unabashed human sexual intercourse. To this, Joyce adds the most obvious and the most touchingly human image of awakening from sleep. However much the other images and actions attest to it, for Joyce resurrection is first and foremost waking up, though to be sure in doing so man is not thought to forget or ignore the world of sleep and dreams. Just as waking is integrally related to sleeping, so in *Finnegans Wake* is revival or resurrection interwoven with death. This explains why Joyce found the dying and reviving god, with his swift ritual transformations, so apt and full a metaphor for HCE's archetypal condition as the quintessential human creature.

A marvelously condensed instance of this metaphor, which also bears on the book's mythopoeic use of metaphor as metamorphosis, comes at the very beginning. The guide on the tour of the museum points out the prominent items and among them draws attention to one of the god's most seminal images: "This is mistletropes" (*FW*, 9:19). Its association with the slaying of the Norse dying god Balder is obvious as is its identification with fertility and life. What is important here, and unique among the varied forms taken by the mistletoe image, is the assertion of its nature as a trope. The expression calls attention to the dual significance traditionally attached to the plant but in a particularly mimetic or ritualistic manner. A trope is a verbal displacement of the literal that energizes or gives life through language to the object or image. By calling it "mistletropes," Joyce similarly reflects the protective and life-conferring properties resident in the death-dealing object of myth while drawing attention to its capacities for metamorphosis. In addition, by identifying it with the verbal realm as well as the natural world of objects, he suggests that, in a century assured of the unreality of magical powers or supernatural properties in things, the metamorphic power to encompass life as well as death lies in language. Thus, the mistletoe is a trope in itself and calling it one results in making it, as it were, a trope of a trope. In substance, this is in miniature or condensed fashion precisely what *Finnegans Wake* as a whole constitutes, a metaphor or trope for the ceaselessly metamorphic actions of life itself.

As if to drive home the point that life's ever-changing pattern is not something dependent on human will or assertions, Joyce begins the *Wake*, as Frazer does *The Golden Bough*, with the significance of trees for man's thrust toward revival of a ceaseless order: "The oaks of ald now they lie in peat yet elms leap where askes lay. Phall if you but will, rise you must: and none so soon either shall the pharce for the nunce come to a setdown secular phoenish" (*FW*, 4:14−17). Influenced by German scholars like Wilhelm Mannhardt, Frazer stresses the vegetative basis of primitive religion and finds one of its earliest expressions in the tree worship he traces throughout Europe. He also stresses that as a result the oak was particularly singled out for worship as a sacred creature by many races including the Celts. As time went on, however, these forests gradually dwindled and with them the worship of the oak. For Joyce, this is ample grounds for imaginative extrapolation so that though the ancient oaks have been reduced to peat and ashes, their vegetative natures persist as growing elms replace dwindling ash trees.

Whether Joyce's botanical theory is accurate or not, he clearly is impressed by two things. The first is the hold trees and vegetation in general had on the primitive reaches of the imagination and the other is the cyclical character of nature and myth alike. Oak, ash, and elm are all forms of the dying and reviving HCE and hence as sacred in *Finnegans Wake* as in primitive religion. The reason for this in both cases lies in their reproductive capacity, which though it is, as it were, a free disposition and so carries overtones of religious sin and downfall, also carries with it the natural imperative to flourish and rise again. Enshrined in this religiosexual metaphor of the course of organic life is the comic release from the essentially tragic notion of finality and termination or "phoenish." What is a farce for the moment is also a perennial comedy because grounded in recurrence, whether of trees or of mankind. Because tragedy is essentially religious and because nature and man are unable to do other than ceaselessly repeat themselves, the drama of man and his environment is irremediably both comic and secular in character. And for such a plot of endless proliferation in a variety of forms both human and vegetative steadfastly viewed by the secular human eye, Joyce could have taken no more instructive model than the narratives of myth.

Later in the first chapter when HCE is being urged to lie quiet and accept his death, one of the things he is told is that his double is already active and alive in the shape of a fish and flourishing like a tree. The fish image obviously aligns HCE both with Finn MacCool and Christ, but there are also other associations as well. *The Golden Bough*, for instance, pays almost as much attention to the reverential attitude of ancient man toward the fish as it does to the tree. In doing so, Frazer is at some pains wherever possible to underscore the parallels between the primitive and Christian responses. Much of the time Joyce follows this lead, working many comic arabesques on the *ichthys* as communion symbol. At this particular point, however, he follows more than the structural ironies of anthropological counterpointing. The double of HCE is reported to have come in a boat which is described in some detail: "this archipelago's first visiting schooner, with a wicklowpattern waxenwench at her prow for a figurehead, the deadsea dugong updipdripping from his depths, and has been repreaching himself like a fishmummer these siktyten years ever since" (*FW*, 29:22–26).

The image of the "deadsea dugong" is both so unusual and so accurate a figure that it seems unlikely Joyce was simply parodying the Christian symbol by an extravagant and outlandish picture. Significantly, *The Golden Bough* recounts the creation of magical models of this bizarre creature as well as the emphatic taboos governing fishing for it. That work also stresses, in its only reference to this body of water, that the Dead Sea both has "sullen waters" and is clearly visible from Jerusalem.[6] When to this are added the male-female sexual aspects concealed in the creature's name, one sees a sharper and more extensive point to the image and to Joyce's deployment of myth as theme. Unlike the Christian version, this emblem of fertility is phallic, recognizing the interdependence of man and woman in life. It functions, however, as a parody since it is only a model or double of the real one and so a resident of that lifeless sea. At the same time, even as a parody it mirrors the genuine and so bodies forth the essential persistence of fertility and revival in the midst of death. The deathlike, stultifying, diminishing character of the parody or model-double, suggested also by his name "Humme the Cheapner" (*FW*, 29:18), explains why he has been reproaching himself for seventy years. On the other hand, his fidelity to the image of the original and his function

6. Sir James G. Frazer, *The Golden Bough* (3rd ed.; London, 1907–1911), I, 108; III, 192; V, 23.

warrant his reiterative preaching of himself as a ritualistic mimer of the symbol of fertility. In terms of Joyce's final implication the Dead Sea's proximity to Jerusalem suggests that the Christian reviving god is relevant but not right because he fails to construe fertility as sexuality in his own person. Only when HCE experiences sexual intercourse with ALP toward morning is he prepared for the man-god's revival in which he awakens to reenter the world of shared dependency.

Joyce, as we have seen, is at some pains to render the archetypal nature of HCE's revival. A further image he utilizes is that which makes the dying and reviving god emblematic of cereals and crops. For Frazer and other anthropologists, this reveals the transition from a nomadic pastoral human life to a more stable agricultural one. It is difficult to tell whether Joyce too is making use of this notion, though it certainly would fasten easily enough onto his general Viconian cyclicism. In any case, the cereal gods mythically reflect the sowing and harvesting of crops together with the ritual customs practiced in these connections. One of these which has continued into more recent, historical religions including Christianity is that of the communion meal. For Joyce it is particularly relevant because it affords him the opportunity to focus on the death and destruction of the god in a way that makes his dismemberment both viable and comic for a modern audience.

At the same time, it allows him to suggest how the god's revival grows out of and is intertwined with his death. Thus, in the second chapter where HCE is being accused of his mysterious crime, it is denied as slander by one who asserts that at least some of the accusers had "that day consumed their soul of the corn" (FW, 34:17–18). Since the first corn cut was used for the communion bread and since John Barleycorn bears a relationship to Tammuz, it is clear that Joyce had warrant for linking one of the sacraments with drunkenness. The reason for doing so here, seemingly, would be to simultaneously aver and impugn. They may have taken communion or simply gotten drunk just as HCE may or may not have performed this or that action in the park.

Less equivocal linkings of HCE with the cereal god occur somewhat later in the *Wake* when Shaun answers the first of Shem's questions about the various members of the family. One set of characteristics attributed to the preeminent myth creator is that he "has his seat

of justice, his house of mercy, his corn o'copious and his stacks a'rye"
(FW, 137:30–31). In this case it is perhaps interesting to note that
Shaun and Shem are often associated with justice and mercy, respec-
tively, and that both are aspects of the father though not identical with
him. Here it is the emblems of rife cereal fertility that complement justice and mercy. This suggests that what distinguishes the father from
the sons is precisely his function as progenitor of the harvest and pro-
vider of the means of subsistence, roles which operate equally on the
human and divine levels.

And in the same chapter Issy sees him in a less august and mag-
isterial guise but no less a representative of the deity of crops: "the
rubberend Mr Polkingtone, the quonian fleshmonger who Mother
Browne solicited me for unlawful converse with, with her mug of October (a pots on it!), creaking around on his old shanksaxle like a
crosty old cornquake" (FW, 144:30–33). Issy's view of HCE is obviously qualified by his identification with aged lechers. Even so there
is no doubt that his genuineness as a corn god is the basis for her savage sexual contempt for him. Her anger is largely that he is not the
young virile revived fertility figure, the god of the young girl's dreams,
but is only a crusty old crow or corncrake. This, however, does not
refute that he is also a quake or turbulent movement in the corn and
associated with or given crosslike qualities. Frazer suggests at one
point in *The Golden Bough* that the wind ruffling the corn fields might
well have been taken by primitive tribes as a sign of the presence of
the spirit or god of the corn. He also copiously illustrates the custom of actually or in mimicry killing the human or animal embodiment of the corn spirit. In particular, he mentions the custom of representing the corn spirit as a dead old man.[7] All of these points bear on
Joyce's image of HCE as the aged cereal god who continues to pursue
his notion of himself as a fertility deity even though he is closer to the
October harvest ritual of death than the spring sowing of life. By this
means Joyce provides an indelible image of the young girl's motivation
for disliking decrepitude's insistence on sexuality. At the same time
he gives the old an archetypal warrant for assuming the role of the
corn spirit.

Ancient harvest scenes of the ritual slaying of the corn spirit blend

7. Frazer, *The Golden Bough*, VII, 132; VI, 97, 106; VII, 149; VI, 48, 96.

fertility and death in a sacrificial emblem that implicitly indicates their interdependence. Elsewhere, as in the accounts of Osiris represented with corn sprouting from his dead body, he makes explicit the sense in which the vegetative fertility of the crops derives from the fructifying presence of divine mortality. In this, as in so much else, *Finnegans Wake* metamorphically mimes in comic accents a central thesis and image of primitive myth and religion. For after dreaming of "the fields of heat and yields of wheat where corngold Ysit" (*FW*, 75:22–23), the ostensibly deceased HCE is given a grave by the society at large. Significantly, this is described in terms which comically mirror both the ritual of Osiris and Frazer's general ironic sense of religious solemnity's involvement with more crassly materialistic or economic impulses: "This wastohavebeen underground heaven, or mole's paradise which was probably also an inversion of a phallopharos, intended to foster wheat crops and ginger up tourist trade" (*FW*, 76:33–35).

Something of the same order occurs in connection with Shem, though here the fertility images are invoked more for comic characterization and to presage the threat of destruction and death. Thus, in "The Mime of Mick, Nick and the Maggies," the program for some kind of drama includes the following: "Tree taken for grafted. Rock rent. Phenecian blends and Sourdanian doofpoosts by Shauvesourishe and Wohntbedarft. The oakmulberryeke with silktrick twomesh from Shop-Sowry, seedmanchap. Grabstone beg from General Orders Mailed. The crack (that's Cork!) by a smoker from the gods" (*FW*, 221:31–36). Though there is much that is obscure here, the complex of the grafted tree, Mediterranean doorposts, the oak, the seedman, and the blow from the gods is enough to suggest a combination of biblical and primitive pagan implications of sacrifice and disaster. It is therefore no surprise to find Shaun a couple of pages later confronting Shem and urging others "to kill or maim him" (*FW*, 223:20). Taken in conjunction, these passages suggest that Shem is here being regarded as the dying god in order to give an aura of rectitude and inevitability to Shaun's personal hostility.

A few lines later this attribution is borne out by the exclamation "O theoperil!" (*FW*, 223:28). This is an anagram for the word *heliotrope* in the children's guessing game. Yet it is also a declaration of the danger in which the god stands from his brother, a relationship which obliquely indicates that Osiris as well as Attis and Adonis are threatened. This phrase is immediately followed by another anagram, "Ethiaop lore" (*FW*, 223 : 28). It is possible that Joyce here is finding a human analogue to the dying god in the priest-kings of Ethiopia who were traditionally put to death. That the peril is, however, mimetic and comic rather than literal and tragic is intimated immediately as Shem endeavors to discover the correct answer to the several versions of the anagrammatic puzzle. One action to which he resorts proves to be a punning parody of the vegetative flourishing of the buried god: "He luked upon the bloomingrund where ongly his corns were growning" (*FW*, 223 : 31–32). Because Shem as the dying god has not really been slain, there is no question of resurrection so that the only growing thing on the fertile ground is his feet, which at the same time signal their vicissitudes by groaning.

Shem's ability to withstand Shaun's attacks is due in some measure precisely to his refusal to accept the myth of the dying and reviving god as anything but a myth, that is, a story about man's projections of his own fears and desire. But Shem is also an aspect of the father HCE so that the same attitude must also be present in him. Later in the book this proves to be the case when the four old men hold their protracted inquest into his death. There in the course of probing and describing and explaining HCE's conflict with the cad or whomever, his opponent is identified as "Patsch Purcell's faketotem" and called "his plantagonist, up from the bog of the depths" (*FW*, 516 : 23–25). The former establishes the fraudulent character and the latter the vegetative nature of the antagonist. Hence in condensed fashion Joyce asserts that HCE's rise and fall are not to be given precisely the same kind of interpretation based on the cycle of vegetative fertility that the dying and reviving god receives in works such as *The Golden Bough*. Frazer, for instance, is concerned to describe and analyze comparatively the religious beliefs of ancient peoples and to indicate to what extent and how these views persist into modern times. Joyce, on the other hand, stresses the comic dimension of Frazer's emphasis. He regards the myths and rituals as stories and actions, as imaginative metamorphoses of existential reality, as archetypal plots and characters on which arabesques of absurdity must be wrought in order to properly capture the full implications of the originals.

Representative of these arabesques is that in which the voice of HCE, speaking in the self-indulgent, pathetic, or bathetic tone of the sentenced Oscar Wilde, says farewell to himself as an Osiris of vegetative and embalmed aspects: "Dear gone mummeries, goby! . . . Nine dirty years mine age, hairs hoar, mummery failend, snowdrift to my ellpow, deff as Adder. I askt you, dear lady, to judge on my tree by our fruits. I gave you of the tree . . . my all-falling fruits of my boom" (*FW*, 535:27–34). On this figure and on HCE in general the old men comment when they declare him a thoroughgoing sceptic in religious or supernatural matters: "How's the buttes? Everscepistic! He does not believe in our psychous of the Real Absence, neither miracle wheat nor soulsurgery of P. P. Quemby" (*FW*, 536:4–6).

To religious belief, whether Christian, primitive myth, modern faith, or mental healing, HCE is completely unreceptive. Part of the reason for this seems to be that they all represent various kinds of violation or suspension of the natural order as known to all men. Instead of spirit or mind or vegetation, HCE finds the real focus for the sacred to lie in woman. In denying that he "did cophetuise milady's maid!" he declares that it is because "in spect of her beavers she is a womanly and sacret" (*FW*, 537:32–33). What makes her so is her sexuality and fertility, though these also make her untrustworthy and depraved to a homosexual like Wilde. Hence he is scandalized by the attempt to "borrough by exchange same super melkkaart" (*FW*, 538:8). This same horror at heterosexuality leads him to a further invocation of Mediterranean fertility worship in the accent of the Church Fathers: "'Twere a honnibel crudelty wert so tentement to their naktlives and scatab orgias we devour about in the mightevil roohms of ancient cartage" (*FW*, 538:10–12). Both Melcarth, the god of Tyre and identified with Hercules, and the religious practices in Carthage are linked with the widespread worship of the dying god.

The striking and, in this instance, highly ironic feature of this treatment is that Carthage is distinguished less for wildly orgiastic fertility rites than for having the rites of Cybele, the Great Mother, observed by effeminate priests. Hercules too was served by effeminate priests dressed as women, who in doing so were recognizing the god's own assumption of female dress. Clearly, Joyce's allusions to Melcarth and Carthage ironically counterpoint Wilde's homosexuality by suggesting that what he is ostensibly disavowing is actually that which he reveres. At the same time it is also the Great Mother who is worshipped there, and HCE as Wilde or Whitehowth concludes his opening appeal with

"Pity poor Haveth Childers Everywhere with Mudder" (*FW*, 535 : 34–35). By this Joyce is also ascribing homosexuality to or aligning it with an infantile attachment to the mother. One recalls Stephen's anguished struggle to emancipate himself from the ghost of his mother in *Ulysses*. As a result Joyce's progression from the theme of the artist as ironically tragic protagonist to the comically emancipated creator is striking indeed. Now the mother-fixated homosexual is accepted as part of HCE, part of mankind because the artist too is seen as included in rather than excluded from the genuine human community which embraces all historical societies.

A particularly clear sense of the unity of mankind and the reconciliation of its opposites emerges near the end of the *Wake* when HCE and ALP are returning downstairs after quieting the upset twins. HCE's description draws together the several strata of his existence— mythic, legendary, literary, and ordinary individual—and shows them not as versions of one another so much as parts of a single creature:

> But. Oom Godd his villen, who will he be, this mitryman, some king of the yeast, in his chrismy greyed brunzewig, with the snow in his mouth and the caspian asthma, so bulk of build? . . . Can thus be Misthra Norkmann that keeps our hotel? Begor, Mr O'Sorgmann, you're looking right well! Hecklar's champion ethnicist. . . . He's the dibble's own doges for doublin existents! But a jolly fine daysent form of one word. He's rounding up on his family. (*FW*, 578 : 3–15)

Among other things he is identified with the vegetative cereal deity and the Persian god Mithra. At the same time, he is the ordinary Dublin tavern or hotel owner returning to bed. The mythic references attach the individual to the archetype. On the other hand, the items of clothing, the greetings, and comments render the gods invoked more homey and domestic in aura. Together these dimensions demonstrate why HCE is regarded as supremely qualified for "doublin existents." Every man, Joyce suggests, exists on more than one level or plane. He also, however, implies pretty clearly by the form of *Finnegans Wake* that this is no astral or spiritualist matter and that perhaps only through literature, that is, the telling of stories, can this multiplicity of existence be truly apprehended.

This in part accounts for the use here of Mithra and the "king of the yeast." Both are selected less for their august roles and ritual splendors than for their relevance to the daily ordinary life of man. The latter is the corn spirit as rising god displaced into a modern reality of chemical knowledge and technology. There the miracle of revival is a natural fact which touches the Christian myth only in its character as a formal ordering of the phenomenological universe. This last explains further the presence of Mithra, who was identified with the Unconquered Sun (his birthday was December 25) and whose worship was a serious rival to Christianity. By embracing in his own person the corn god of the earth and the sun god of the sky, HCE subsumes not only aspects but regions of the natural order necessary to revival and the continuance of life. Implicitly he also suggests that he is the rival of the supernatural Christ, whose institution has left him bereft of his roots in primitive nature worship. One of his garments is described as "chrismy," which clearly seems designed to suggest the birthday of both gods. In addition, he is called a "daysent form of one word," which indicates that he is a solar-produced Logos, a miracle immanent in, not transcending, the natural world. He is "daysent," not the "Dayspring," that is, the product rather than a metaphor drawn from the diurnal cycle. In short, HCE is Joyce's answer to the Christian dying and reviving god who miraculously claims to transcend the natural universe and to reveal another one attainable by man. The flourishing of corn, its transformation into bread, the warming sun on the earth— these, Joyce says, are the real divinity of the word for the artist. They constitute the joyous, splendid, decent expression of the one word, *life*, which the metamorphic esthetic imagination prismatically renders.

*

We have seen how Joyce brings vegetative and animal emblems of fertility to bear on his rendering of the myth of the dying and reviving god. Yet as has been suggested earlier, for Joyce all of these, even the myth itself, are ultimately metaphors for human fertility and the only death from which man indeed can revive and awaken. The rendering of these twin ultimates in their multitudinous and metamorphic forms occupies a great deal of *Finnegans Wake*. Yet strikingly enough, the vast majority of the sexual encounters seem to be memories, rumors, suppositions, jokes, slander, or wishes rather than experiences immediately and physically rendered in the present. The effect of this is to suggest two things. First, it shows dramatically, with a range that carries from the tragic to the comic, the full extent to which the sexual fulfillment of the individual dominates the mind of the race. Second, it conveys how extraordinarily infrequent is that consummation which issues in the microscopic version of the archetypal movement of the man-god from triumph and fertility to decline and death-with-the-anticipation-of-revival.

The chief difference in this regard between the *Wake* and the scholarly encyclopedic fertility drama wrought in something like *The Golden Bough* lies in narrative attitude and character creation. In the former, the degree of involvement is much greater on the part of the narrator. Joyce here asserts the artist's commonality with mankind implicitly but relentlessly by refusing to permit the order of his words to create a distinct narrator who is distanced from the ritual drama of death and revival. Frazer, by contrast, always maintains a clear sense of the difference between himself as author and the persons and behavior he seeks to render with neutrality and objectivity. The difference is essentially that between the ironic and the comic stances, which also marks the crucial difference between *Ulysses* and *Finnegans Wake*. Instead of holding the artist aloof and more than faintly contemptuous of the human whirligig of impulse and aspiration, Joyce plunges him into it at its most crucial point, into a wake, which is simultaneously a ritual of mourning and of resurrection operating through the action of memory.

To convey man's intense concern for and concentration on sexual intercourse and fertility, the *Wake* adopts what might be called a post-Freudian perspective on both human behavior or consciousness and the myths and rituals of primitive mankind. With it he achieves the annihilation of time, the sense of language as a clue to unconscious motivation, and the interiorizing of natural emblems into archetypal rituals for the individual. The main thrusts of *The Interpretation of Dreams*, *Wit and the Unconscious*, and *Totem and Taboo* are, in effect, deployed as structural perspectives on the rationalistic interpretation of the history of the myth and ritual of the dying and reviving god. As a result, gods, legendary heroes, and historical figures from different periods freely commingle. They betray by speech impediments, puns, jokes, and lies their desire for the sexual ritual of consummation and detumescence, which is the physical mirror-image equivalent of the psychic archetype of death and revival whose symbols range from the diurnal to the seasonal. This is not to say, of course, that many of these symbols did not already exist in their essential meanings long before a Freudian orientation was available. What it does mean is that Joyce reflects that orientation, at least in a macroscopic, possibly vulgarized fashion. By doing so, he locates *The Golden Bough*'s quest romance treatment of what it considers to be the essentially tragic drama of mankind in an encyclopedic comedy of recurrence and open-endedness. It becomes, for Joyce, the means to reconciling the obscene or profane and the pure or sacred, a task which even *The Golden Bough* completed only on the level of concept and theory.

Of all the indices of life and fertility in *Finnegans Wake*, probably none is more frequently invoked than that of the erect phallus or its equivalents. Joyce, however, is concerned to write a comic epic rather than a medical textbook or a pornographic novel. Hence he avoids the literal image in favor of figures which possess some humorous possibilities, no matter how slight. Some of the most often used metaphors for the phallus derive from ancient tree worship, a belief that obviously lies as close to literalism as emblems can conveniently go. Thus, very early in the *Wake*, just before the text of "The Ballad of Persse O'Reilly" is sung over the scapegoat HCE, the leader of the singers lifts his hat as a signal to begin. About this the narrator observes parenthetically: "our maypole once more where he rose of old" (*FW*, 44:4). Among the various May rituals and emblems trees and poles play a major role. It is clear that they were regarded as fertility symbols with magical powers affecting both women and cattle. From this it is obvious that though HCE is here enduring the ritual of the scapegoat, the vegetative sign of sexual prowess serves as an implicit guarantee of his revival. As if to make sure that this embodiment of life in the midst of death is not overlooked, Joyce sets beside it another which indicates that the vegetative image is a human analogue. The leader's sign for the scapegoat ritual is unabashedly phallic: "'Ductor' Hitchcock hoisted his fezzy fuzz at bludgeon's height" (*FW*, 44:2). The equating of sexual fertility and resurrection is sharpened a few pages later when the story of HCE's fall and rise is promised and listeners told that if they emulate his affirmative sexuality "paradigm maymay rererise in eren" (*FW*, 53:13). This is followed by an injunction to observe a vegetative image or scene containing the full ambivalence implicit in primitive tree worship: "The augustan peacebetothem oaks, the monolith rising stark from the moonlit pinebarren" (FW, 53:15–16). The phallic nature of the monolith is identified by its being stark, as with a naked body, but on either side it confronts the god's threatening antagonist, sterility, and also the ground of fertility, continuity. The barren pine epitomizes the Attis myth of emasculation and sacrificed sexuality, while the oak traditionally was revered as the home of the mistletoe, which represented the deathless persistence of life. The scene, then, which observers are enjoined to "bebold" (FW, 53:14) is a vegetative symbol, cast in a faintly eighteenth-century or Augustan pastoral mode, of HCE's sexual challenge.

That he answers or has answered it successfully (and the two are the same thing in the Wake) on the side of life, fertility, and sexuality is indicated at the end of Book I. There the two old washerwomen explore ALP's sexual life and remark that her first lover was a vigorous man of Curragh who was "making his hay for whose sun to shine on, as tough as the oaktrees" (FW, 202:29–30). Clearly, on the archetypal level in which HCE subsumes all men, the perpetuity of sexual vigor is assured. Even Shaun joins in a tribute and quasi prayer to the fertility and life of his parents: "Their livetree (may it flourish!) by their ecotaph (let it stayne!)" (FW, 420:11–12). Yet even he indicates that the symbol of fertility is aligned with that of death as if to suggest that they are not so much alternative paths as that each grows out of and in some sense is interdependent with the other. The flourishing of the "livetree" and the remaining of the "ecotaph" are concomitant. The mythic, archetypal nature of both is revealed by the epitaph's being not only permanent but a stain. This links it with the dying god whose place of death is perdurable because it exists in the indestructible metamorphic world of the narrative imagination and is marked by the god's immortal blood staining the earth, water, and vegetation where he suffers his demise. The signs of the god's death are thus promises, in effect, of his resurrection and restoration to the full vigor of his fertility. The interrelation is, however, symmetrical. That is, the representative of the god in the mature exercise of his powers may also be seen as a rather sinister figure capable of conferring death upon his opponents.

Such a role is clearly rendered by The Golden Bough's celebrated account of the King of the Wood at Nemi, who prowls the goddess' sacred grove, protecting it by dealing death to all who challenge him so long as his strength survives. His equivalent in the *Wake* may be found in the same context with Shaun's expostulation: "And why there were treefellers in the shrubrubs" (*FW*, 420:7–8). The furtive lurking air they possess conveys a hint of violence altogether appropriate to would-be Kings of the Wood as well as to the three soldiers supposedly accosted by HCE in the suburbs of Phoenix Park. Since these three include Shem and Shaun, the inveterate father-son conflict functions on the archetypal level as the struggle for the right to represent the mythic dying and reviving god. When the struggle is joined, the loser is the old, impotent representative. But because he is who he was, his death is a ritual of departure and return, like the seasonal course of vegetation, and must be so symbolized. This occurs at the beginning of Chapter XIV in which Shaun functions as the old, sterile dying god. While he is "amply altered for the brighter," he is also called "the graven image of his squarer self" (*FW*, 429:25–26). And he leans against a policeman, who is an earlier version of himself and who is "buried upright like the Osbornes" (*FW*, 429:33–34). Were the identity of the Osbornes known, the act might have Irish as well as anthropological significance. Still, it is clear that particular burial position is meant to suggest the dying and reviving god's vegetative symbol, the tree or perhaps the Yule log, with its attendant intimation of resurrection.

As we have observed earlier, no matter how much Joyce relies on vegetative emblems he never ceases to regard them as metaphors for human sexuality. This is graphically conveyed in Book III where Shaun at one point urges intercourse most vigorously on Shem and Issy. Thus, just after saying, "Hatch yourself well! Enjombyourselves thurily!" he declares, "Let us be holy and evil and let her be peace on the bough" (*FW*, 465:13–14). Later on the same page he further remarks: "There's nothing like the mistletouch for finding a queen's earring false" (*FW*, 465:26–27). The general sexual character of the monologue and the pun on *peace* in conjunction with the phallic bough show unmistakably that vegetative and human forms of fertility are intertwined here as expressions of all life. The peace wrought by the woman between the brothers, one of whom is holy and the other evil, indicates also that the sexual relation is not only a battle or war, as is suggested by the opening of the *Wake*, but a cessation of all hostilities in a death that is also revival. The peace conferred by sexuality is represented by the piece of mistletoe on the bough. In effect, then, Joyce has affirmed what a book like *The Golden Bough* left implicit. The external soul or life of the individual, what preserves him in spite of all vicissitudes and disasters, is nothing other than his capacity to sexually experience the myth of death and resurrection. And in so doing, Joyce also affirms as reality what Frazer is content to observe as fact, that is, the earliest and fundamental impulse of man is to identify the sacred and the unclean, the holy and the evil, the divine and the sexual. This affirmation is exactly what Joyce presents at the end of the page in the dramatic alignment of "the leady on the lake and the convict of the forest" (*FW*, 465:36). The sinister criminal King of the Wood and the pure woman, representative presumably of Diana the fertility goddess and the mate of the King of the Wood, are both equally essential to the ritual as well as the myth of fertility at the core of which is the metamorphic action of the human figure. It is both the centrality and the metamorphosis that lead Shaun to exclaim in surprise: "Why, they might be Babau and Momie!" (*FW*, 466:1).

Joyce, however, does not rest content with metamorphosis as a function of historical genealogy. He also makes it a biological phenomenon as well. He does so because just as sexuality is the ground of phenomenological reality so metamorphosis is of imagination and the verbal world. And if he wishes his work to fully encompass that reality, it must verbally enact the merging of identities that sexuality represents. Some sense of this esthetic disposition emerges from the Circe chapter in *Ulysses*. There, however, the sexual metamorphoses are demoniac, inverted mirror images, ironic parodies of the comic changes wrought on the human sexual character in *Finnegans Wake*. In the latter, biological metamorphosis is part of the human comedy, whose ultimate source of amusement is that it is being written as well as lived. Nowhere is this more explicitly seen as a verbal event than in the baffling section of Book III where Shaun talks of his brother and himself as Browne and Nolan. At one point he declares: "O Tara's thrush, the sharepusher! And he said he was only taking the average grass temperature for green Thursday, the blutchy scaliger! Who you know the musselman, his musclemum and mistlemam? Maomi, Mamie, My Mo Mum! He loves a drary lane. Feel Phylliscitations to daff Mr Hairwigger who has just hadded twinned little curls!" (*FW*, 491:26–31).

Much is unclear here, but there is no doubt that HCE is declared to have given birth to twin girls, an action that in comic terms obviously carries far beyond the primitive custom of *couvade*. The motives for this are murky, but there are signs that the event is not unrelated to those vegetative and animal representations of fertility that mythically align with human sexuality. Thus, the metamorphosis of HCE from man to woman moves from a muscular fishman to a maternal mistletoe. Instrumental in this perhaps is the expletory "Tara's thrush," for the thrush was generally regarded as the chief means of transmitting the mistletoe seeds from one tree to another. In effect, Shaun is exclaiming that the thrush (perhaps a songbird image for Shem the artist-poet aspiring to sing for his nation) was really carrying the means of life and fertility to HCE when he purported to be merely preparing for Maundy Thursday and the death of Christ. This last also suggests that the fishman is the sacrificial Christ who must be transmuted into an emblem of fertility and life if the perpetuation of man is to continue. Since Christ is also the Word, he is invoked here as the prime symbol of the sexual metamorphosis that marks the movement from death to life. That is, such a transmogrification can occur only through the word, through language, which enables "musselman" to become "mistlemam" without violating or transcending the natural world of possibility, which is man's only residence.

*

Having shown how the tree and the mistletoe serve as archetypal symbols of fertility and sexuality and how man and woman become one in function, Joyce, then, brings the two motifs together. Shaun's attack on Shem is followed by the four old men's inquest into HCE's death at which he once again stirs toward life while they endeavor as usual to restrain him. His attempts at revival are recognized to be the result of his retention of sexual vigor, for one says: "But there's leps of flam in Funnycoon's Wick. The keyn has passed. Lung lift the keying" (*FW*, 499:13–14). In doing so, he reveals Joyce's continued weaving of mythic elements into the narrative as a means of emphasizing the primordial nature of the human effort to see symbols and portents of continued life and sexuality. In this he is at one with both Frazer and Freud. *The Golden Bough*, though neither as explicit nor as categorical as Freud on the subject, nevertheless indicates unmistakably the sexual aura that fire possessed for man from almost the earliest times.

Similarly, the transmuting of the king into a key is as Frazerian as it is Freudian. For numerous races and tribes, the key is often held to be a symbol of birth, while locks are thought to prevent sexual consummation. When one also finds that the mistletoe is regarded as a master key which opens all locks, Joyce's reasons for making HCE a "keying" become obvious.

Taken together, these items emphasize two things. The first is that human revival or resurrection is a matter of sexual potency. The other is that the ritual wish for long life to the king is observed because he is the human representative of the dying and reviving god of fertility whose vegetative emblem assures all births and rebirths. As if to render the point both unmistakable and a cultural universal, Joyce has one of the old men remark a couple of pages later that one summer "there were fires on every bald hill in holy Ireland that night" (FW, 501:24–25). Such an observation ritualizes and publicizes HCE's efforts to reassert his living sexuality, for it links "his flam" to those needfires offered in ancient Ireland and elsewhere on Beltane or May Day to encourage fertility in the coming season. The function of these fires for human beings is underscored by the transposition of the lady of the lake and the King of the Wood to figures in the ritual mating of earth and sky. These fires operate as one of the constituent elements in primitive cosmology:

> — Was our lord of the heights nigh our lady of the valley?
> — He was hosting himself up and flosting himself around and ghosting himself to merry her murmur like andeanupper balkan. (FW, 501:32–35)

The fire ceremonies indicate how the tree and the mistletoe together proclaim the resurgence of sexuality. In the final reference to the lord and lady, they also adumbrate the unifying of human sexuality in a single image which follows. After some discussion of the weather, which also seems pointedly concerned with fertility, the question is raised as to "where the illassorted first couple first met with each other" (FW, 503:9). The answer, of course, proves to be that it was by a tree, the tree of life as compounded by Joyce's comparatist comic perspective:

> — There used to be a tree stuck up? An overlisting eshtree?
> — There used, sure enough. . . . Oakley Ashe's elm. With a

snoodrift from one beerchen bough. And the grawndest
crowndest consecrated maypole in all the reignladen history
of Wilds. . . . The cran, the cran the king of all crans.
Squiremade and damesman of plantagenets, high and holy.
(*FW*, 503:30–504:2)

Like Mannhardt, Frazer, and others, Joyce finds the sacred tree to
have a number of generic representatives which taken together testify
to its "high and holy" nature. It is difficult to be sure to what extent the
Wake attaches to its specimens the significance found by, say, Frazer in
the various species. There does, however, seem to be a general coher-
ence of meaning in Joyce's selection, which would suggest that he is
trying to make the image subsume the various symbolic roles of the
tree. Thus, the ash is primarily curative in function, the birch linked
with woman, the elm forms the needfire, and the oak carries the mistletoe and is associated with thunder. Such specializing of function is,
of course, very loose and not to be regarded as anything more than
approximate. Neither *Finnegans Wake* nor *The Golden Bough* is *The
White Goddess* and neither attempts to codify the symbolic or magical
properties of the forest with anything of Graves's ingenious and dogmatic finality. Nevertheless, within this approximate and overlapping
range, the above passage may fairly be viewed as Joyce's effort to show
how the tree-of-life metaphor may be worked out in archetypal terms.

It itself is life with its fall or loss of innocence, its sexual antinomies, its temptations and redemptions, and its healing powers. Similarly, in relation to man, it has a dialectical ambiguity whose ultimate
humor does not attempt to gainsay the implicit threats and fears it
holds. Thus, the question as to its function is answered with an oblique-
ness whose ominousness is only redeemed by the delightful transmuta-
tion of the language itself:

What was it doing there, for instance?
— Standing foreninst us.
— In Summerian sunshine?
And in Cimmerian shudders. (*FW*, 504:3–7)

The tree of life is both for and against us, light and dark, warm and
cold, cultivated and barbaric, joyous and fearsome. What makes the
first and all subsequent couples able both to live beside it and to leave

it is, Joyce intimates, the capacity to perceive its lambent fluidity and contradictions as an organic whole, as the unity of the metamorphic.

Nowhere is this unity more pointedly connected with mankind than in the identification of the tree as "squiremade and damesman of plantagenets" and in the immediately following pages where the tree not only swarms with persons, birds, fruit, and vegetation but also becomes both male and female. It is the latter when there are "woody babies growing upon her" (*FW*, 504:22), when the snake of the Fall slides down the trunk tempting her into "a fashionaping sathinous dress" (*FW*, 505:8), and when one finds "burstall boys with their underhand leadpencils climbing to her crotch for the origin of spices" (*FW*, 504:26–28). The tree becomes masculine in the same sentence when warriors are "snoring in his quickenbole" (*FW*, 504:25), when there are savage "creatures of the wold approaching him" (*FW*, 505:2), and when one discovers "handpainted hoydens plucking husbands of him and cock robins muchmore hatching most out of his missado eggdrazzles for him" (*FW*, 504:34–36). Reproduction and child rearing, war, beauty and ornamentation, temptation and self-defense—all are intertwined in life no matter how much they may individually characterize one of the sexes. Hence the tree itself must intertwine the sexes in precisely the same manner.

The use of the primordial association of human and natural fertility is, of course, important. But what is particularly significant for our purposes in all this is the responses to the efforts to name the tree and so establish the truth:

> — Telleth that eke the treeth?
> — Mushe, mushe of a mixness.
> — A shrub of libertine, indeed! But that steyne of law indead what stiles its neming?
> — Tod, tod, too hard parted!
> — I've got that now, Dr Melamanessy. Finight mens midinfinite true. The form masculine. The gender feminine. I see.
> (*FW*, 505:19–25)

Here the truth about the tree, which is itself apparently tantamount to the truth of life, is extremely complex at the same time as, as the *Alice in Wonderland* phrase suggests, it is all of a piece. Joyce here brings into conjunction the truth of life as seen from the perspectives of

Christianity and modern anthropology. The tree is both freedom of the will and constraint of the law, the dynamic power of "deed" and the static quality of "dead," the organic "shrub" and the inanimate stone. In all of these, the changing and limitless encounter the fixed and immutable. Growth and action meet the stain of death. The ineluctable quality of space and time perceived by Stephen in *Ulysses* seems to carry here into an inexorable confrontation with mortality. From this there seems no relief save in the Christian paradox that conceptualizes the temporal existence into an infinite truth forever beyond the human finite mind.

Such a notion is a direct challenge to Joyce with his conviction of the artist as a creator for whom nothing is impossible. He does not, however, reject the Christian view in the way he does in *Stephen Hero*. Rather he transmutes and absorbs it into something he feels to be both larger and less at odds with human experience in the twentieth century. *The Golden Bough* expands the Christian story by contextualizing it among the plethora of dying and reviving gods found in history and custom. In the same way *Finnegans Wake* here offers its own anthropological frame for the Christian sense of human finitude and transcendent immortality. The limiting answer to the question of the tree's name is "Tod, tod, too hard parted!" What is *death* in German is *father* in Welsh, and between them they encompass man's death and the state which naturally and psychologically presages it. To become a father is to attain a maturity beyond which lies only death. At the same time, as the *Wake* dramatically and vividly shows, the state of fatherhood inaugurates the individual's symbolic death through supplantation by his children.

Yet the limiting answer is not the only one or even ultimately the human one, as Joyce subtly indicates. The emancipatory answer lies within the question itself, "But that steyne of law indead what stiles its neming?" The natural law of death generates its own stain, but when it is named or styled according to human law, it loses its linear, dead-end form and takes on the cyclical, recurrent, and therefore ultimately comic nature of the imagination and language. For Joyce, the only human law which is not confining to the imagination is ritual. It was the several rituals of the Church, its intricate patterns of voice, action, and person, in short, its drama that Stephen clung to longest and that Joyce never ceased to weave adaptively into the fabric of his works.

Here, however, the ritual is not that of the Roman Catholic church. Instead it is the same one which opens and closes *The Golden Bough* and whose explanation its author felt was tantamount to the whole enormous corpus. In other words, the name of the tree of life is Nemi, and Joyce conceals it as artfully as ever any other worshipper did the name of his god. The ritual of Nemi is that of protection, conflict, death, and continued protection of the divine tree associated with fertility and sexuality. Thus, the Christian notion of "the form masculine" is transmuted into the King of the Wood, the lone, former slave, criminal guardian of fertility who too must take for his only weapons silence, cunning, and exile. "The gender feminine" is that which the priest and husband protect and revere, the flow of life on and on without stopping, form, or limit. The one is finite, the other infinite. Together they shape the existential threat of mortality into an imaginative guarantee of endless life. They do so, however, unlike the Christian view, without postulating a transcendent realm requiring an act of faith at odds with one's most intimate experience.

As if to show the antinomic character of life, Joyce immediately balances the tragic solemnities of Nemi's ceaseless struggle to protect the spirit of fertility. He follows them with broad strokes of low comedy which vigorously assert the sexual basis of human fertility:

— Woe! Woe! So that was how he became the foerst of our treefellers?
— Yesche and, in the absence of any soberiquiet, the fanest of our truefalluses. (*FW*, 506:15—18)

Here HCE's dual nature as well as his irremediably phallic character are stressed. By virtue of the German pun combined with a semi-anagram he emerges as a human being, a somewhat legendary prince of the forest. As the first of (as well as a forest of) that long line of incarnations of vegetative fertility traced by *The Golden Bough*, he also is a god like them. As with Frazer's, though, he also is one considerably reduced in scale by the viewpoint of ironic comedy. To see the vegetative dying and reviving god as the foremost of "our treefellers" is to view him from the eyes of the twentieth-century ordinary man. This individual is, as it were, the lineal descendant of the rational, sceptical, empirical author of *The Golden Bough*.

It is precisely such an attitude that makes possible the directness and the humor about HCE and the tree god's sexual role. And here too Joyce continues to show the metamorphic nature of language and life by simultaneously providing two appraisals of HCE's behavior and reputation. On the one hand, apparently so long as there are no nicknames or aliases about to conceal his identity and reality, he is the finest of fertility spirits. On the other hand, whenever there is an absence of sober quiet, then he is the most willing and eager of phallic forces. Thus, he embraces both the qualities of Osiris, the dying and reviving god as civilizing power and culture hero, and those of Dionysus, the deity as releaser of orgiastic frenzy and ecstatic sexuality.

As if to complete this comic revelation of the relation of man to the tree or vine, Joyce turns the questioning to old Tom. So far as one can tell, he is an aged, less vigorous figure than HCE but in reality is actually a version of him. Since he also may be Joyce himself, the decline is both archetypal and historical. It is a record of the inevitable aging of the gods and also an account of what a fertility deity of death and revival would look like had *The Golden Bough* carried its researches down into the twentieth century itself. Tom is a dirty old man with a fishy stare who drinks tea mixed with milk and whisky and who is slightly demented or mentally unbalanced. The truly significant thing, however, is that he spends "most of his time down at the Green Man where he steals, pawns, belches and is a curse" (*FW*, 507:4−5). His tavern home is also a means of identifying him as one of the leaf-clad mummers of Europe who traditionally participated in rituals such as magical dramas and contests of the seasons in order to encourage fertile crops and vegetation generally. To have fallen on such hard times is an index both of his aged, less than potent nature and of the historical disintegration or dwindling of religious rites and customs. At the same time, the gaiety of the language and the energy of Tom himself show unmistakably that he is not so much to be pitied as laughed at for the strange, crazy, comic figure that Joyce shows him to be.

The vigor of language and character alike naturally intensifies enormously when one moves from a figure in decline to a resurgent creature in full possession of his sexual potency. A particularly moving sense of the world's and life's desire for such an individual is conveyed in ALP's consideration of her own physical decline as a woman and river, both emblems of fertility, which issues in an intense longing for HCE's return: "*For the putty affair I have is wore out, so it is, sitting, yaping and waiting for my old Dane hodder dodderer, my life in death companion, my frugal key of our larder, my much-altered camel's hump, my jointspoiler, my maymoon's honey, my fool to the last Decemberer, to wake himself out of his winter's doze and bore me down like he used to*" (*FW*, 201:7–12). The sexual nature of a large part of her desire is clear, but it is equally true that the desire is both archetypal and personal. He is not merely a dead husband. He is also the dying and reviving god, who is alive and vigorous in May, becomes the festive fool at the end of the year, and then retires to sleep in the winter.

The desire for his return is soon met, though not quite perhaps in the fashion she was envisaging. In "The Mime of Mick, Nick and the Maggies," as Adaline Glasheen has observed, the children's games are treated in Frazerian fashion as survivals of fertility rites.[8] Here the young woman serves as the temptress who tries to coerce the twins into sexual behavior. In order to do so, she even divides into a series of girls who perform Moslem ritual prayers that involve their "prostitating their selfs eachwise and combinedly" (*FW*, 235:2). When at the end of the same page one of them is also described as wearing "her necklace of almonds" (*FW*, 235:33–34), the ritual clearly assumes anthropological relevance as well as Eastern religious significance. The almond was thought to have the capacity to make virgins conceive and so was held to be the father of all things. It also was identified with Attis through his mother and associated with the mistletoe. The girl with the necklace clearly is a precocious worshipper of the handsome, young dying god, that is to say, a girl like Issy becoming aware of her sexual impulses, fascinated by them, and endeavoring to gain their fulfillment. This explains too why the religious ritual prostration also embraces the notion of prostitution. Adonis, who sometimes was identified with Attis, was especially closely connected with the ancient custom of sacred prostitution, which brought neither stigma nor punishment but was treated as an essential part of the maturation of the female.

This archetypal incitement to sexual rituals of fertility ultimately has its effect, at least on the mimetic or symbolic level. HCE has been aware of what was being performed before his eyes. Hence when ALP

8. Adaline Glasheen, *A Second Census of Finnegans Wake* (Evanston, 1963), xxxix.

calls Issy into the house, he picks her up, carries her inside, and slams the door behind him, an act which is greeted by the twins as sexual in nature. During this scene, both HCE and ALP assume the lineaments of myth and anthropological ritual. She becomes "Gran Geamatron" (*FW*, 257:4–5), the classical earth mother and fertile ground of all existence. He takes on a variety of agricultural names such as "old Father Barley," "bold Farmer Burleigh," and "Wold Forrester Farley" (*FW*, 257:10, 17, 24). Issy, in turn, is identified as "Ruth Wheatacre" (*FW*, 257:21), a name that taken in conjunction with those given HCE obviously establishes them as Joyce's adaptations of vegetative fertility representatives like the Old Man, the Hay-man, and the Wheat-woman.[9]

The incestuous overtones in the scene are undeniable and bear out the earlier comment on his giving lollipops "in presents to lilithe maid-inettes for at bloo his noose for him with pruriest pollygameous in-atentions" (*FW*, 241:4–5). Both here and throughout the book, the theme of incest may owe something to the horror and the punishment with which it was greeted by many primitive peoples and also to its observance among royal families as a ritual guarantee of lineal succession. The act, however, does not transpire but is only a subliminal impulse or fantasy. And Issy is, as the twins are to HCE, an aspect of ALP. Consequently the scene and the motif underline rather more emphatically myth's more general dramatizing of the concentration of the cycle of sexual fertility in the young, the recently married, and the pre-eminently physically attractive. HCE's symbolic sexual assault of Issy is, then, an incestuous fantasy because she is ALP as emergent object of sexual desire rather than because HCE is preternaturally predisposed to incest itself.

In reality this scene presents a child's view and version of sexual vitality, its development and arousal. It is therefore much given to ignorance of details, sniggering innuendo, and vague anticipation. The sexual act is still in effect an awesome mystery performed behind closed doors and equated with the cataclysmic and only imperfectly apprehended thunder word. The other chief instances of sexual vigor resurgent afford additional perspectives—principally those of Shaun, the four old men, and HCE himself as well as ALP. Together they indi-

9. See Frazer, *The Golden Bough*, VII, 136–39, 148, 218; IV, 253 ff.

cate that Joyce means to suggest that human sexual vigor and fertility
are both dynamic and prismatic. It is an activity that is neither fixed
nor continuous but a developing phenomenon with changing forms,
manners, and attitudes. Thus, to see what Joyce means by sexual fertility and why it is the human ritual that enacts the myth of the reviving
god and in so doing transcends the experiential fact of mortality, one
must coalesce all of the instances of sexuality in the *Wake* into a single
composite, complex vision of life's central drive, namely, metamorphic
objective creation.

The child's view of sexuality is followed by that advanced by the
young man. Since, however, he is Shaun, the attitude is warped and
constrained by attitudes that are imaginatively, physically, and morally
sterile. Shaun's efforts to preach chastity and the spiritual pleasures
and rewards of an afterlife are quite unable nevertheless to conceal the
pronounced virility of his nature. The phallic significance of his lean-
ing against the policeman buried upright has already been mentioned.
In the same chapter in Book III he threatens the girls with beatings if
they indulge their romantic sexual feelings. Yet he also indulges in
erotic protestations like the following: "Iy wacount yiou! yore ways to
melittleme were wonderful so Ickam purseproud in sending uym love-
liest pansiful thoughts touching me dash in-you through wee dots
Hyphen, the so pretty arched godkin of beddingnights. If I've proved
to your sallyfashion how I'm a man of Armor let me so, let me sue, let
me see your isabellis" (*FW*, 446:2–7). The "pretty arched godkin" is
manifestly a coy allusion to Cupid in his classical guise and role. But
latently, as the substitution of "beddingnights" for wedding nights and
the eighteenth-century use of "Armor" substantiate, the "arched godkin" is also the phallus itself.

Joyce is careful nevertheless to show that this is more than covert
sexual joking and erotic inducement. On the next page he has Shaun
call attention to "our priest-mayor-king-merchant, strewing the Castle-
knock Road and drawing manure upon it" (*FW*, 447:15–16). Then
he demands of his female audience that they "explain why there is
such a number of orders of religion in Asea!" (*FW*, 447:24–25). And
later in the same harangue he declares: "For I sport a whatyoumacor-
mack in the latcher part of my throughers. And the lark that I let fly
(olala!) is as cockful of funantics as it's tune to my fork. . . . What's

good for the gorse is a goad for the garden" (*FW*, 450:25–30). This
rises to a crescendo of self-advertisement and bluster when he goes on
to predict his success economically and sexually:

> To funk is only peternatural its daring feers divine. . . . I'd be
> staggering humanity and loyally rolling you over, my sowwhite
> sponse, in my tons of red clover, nighty nigh to the metronome,
> fiehigh and fiehigher and fiehighest of all. . . . Not a spot of my
> hide but you'd love to seek and scanagain! There'd be no standing
> me, I tell you. And, as gameboy as my pagan name K. C. is what
> it is, I'd never say let fly till we shot that blissup and swumped
> each other, manawife, into our sever nevers where I'd plant you,
> my Gizzygay, on the electric ottoman in the lap of lechery. (*FW*,
> 451:16–31)

The unrestrained physicality and specificity of the remarks are
clearly augmented by such mythic elements as priest-kings, garden
gods who mingle vegetative and human fertility, sowlike spouses, and
pagan names. These latter serve to move Shaun's animalistic rutting
talk to a level of irony and archetype simultaneously. His distortions,
even of them, together with the tone used, reveal strikingly the extent
of the distortion of his essential nature. His quasi-Christian Puritan-
ism insistently impels him to deny the limited human physical immortality in the hopes of an unlimited divine version existing only in a
conceptual realm. Yet the references to the aforementioned elements
also manage to invest even Shaun's perverted hedonism with a kind of
residual or root mythic quality. In effect, what he dramatizes is less the
nature of a particular fertility deity or even the myth of the reviving
god than, somewhat as Molly does in *Ulysses*, the primal energy of life
in raw, undifferentiated form. The central difference, of course, is that
Shaun is an ironic, demoniac version of human sexuality whereas
Molly is not its parody but its reality. Both the primal and the demoniac facets of Shaun's nature are perhaps best rendered near the end of
this section when he urges Shem and Issy into sexual relations. There
he reveals graphically both the torrential instinctual energy and the
callous, cynical indifference to the individual: "Shuck her! Let him!
What he's good for. Shuck her more! Let him again! All she wants!"
(*FW*, 466:15–17).

In this attitude to sexuality one sees both its proximity to that evinced by the four old men in the "mamalujo" chapter and its contrast to that presented by HCE and ALP in their intercourse near the end of the book. Before that, however, HCE declares what he has achieved. Part of this is the transformations he has wrought in connection with ALP seen as the natural world and the Liffey that stretches out to the sea. In the guise of King Canute (his pagan name), he "upreized my magicianer's puntpole" in order to "abate her maidan race, my baresark bride, and knew her fleshly when with all my bawdy did I her whorship" (*FW*, 547:23, 27–28). As a result of this control of the sea, of the elements of nature, by the magical authority of sexual power, HCE engages in an act that reveals the ultimate value of sexuality for Joyce: "And I cast my tenspan joys on her, arsched overtupped, from bank to call to echobank, by dint of strongbow (Galata! Galata!) so streng we were in one, malestream in shegulf" (*FW*, 547:30–33).

The careful interweaving of sexual and architectural phrases is not merely a technical device for telling two disparate stories of coition and bridge building simultaneously. It is more importantly Joyce's declaration in the most dramatic fashion devised by an artist of the universally creative character of sexuality. This creative nature, however, is more than just the capacity to engender and bring forth a new life. It is also the capacity to construct, to build slowly and painstakingly structures not seen before in the world of man. These bridge and channel the irresistible forces of time and mortality, thus allowing man to institute civilizations capable of serving as the fertile matrix necessary to the perpetuation of the human experience and the transcendence of its individual physical limitations. This same capacity can, Joyce suggests, be equally utilized in the imaginative world of language as in the physical universe of bridges and ships and machines. Precisely how it is deployed, *Finnegans Wake* demonstrates with supreme and convincing artistry. And in doing so, it articulates the theme that the civilizations of man are infinitely complex and, when viewed from a sufficiently inclusive perspective, emerge as creative works of metamorphosis, even as works of art are. It is this which places Joyce at the center of his age, that he should have seen and so effectively employed the identity of nature existing between the encyclopedic verbal form and the welter of experience that shapes twentieth-century man into the protean creature that he is. And in perceiving this identity, Joyce also perceived that forging this identity was the creative metamorphic power of myth both as verbal fact and as imaginative play so that ultimately myth and mythmaking are indissolubly linked.

My soul, do not seek immortal life,
but exhaust the realm of the possible.

PINDAR

FOUR · Myth and Character: The Dialectic of Scapegoat and Reviving God

THE QUESTION of the relationships between myth and character in literary works presents at once a more sharply drawn issue than those involving structure and theme. In the latter instances, as we have seen, myth may serve in a variety of ways and guises—as a kind of subterranean paradigm of narrative and imagistic sequences, as a sustained analogy of a hypothetical order, or as a reflexive commentary, ultimately ironic in nature, on itself. But with the issue of character we confront, in some sense, not speculative or conceptual topics so much as concrete matters of actual presence and verisimilitude. A story or action may resemble a myth or an event central to a myth without raising ontological questions about the referentiality of the narrative or incident. This is because the reference occurs within the same mode, namely, language. That is, the literary narrative refers, by virtue of its resemblance, to the narrative of myth; both are subtended within a linguistic frame. In the case of character, however, the issue seems more problematic. The question is whether for us today representations of human beings can also be renderings of mythic personages when in the twentieth century we deny the very existence of such creatures as gods, demons, and creatures half-human half-animal.

On the other hand, if we assume that a character possessing a number of traits or properties of a mythic personage is merely being given a verbal or linguistic reference, we find ourselves essentially in the realm of allusion. This, however suggestive, does not carry the same weight as the ontological stipulation of even fictive existence. In point of fact, very few modern writers have sought to present characters, directly or indirectly, as specific mythic personages who exist either apart from or in conjunction with the character conceived as the product of the loose realism of verisimilitude. Mythic personages have, of course, been presented as characters, as witness the works of Naomi Mitchison, John Cowper Powys, Henry Treece, and Mary Renault. When they are, however, it is with a complete congruence between character and mythic personage. What is being presented is a tale about someone depicted as living in an ancient or even mythic period, which last is treated as essentially prehistorical. The difficulty comes when a writer has a specifically identified character set in a historical period whom he also wishes to represent as a named mythical personage. Here he confronts challenges not only to verisimilitude but also to what one might call existential plausibility. That is to say, if credibility is threatened by the appearance of a character from an ancient epoch in a significantly later period, it is all but annihilated by a character's being rendered as two entities simultaneously—one mythic and the other what can, for lack of a better term, be called realistic. Perhaps the one major writer to essay rendering the ontological as distinct from the psychological duality of a character is D. H. Lawrence and even he does so in very few instances, of which the most notable is his treatment of the central characters in *The Plumed Serpent*.

There is, however, a strategy different from Lawrence's attempt to postulate ontological duality, from that of novelists like Treece and Renault to, as it were, historicize ancient mythic figures through scenic detail and narrative event, and from the endeavor of fabulists like John Barth to deflect the issue of verisimilitude through contemporaneity of dialogue and temporal interfacing. It can be found not only in Lawrence himself but also in many other writers from classical tragedy to the present. It consists not of personal identification between character and mythic personage but rather of functionally homologous assignment. That is to say, instead of doing as Lawrence does and trying to link Don Ramón Carrasco and Quetzalcoatl, the focus falls on the functional relationship obtaining between the character and the chief figure in a metamyth, such as the dying god. Such a strategy places the emphasis on the character's functions rather than on static essentials of his nature. As a result, the artist gains immeasurably in flexibility. He is able to construe and render characters of differing qualia such as sex, age, social status, and even role conformity while still preserving their homologous relationship to the metamythic figure. In addition, this figure becomes the locus for whatever narrative it appears in since all the possible narratives have a paradigm consisting of the events articulated in the metamyth. As a result, the narrative developed in any specific case may vary widely in event, action, and order from others entertainable. The only limiting condition is that the narrative elements preserve the structural, functional, homologous relationship to the paradigm.

Obviously any number of metamythic figures might be considered in relation to selected fictional characters. For our purposes, two will suffice to illustrate some of the ways in which literature has utilized mythic figures in generating highly individual and concretely realized characters who move through diverse plots and give rise to a surprisingly varied order of attitudinal responses. The figure of the reviving god affords us an opportunity to examine character in relation to psychic integration, social transformation, and personal survival or achievement. In the same way, the figure of the scapegoat possesses multiple points of alignment with characters who suffer psychological disintegration, social or cultural abasement, and even in some instances physical destruction. To this end, we will turn first to Lawrence's *The Plumed Serpent* once again and then to a series of examples ranging from August Strindberg to James Baldwin that illuminate the fertile possibilities inherent in the figure of the scapegoat.

*

Perhaps the most important contribution myth makes to *The Plumed Serpent* is the organizing principles for the novel's characters, themes, and controlling rhythms. What is most significant about its major characters is that they exist on three different levels each of which provides a different function and form of behavior. On the most plausible level, they exist as human beings, as persons named Don Ramón Carrasco, Don Cipriano, and Kate Leslie who are engaged in social and personal struggles that bring them into contact with a number of minor characters in ways that largely conform to the convention of realism. On a second level, without ceasing to be recognizably individual, the three main characters depart from the conventional range of human response and gesture to become human representatives of ancient Mexican deities, actor-priests whose behavior makes them different from the ordinary person. Finally, on the third level, which is attained only fleetingly and in those scenes most freighted with ritual, they cease to be human beings and become mythical creatures, deities appearing to men through what one scholar describes as temporary incarnation. It is exactly this triad of roles—of persons singled out from the group because of birth, special attainment, or sense of vocation to act the part of and so become identified with the deity—that emerges as one of the dominant features of primitive society. And to be aware of it as an organizing principle is to avoid a number of critical misconceptions about the nature of the major characters.

In this notion of the mimetic relation between human and mythical affairs also lies a major clue to the book's theme and structure. In effect, *The Plumed Serpent* consists of two complex patterns, the human and the mythical, which reflect one another in such a way that each emerges as the cause of the other. By providing the individuals and the basic setting, the human pattern functions as the material and efficient cause of the mythical pattern. At the same time the latter's provision of meaningful actions and an inclusive perspective makes it the formal and final cause of the former. In the human pattern, there are three distinct strands: first, there is the psychological self-discovery embodied in the personal experiences of the character Kate Leslie; second, there is the issue of social revival which centers in the problems and destiny of Mexico; and third, there is the activity of what might be called analytic exposure, expressed both by characters and by author, in which the modern world is subjected to a satiric excoriation. Because Kate is in Mexico in the twentieth century, it naturally follows that there should be a revival of the myth of Quetzalcoatl. Similarly, because the mythical pattern of the novel embraces such notions as those of the dying and reviving god, the marriage of sky and earth and sun and moon, the symbolic character of snake and dragon, and Cronus' swallowing a stone, the characters not only act but also think in terms which lead them to conform to or to imitate these controlling myths. Thus, what Lawrence seeks to do is simultaneously to affirm the truth of myth and to reveal its roots in the needs of actual living human beings.

A similar counterpoint exists in the controlling rhythms of the novel. Both patterns have their own individual rhythm, but in this case they contrast rather than complement one another. While Kate's course of thought and action is the most obvious example, there are a number of others that reinforce the conviction that the human rhythm in the novel is oscillatory. Don Ramón accepts his role as leader and savior of his people and then recoils from it momentarily several times in the course of the book. Carlota cannot stand her husband's beliefs about Quetzalcoatl and yet cannot refrain from discussing or witnessing his religious practices. And preeminently, Kate oscillates, as we have seen, between attraction to and repulsion from Mexico, its people, Cipriano, the modern world, and primitive deities. In contrast to this, the mythic pattern possesses an essentially cyclical rhythm. The departure of Christ and the arrival of Quetzalcoatl are pointedly seen as but the latest phase in a round of religious conviction. As the hymns and other comments make clear, in the distant past the roles of the two divinities were precisely reversed, with Christ supplanting his aged brother. And since neither of them dies completely or absolutely—they merely partake of a revivifying bath and sleep—the cycle is bound to be sustained.

Though *The Plumed Serpent* deals with the myth of the reviving god, one would not think so at the beginning of the book. The first three and a half chapters concentrate on a bitterly satiric disavowal of Mexico, America, and the modern world in general. To Kate, America is dominated by egocentric sensationalism, Mexico by a squalid evil and fatalistic apathy, and men by a "soft rottenness of the soul" (*PS*, 27). In the world of Americans like Owen and Villiers or of Judge and Mrs. Burlap and of the Mexicans at the bullfight, there is nothing to offer any hope of a revival of a divine savior. This opening, however, is central to Lawrence's conception of his mythic theme and its relation to the human drama of the individual character. Beginning as he does, before the revival and return of Quetzalcoatl, Lawrence plunges his reader immediately into a dark night of the soul which is both personal and societal in its scope. Significantly enough, Mexico in the early chapters is largely seen through the eyes of Kate, and it is not long before we realize that the country serves as a projection of her own psychic state. Through this connecting of character and scene, Lawrence is able to dramatize the coordination between the myths of the one and the rituals of the other. In addition, this reveals that the relation between the individual and the society is not merely one of impingement but also a matter of genesis. Kate learns from the public myths of Mexico, but she also generates them, or contributes to their generation, at least as dynamic cultural forces, by her personal experiencing of their paradigmatic pattern in her own psychological development.

Her responses to this strange country and landscape are essentially valid so that they mirror the desperate straits of a nation which is on the verge of extinction. Thus, the controlling image with which Lawrence begins is that of death and the dead god. Kate witnesses the initial rites of the death of the bull at the same time as her consciousness is dominated by the memory of her husband's death and the awareness of her own psychological extinction "in a kind of death agony" (*PS*, 53–54). Essentially, then, the book begins, as we have noted earlier, like *The Waste Land*, prior to the god's resurrection or even man's hope of such a revival. Kate sees in the external world what she herself is: the nadir of life, existence on the lowest point in the cycle of creation and death. What she faces is not so much a descent into the terrors of death as the challenge of an ascent through the horrors of an alien culture to a life that is genuinely integrated.

In dramatizing the nature and function of nescience, Lawrence utilizes elements of myth and ritual. The first of these appears in the opening phrase of *The Plumed Serpent* which places the novel's first scene, that of the bullfight, on "the Sunday after Easter" (*PS*, 7). On this occasion such rituals as the Carrying Out of Death and the Return of Summer were celebrated by many communities. Both figures, those of Death and Summer, were thought to possess a vivifying and fertilizing influence. Both here and in "The Man Who Died," Lawrence implicitly agrees with *The Golden Bough* that the figure of death "represented in these ceremonies cannot be regarded as the purely destructive agent which we understand by Death" but there must also be ascribed "a life-giving virtue to the figure of Death."[1] It is precisely this perspective that Kate achieves near the end of the novel when she contemplates Huitzilopochtli and sees in Cipriano, his incarnation, not only a bloody, savage executioner but equally a quickening, godlike power who gives her renewed life through the phallic restoration of her maidenhood. Thus, in opening the novel on the Sunday after Easter, Lawrence both ironically juxtaposes the resurrection of Christ and modern nescience and also hints at the positive values inherent in

1. Sir James G. Frazer, *The Golden Bough* (3rd ed.; 12 vols.; London, 1907–1911), IV, 250.

death. This creative quality inherent in death is presented contrapun-
tally and in a minor key through Don Ramón and his wife, Carlota. In
order to become the manifestation of Quetzalcoatl, Ramón has had to
undergo a spiritual death that separates him from his wife and family
and from such beliefs as love and human liberty. All of these are related to his old body which has now been replaced by a new one conscious of its own intrinsic manhood. Carlota, on the other hand, has
let life kill the goddess in her. Hence she is unable to recognize the vivifying power to be found in the death of a god, the image of a husband,
or ancient concepts such as the sexuality of religion.

The fusion of death and creation is equally important for the structure of the book and for the characters. *The Plumed Serpent* begins by
recording the state of death and destruction as it manifests itself in individual (Kate) and social (Mexico) forms. Then it moves to a lengthy
and complicated transitional period of external and internal struggle
in which Ramón tries to bring Quetzalcoatl alive in the hearts and
minds of his people and Kate endeavors to free herself of her European
and modern prejudices and to find her own true womanhood. Following this period, marked by the oscillation of human impulses and
politicomilitary power, is the third and final stage of the novel which
ends on the verge of resurrection and creation. There emerge the outlines of a new theocracy in Mexico which, however tentative and uncertain, is nevertheless a living community. Concomitant with this is
the appearance of the new Kate who, having barely emerged from the
shell of selfhood, is still hesitant and unsure but who, for the first time,
finds it within her power to request rather than demand and to acquiesce rather than resist. Viewed in this light, *The Plumed Serpent*
reveals a structure that matches in striking fashion the mythic pattern
of the reviving god: death, seen as the mindless stupor of peons and
Christ alike, and as the dismemberment of both an individual psyche
and a nation; the involved and anguished transition of resurrection;
and at last the sense of creative powers focused on the task of moving
toward a life of harmony, integrity, and reverential awe despite a
swarm of antagonists.

With Kate's ultimate return as a creature possessed of life-giving
power, her role as the mimetic figure of Summer is justified. For as critics have pointed out, it is a matter of crucial significance that she
should be a woman of forty for whom "the first half of her life was

over" (*PS*, 54). In bringing to light the second half of her life from the darkness in which it was shrouded at the beginning of the book, Kate demonstrates her capacity for growth and her role as Lawrence's version of the ritual image of Summer. This, however, leads to the question of what constitutes the parallel to the figure of Death. The old self of Kate certainly constitutes part of this figure, at least on a metaphorical level. But the major parallel is clearly the bull which Kate, significantly enough, doesn't want to see killed. The bullfight obviously arouses a deep and profound response which engages her in the complexities of her own and Mexico's nature. It begins her education in the nature of death as a result of which she is able to utilize the principles of her subject for a viable goal.

The satiric quality of the first part of the novel has already been mentioned, but it is important also to see how this reflects the mythic pattern. Intuitively, Lawrence recognized that satire is the literary mode which most closely parallels destruction and disintegration as a mode of action. Consequently, when he places his characters in the bullfight scene he permeates its images with a satiric aura. The "gallant show" expected by Kate is found to be redolent of "human cowardice and beastliness, a smell of blood, a nauseous whiff of bursten bowels!" (*PS*, 16). The bull itself becomes an ironic reversal of the mythic beast symbolic of fertility and the sun. "In spite of his long horns and his massive maleness" (*PS*, 17), the bull appears merely a stupid fool unable to determine the real source of his humiliation. The ironic perspective is not, however, confined to Kate's view of the proceedings; it also envelops her actions as well. She thinks of the bull as "the great Mithraic beast" (*PS*, 17) and, in so doing, draws the primitive religion of Mithra into the fabric of the novel.[2] This cult was strikingly similar to both Christianity and the religion of the Mother of the Gods which existed in Mexico. As such it was regarded in Mexico as a diabolic parody of the true religion. In its ritual sacrifice the god himself plunged a knife into the bull which was regarded as an incarnation of the spirit of things rooted in and growing out of the dark soil.

Putting these together, one can perceive in Kate's contempt for the bull and her refusal to witness its death the same dogmatic rejection of a religion alien to her experience as exhibited by the early Christians

2. For pertinent details of the cult, see Frazer, *The Golden Bough*, V, 302; VIII, 10; IX, 289.

of Mexico, a point that reveals a striking affinity between her initial attitude and that of Carlota. These actions also shed an ironic light on her refusal at this point either to accept the fact that the god himself must be capable of taking life if he would preserve it or to acquiesce to the necessity of a mimetic slaying as part of the novice's initiation into the inner mysteries. Fear of the country, revulsion for its habits, and a snobbish humanitarianism are the inhibiting strictures of character from which she must free herself before she can begin the second half of her life. In effect, with the bullfight she is running away from the very thing she needs if she is to emerge from "the bottom of some dusky, flowering garden down in Hades" (PS, 48), which life among Americans in Mexico appears to be at the outset.

Lawrence also makes her a widow, which in a primitive land leaves her subject to the conviction that she is tainted with death and needs purifying by a scapegoat. And since bulls were traditionally utilized as scapegoats, her flight is clearly to be construed as a flight from her own purification. She needs to be purified of essentially the same lust for sensation as she accuses the bullfight spectators of being prey to. Her only difference from them is that her passion for sensation is not visual but tactual, as her final renunciation of the orgasm indicates. Hence she excoriates her companions for sensation-mongering without realizing that her indicting the genus subsumes her own species of lust.

The bullfight, then, is a microcosmic image that organizes the theme of Kate's personal alienation and Mexico's nihilism and the corrosive perspective of satire and irony into a crisis situation for all. This produces the question of how the protagonists are going to cope with this critical problem. On both personal and national levels, the answer is the same: they must become something other than they are. Thus, Kate recognizes that at forty "one had to cross a dividing line" (PS, 52) and that since hitherto "she was never *in* any society: too Irish, too wise" (PS, 44), she must undergo rites of passage which will make possible her transition and incorporation into a new life and community. Before such a change can be inaugurated, however, the individual must detach herself from her former world. Kate follows the traditional threefold ritual of separation, transition, and incorporation.

She separates herself from her old world by coming to Mexico from Europe, from her blood relative and acquaintance by leaving the bullfight, from the vestigial remnants of Europe by insulting the Pole and

Spaniard who stop at their dinner table, and from casual Occidental acquaintances like the Burlaps by her assessment of them as an "'awful ill-bred little pair'" (*PS*, 50). The effect is to cut her off from everything in any way connected with her physical past—country, relatives, culture, and race. This is further accentuated when she determines to stay in Mexico without Owen and then retreats into the countryside. In physical terms the separation is effected without much trouble, but psychologically Kate finds more difficulty in shedding the welter of associations and convictions that constitute the first half of her life. It is this protracted struggle to renounce the old and familiar and to accept the new and alien that constitutes Kate's rites of transition. These begin in reality after she is established in her village home, but they have been prepared for by a series of events which have roused Kate to a renewed sense of her own spiritual incompleteness and of the possibility of an integrated life.

The first of these events is the newspaper story of the Return of the Gods in which Don Ramón appears as a historian and archeologist rather than as a deity; its effect is threefold. It makes Kate realize "a strange beam of wonder and mystery, almost like hope" (*PS*, 62); know "in her vague, woman's way" that "ye must be born again. Even the Gods must be born again" (*PS*, 63); and desire "the presence of that which is forever unsaid" (*PS*, 64). This hope for the inarticulate mystery of rebirth is stirred further by the dinner table discussion at Don Ramón's in which talk of the gods mingles with expressions of concern about the revival of Mexico. There is more than a passing significance in the emphasis here on talk or speech, for the young Mirabel introduces a principle not only derived from primitive myth but also vital to Lawrence's technique in subsequent portions of the novel. Mirabel insists that "the *names* of the gods! . . . the *names* are like seeds, so full of magic, of the unexplored magic. . . . I believe in the fertility of sound" (*PS*, 66). This reflects the ancient belief that the mere mention of the names of the powerful beings who govern growth and life is sufficient to produce a magical fertility.

This belief also contributes to Lawrence's technique in presenting Quetzalcoatl and his myths. The telling or reciting of legends or tales of olden times is designed in both cases to produce a fructifying effect, the difference being that in Lawrence the goal is psychological or spiritual, while in the savage it is physical. Lawrence's genuine concern to change the course of human affairs makes him imitate the primitive enchanter whose narrative legends were also spells. And like him, Lawrence found his prayers and spells, his imperatives or requests (depending on his mood), and his narratives following the pattern suggested by Frazer when he remarked that "prayer and spell, in the ordinary sense of the words, may melt into each other almost imperceptibly."[3] In effect, Mirabel's outburst defines the manner in which Kate is to be affected by the worship of Quetzalcoatl: through sound that reverberates in the depths of her consciousness. Her reluctance to submit to this kind of spell and her inability to avoid it can be seen by juxtaposing her conversation with Ramón in Chapter IV about the search for God against her reactions to her first participation in a drum-filled, hymn-singing, dance-entranced meeting of Quetzalcoatl's followers. When Ramón attempts to define his search for God she retreats into the banalities of her ordinary sophisticated woman's conversation, but to the drums and dancing she responds fully, acquiring "the strange secret of her greater womanhood" (*PS*, 141).

This last, which marks the beginning of her transition, has been prepared for, however, by a scene in which sound is secondary to the visual world and the capacity for intuitive sympathy. On her way down the river to the hotel on the lake, Kate, conveyed by a crippled boatman, is struck, as she was when reading about the Return of the Gods, by the fact that "earth, air, water were all silent with new light. . . . The great light was stronger than life itself" (*PS*, 97). This image of a new light serves as a prelude to her encountering a stranger bathing in the water who demands she make a tribute to Quetzalcoatl before going on the lake. Intuitively she senses the connection between the morning star "hanging perfect between night and the sun" (*PS*, 99) and the look in the eyes of the natives who are aware of Quetzalcoatl. In both there is a sense of being "perfectly suspended between the world's two strenuous wings of energy" (*PS*, 98). The polarity of life emerges for Kate here from a setting which is an intricate combination of the natural and the human, of the static mystery of distance and perspective which is "yet sharp-edged and clear in form" (*PS*, 100). The natural description releases even as it impels Kate's imaginative

3. Frazer, *The Golden Bough*, VII, 105.

perception so that the two formulate the goal of her quest in images which are equally natural and mythic:

> And for the first time Kate felt she had met the mystery of the natives, the strange and mysterious gentleness between a scylla and charybdis of violence; the small poised, perfect body of the bird that waves wings of thunder and wings of fire and night, in its flight. But central between the flash of day and the black of night, between the flash of lightning and the break of thunder, the still, soft body of the bird poised and soaring, forever. The mystery of the evening-star brilliant in silence and distance between the downward-surging plunge of the sun and the vast, hollow seething of inpouring night. The magnificence of the watchful morning-star, that watches between the night and the day, the gleaming clue to the two opposites. (*PS*, 100–101)

This sense of a living world and a people in a natural relationship with it is not, however, sustained once the experience of mythic and ritualistic participation concludes. Thus, after her contemplative vision of her quest's goal, experienced on the water voyage to the hotel, she is immediately aware again of the "vacuity, arrest, and cruelty" (*PS*, 103) of her surroundings and of "the malaise which tortures one inwardly" (*PS*, 104) as a result. Before her boat trip she was struck by "the strange emptiness, everything empty of life" so that "the stones seemed dead, the town seemed made of dead stone" (*PS*, 94). And here again at the hotel her dominant impression is of "an aboriginal, empty silence, as of life *withheld*" (*PS*, 104). What begins as an estimate of Mexico broadens until it includes all of modern life. After listening to the hotel manager's cynicism about Mexico and Don Ramón's Quetzalcoatl, she realizes that it is "this sterility of nothingness which was the world, and into which her life was drifting" (*PS*, 112). And from this, she turns determined to believe in Ramón and Cipriano, "to let the sunwise sympathy of unknown people steal in to her" (*PS*, 112).

In stressing the nothingness and emptiness of this life of Kate's, Lawrence appears to be adapting an Aztec observance to the requirements of character and symbol. A number of peoples, including those of Mexico, associated the intercalary period of their calendar with certain superstitions. It was variously regarded as unlucky, evil, and outside the regular order so that communities were abandoned to riot, turbulence, and disorder and individuals unrestrained by customary morality. As an approximation to the modern world chronicled by Lawrence in *Women in Love*, *Aaron's Rod*, and *Kangaroo* this image is remarkably apt. But even more striking in this regard is the fact that the Aztec name for this period means "vacant," "superfluous," or "useless," essentially the same terms as Lawrence reiteratively applies to the world and life Kate sees around her. Clearly, she is part of a time between the old and the new orders. And as a description of life during Lawrence's version of this interregnum, it would be hard to better the following remark on its Aztec prototype: "People abstained from all actions of importance and confined themselves to performing such as could not be avoided, or spent the time in paying visits to each other."[4] It is from the emptiness of such a life that Kate flees down the lake to her own house. The interregnal quality is underlined by the momentary sense of fulfillment which descends on her in the boat.

Once settled into her own home in the heart of Mexico, Kate is in a position to begin her actual rites of transition by which her character transformation is to be effected. It is worth recalling at this point, however, that she is not alone in trying to move from a state of death and destruction into a creative world. Mexico itself is endeavoring to revive from its contemporary deathlike stupor. Lawrence puts the ancient belief in the relation of the individual and the community, the hero and his people—the sense of their fates being bound up with one another—to characterological and "sociological" uses. Thus, not only does another mythic aspect of *The Plumed Serpent* emerge but the function of a number of otherwise gratuitous episodes is determined. For instance, Kate's violent revulsion toward the new frescoes at the university constitutes a recognition that social and political sympathies are inadequate to heal the wounds of the soul shared by her and Mexico. Similarly, when she meditates upon the continental differences between America and Europe and feels that the former is "the great death-continent" that opposes "the creative continents" and makes "all its peoples the agents of the mystic destruction" (*PS*, 83), there is a clear sense of the mythic cycle of creation and destruction. And when she recalls the words of Don Ramón, she acts on her identi-

4. Frazer, *The Golden Bough*, IX, 339, 340.

fication of Mexico and herself. Both need to utilize the weight of psychic gravity, to understand that " 'men are still part of the Tree of Life, and the roots go down to the centre of the earth' " (*PS*, 85) and all that matters is " 'the roots that reach down beyond all destruction. The roots and the life are there. What else it needs is the word, for the forest to begin to rise again. And some man among men must speak the word' " (*PS*, 86). It is this word that Kate and Mexico alike both begin to hear and heed in the chants and hymns of Quetzalcoatl.

Even more striking examples of this identification of interests occur in the opening scenes of Chapters VI and VII. In the one, Lawrence devotes considerable space to chronicling the past history of Orilla, the resort town by the lake, with its incidents of murder, dismemberment, and robbery. In the other chapter he dwells at length on the ordinary social life of the inhabitants of Sayula, on the differences of attitude and the resultant tensions between the peons and the Indians on the one hand and the flappers and fifis on the other. In both cases, the scenes dramatize the moral, social, and spiritual state of the nation and its inhabitants. The strange combination of apathetic indifference and aggressive hostility toward the outside world manifested in these scenes mirrors almost exactly Kate's weary detachment from and virulent scorn for life around her. It is from this state that both must be aroused if resurrection is to be achieved.

It is significant, therefore, that Kate's first actual glimpse of the Quetzalcoatl world and ritual should occur in a communal situation while she is accompanied by her housekeeper, Juana, who epitomizes the ambivalent polarity of the natives and of Kate herself. Both are torn by their own inability to achieve that balance of opposites which the worship of Quetzalcoatl celebrates. Thus, they are drawn in fascination of the ceremony of Quetzalcoatl's men partly because of its novelty and color but more especially because of the performers' sense of equilibrium and purpose. What gives them this quality is their being united in an intricate series of ritual acts. They constitute, as Kate sees in the course of the ceremony, "a darkly glowing, vivid nucleus of new life" (*PS*, 130). And so they reflect one of the things stressed in Lawrence's anthropological sources, namely, that ritual is a means of achieving and renewing the living community through emotional participation. Kate, likening the Quetzalcoatl drumming to that of the Indians of Arizona and New Mexico, "instantly felt that timeless, primeval passion of the prehistoric races, with their intense and complicated religious significance" (*PS*, 126). In this, she is not only reiterating the views of Lawrence in *Mornings in Mexico* but also reflecting the anthropological view that ancient songs and dances were part of sacred dramas. Similarly, Lawrence's notion of the purpose of Mexican rites, that the natives dance to gain power, power over the *living* forces or potencies of the earth, mirrors the scholarly conviction that "the aim of these elementary dramas . . . was the acquisition of superhuman power for the public good."[5]

More specifically, the first dance in which Kate participates clearly resembles that of the Indian festival of the first fruits. In both cases, two circles, one of men and the other of women, of firelit dancers revolve in opposite directions with great solemnity to the time kept by a drum. Clearly, Lawrence utilizes this dance form because of its symbolic appropriateness. His seerlike singer, who carries the banner of Quetzalcoatl and whose gaze is sightless either through blindness or concentration, narrates the myth of Quetzalcoatl in its cyclic form whereby he passes from culture hero into decline and thence to replacement by Christ, who in turn yields to the reviving Morning Star.

In this there may be an attempt to underline the cyclic nature of the myth by the use of the wheel pattern in the ritual. More important, however, is the fact that the ritual celebrates the omnipotence of the sun. It is this as the source and support of human life that Lawrence symbolizes by the image of the wheel composed of the dancing figures. In focusing on the sun here and throughout the novel, Lawrence is deliberately employing a mythic image to reinforce his concern with the interrelationship of sacrifice and creation in the formation and transformation of character. He knew from his sources that the sun was created by the gods leaping into a fire and that the sun's perseverance and sustenance depended on human sacrifice. The point that a creative life is attained only through a submissive sacrifice—which the rites of transition seek to teach Kate—is here presented implicitly in the symbolic images of wheel, sun, and fire that appear in the ceremony.

The nature of this submissive sacrifice in Kate's case is also suggested by the symbol of the sun and the ritual chant that accompanies the dance of the men and women. The sun was a mythic participant in the fertility ritual of the sacred marriage, and so adumbrates Kate's

---

5. Frazer, *The Golden Bough*, IX, 375.

later role with the living Huitzilopochtli. Moreover, the sun was thought to marry both the moon and the earth. Lawrence echoes this mythic plurality by making Kate emblematic of both. When during their discussion she was overcome by sorrow at her husband's death, Cipriano felt "he was in the presence of the goddess, white-handed, mysterious, gleaming with a moon-like power and the intense potency of grief" (*PS*, 76). Then by participating in the dance, she becomes a part of the myth that the ritual chant iterates even as the dance re-enacts it. In the image of the sunbird treading the earth at dawn like a brown hen under his feet, the myth of the union of sky and earth, which figures prominently in the novel, is first introduced.

The purpose of this duplication, however, is not simply to empha-size the centrality of the sacred marriage ritual; it is also an effort to illuminate the nature and facets of the relationship between myth and the human character. Thus, the joining of the core of existence to the moon goddess—woman dramatically reveals that tenderness and grief are a part of the union. Similarly, the linking of sun or sky with the earth and water shows that creation and passion, too, are aspects of the sacred marriage. In effect, from its biblical or Christian form and from primitive fertility myths, Lawrence evolves his own creation myth, something we earlier have seen him doing in his poetry.

From this scene Kate learns two things in particular: first, that "faith is the Tree of Life itself" (*PS*, 135), as a result of which it is the roots of faith that man must rely on; and second, that her salvation lies in the ritual of sacred marriage. This is the personal epitome of the principle of polarity which is embodied on the cosmic level in the con-cept of the morning star. She has, therefore, in one sense, been pre-sented with all that is requisite for her incorporation into a new life. But the transition from fact to psychological acceptance of the fact, much less to existential enactment, is a difficult, slow, and long pro-cess. Realizing this, Lawrence organizes *The Plumed Serpent* so that Kate's exposure to the mythic world of Quetzalcoatl is gradual with ample periods intervening for meditation and application of what she has learned. Thus, following the scene just discussed, she is left quite free for three chapters from any further symbolic indoctrination. In-stead, she lives quietly in her house with her servants, who protect her from the night which "began to be full of terrors" (*PS*, 142) since in it "primitive darkness reigned" (*PS*, 143).

During this time she contemplates the Mexican mind as she sees it manifested in those around her and relates it to the views of Ramón concerning the value of strengthening faith and restoring manhood through myth. The extent of the impression made on her by the rituals of the men of Quetzalcoatl is evidenced in two ways. For one thing, her assessment of the ultimate spiritual problem of the Mexican culminates in an image that harks back to the chant of the dance. To her, "they are caught in the toils of old lusts and old activities as in the folds of a black serpent that strangles the heart" (PS, 144). The "black serpent" is the demoniac antithesis of "the snake of the world" that is also "the heart of the world" (PS, 137). And in the second place, she explicitly endorses Ramón's return to old life-modes when she declares: " 'We must go back to pick up old threads. We must take up the old, broken impulse that will connect us with the mystery of the cosmos again, now we are at the end of our own tether' " (PS, 147).

Having witnessed an introductory Quetzalcoatl ceremony and decided that it represents a possible hope for herself and Mexico, Kate is then ready to explore the ritual in greater detail. In particular, she needs to experience the incarnation of god in man and to witness the power and scope of faith in a world and life greater than the human. It is this that occurs in the subsequent three chapters, "Lords of the Day and Night," "The First Waters," and "The First Rain." The first of these, however, introduces a significant change in point of view. No longer are the myth and ritual of Quetzalcoatl seen solely from Kate's standpoint. Instead they are presented from an objective, detached, third-person perspective. The effect of this is to change the structure of the audience or the position of the reader. Hitherto, the reader has been viewing the drama of Kate's relation to the ritual myth. Now he is brought into direct contact with the myth and its performers so that they work immediately upon his sensibilities. As such, it forms part of Lawrence's concern to change the world in reality rather than simply mirroring it in imaginative literary form. Here he seeks to convert his readers just as he has already indicated his characters' quest for transformation, though to be sure the conversion aimed at is psychological rather than political.

He begins by presenting the manner in which Don Ramón prepares for the private religious ceremony. And while the exercises he performs may be modeled upon those of yoga and the theosophists, it is worth noting too that they reflect also the basic pattern of shamanism.

Generally speaking, in both cases "one finds the recurring series of trances, death, voyages of the soul to the other world, return, and application of the knowledge acquired in the sacred world to a particular case." Back of this reliance on the Eastern rites of theosophy may be Lawrence's awareness of the interrelation of magic and religion and "'the agreement between the magic ritual of the old Vedas and the shamanism of the so-called savage.'"[6] By so doing, he meets head on one of the major prejudices of most of his readers and implicitly asserts that it, like those of Kate, must be sloughed off if the integrated individual is to emerge. How this is to be done forms the text of Ramón's sermon to his disciples following his prayer and their antiphonal response.

After the private ceremony, Ramón returns to the daily world where his nakedness, a reminder of his ritual divestiture, stirs Kate to imagine "a knife stuck between those pure, male shoulders" (PS, 195) and to recognize that "this was how Salome had looked at John" (PS, 196). The clarity of this perception of herself as the temptress and voluptuary provides its own purification so that she grasps the necessity of abandoning the assertive self and "'the desire that works through the eye'" (PS, 197). In this same chapter, she is first approached by Cipriano with his proposal of marriage and stirred by it against her will. More important, she begins to clarify her relationship to Ramón and Cipriano. In the former, she sees "the mystery, the nobility, the inaccessibility, and the vulnerable compassion of man in his separate fatherhood" (PS, 201), a fact that explains both her attraction to him throughout the novel and his avoiding of any close sensual contact with her.

By way of contrast, she is struck by "the incompleteness in Cipriano that sought her out, and seemed to trespass on her" (PS, 201). Here her earlier general intuition about the incomplete selves of human beings is given a specific and somehow personal reference. It marks a further stage in the focusing of her vision of the sacred marriage, now seen as the creation of total contact between two inevitably incomplete human beings. Kate accepts Ramón first and from his precepts and examples then learns to accept Cipriano. In this she follows the pattern of maturation found in many rebirth rituals of initiation.

6. Arnold van Gennep, *The Rites of Passage*, trans. M. B. Vizadom and G. L. Caffee (London, 1960), 109; Frazer, *The Golden Bough*, I, 229.

The dance, which we have already identified as a symbol of creation, gives her the feeling of being virginal again, which is equivalent to a rebirth into innocence. Then, in Don Ramón, she encounters a father who educates her in what she needs to know to face the strangeness of the new world. And finally, in Cipriano, she finds the lover-husband who fulfills her, a fact symbolized by her ability to live apart from others with him and even to live alone but in his aura when he is away.

The relationship between Kate and the two men is further developed in "The First Rain." Here Kate witnesses another Quetzalcoatl ceremony, but this time it involves not simply followers celebrating their cult but the priest who exhorts and informs his audience. Don Ramón, like ancient divine kings, derives his power from contact with "the dynamical centre of the universe."[7] Following the initial song of challenge to the worshippers, he begins a prayer which also serves to introduce the cosmogonic myth underlying the worship of Quetzalcoatl. Central to this myth is one already mentioned, that of the sky and earth, but in this context both bodies are transformed into living creatures. The earth is dominated by a great serpent "that lies in the fire at the heart of the world" (*PS*, 210), while the sky is the mythical dark thunderbird, an image that completes and reiterates the eagle-serpent complex of Quetzalcoatl's banner.

Both these images have a complicated background. Traditionally, the snake plays a part in initiation, purification, and fertility rituals. It also is prominent in the worship of Demeter (the ancient mother-virgin figure whose role Kate parallels in the novel). All of these have a general significance for this particular scene and for Kate's transition from the profane to the sacred world. In addition, Lawrence carefully follows his reading by suggesting that the god of the upper air, of thunder and lightning, emerged from an ancient serpent divinity of the lower world. Quetzalcoatl is a god of wind and lightning whose name itself indicates his ophidian aspects and antecedents. To his believers, he is the animating principle both of the external world, symbolized by sky and bird, and of the individual himself, symbolized by the snake coiling at the base of the human spine. Thus, though theosophical notions enter into it, the controlling idea is found in myth itself. This cosmogonic myth of *The Plumed Serpent*, as it is ceremonially

7. Frazer, *The Golden Bough*, III, 1.

rendered, culminates with a torrential downpour, thereby naturalistically authenticating the fact that the thunderbird invoked by Ramón traditionally played a prominent part in rainmaking ceremonies.

In the conversation that follows this freeing of the waters and the dramatic rendering of the magical qualities of the myth to manifest what it describes, Kate becomes aware of the inherent positive value of fear and of the nature of belief as something compelled, as an inescapable destiny but not a universal one. Following this combination of mythic image and overt doctrine, Kate returns home to Sayula, where her growing attachment to the world of Quetzalcoatl is confirmed by her reaction to the ordinary world: "Her own house seemed empty, banal, vulgar. For the first time in her life, she felt the banality and emptiness even of her own milieu" (PS, 226). The crystallization of her vision of a life devoid of a sacred power or presence occurs in a series of brief scenes in this chapter. First, there are Juana's sneering questions about "gringos" on the other side of the world. Then, there is her housekeeper's daughter's raucous insistence on Kate's eating a tortilla. Next comes Concha's tormenting of her slow-witted sister, Maria. And finally, there is the Indian urchin who tethers a black mud-chick in the water at the edge of the lake and then stones it.

In all of these, Kate senses that the fundamental relationship in each case is that of "the victim, the inevitable victim, and the inevitable victimiser" (PS, 229). The apparent inescapability of this pattern is dramatized in the final scene when after having chased the boy away and freed the bird, Kate is horrified to see that the bird had let itself drift back to shore, where an older youth turns it over to its original tormenter again. At this point, Kate sees the pattern as typical of the continent at large: "This country would have its victim. America would have its victim. As long as time lasts, it will be the continent divided between Victims and Victimisers" (PS, 233–34). In effect, Kate here creates her own myth corresponding to that of Quetzalcoatl which Ramón is refurbishing. Significantly enough, her creatures lack names and are identified only by their roles. It is as if they are denied the creative potency Mirabel attaches to the names of Ramón's pantheon.

This contrast between the two myths is heightened by the structure of this section of the novel. The four scenes of victimization in Kate's myth are matched in the next three chapters by the four hymns of

Ramón's invention, thereby emphasizing their differences as characters. The hymns recount the death, resurrection, and imminent return of Quetzalcoatl, the dying and reviving god of Mexico. But Kate's myth is a demoniac or diabolic parody of this, for in it nothing dies or revives, nothing changes, and nothing—apart from bare survival—is achieved. Instead, the participants remain locked in a static tableau of scapegoat and assailant, which implicitly denies the connection of scapegoat with dying god. The aim of this parody of man's expulsion and purification of evil is cruelty and torment rather than the effecting of death as in the ritual itself. The dedication of Juana, Concha, and the unnamed urchin to prolonging suffering and vengeance is ample testimony to the diabolic character of Kate's Mexican myth.

Yet Lawrence and Kate do not leave matters wtih a simple indictment of "the horrible uncreate elementality, so uncouth, even sun and rain uncouth, uncouth" (PS, 234). The chapter concludes with Kate's striking intuition of the essential world view and feelings of the urchin, who is regarded as typical of his race. In seeing that he views the entire world as a place where "the elements were monstrous and cruel" and "an uncouth, monstrous universe of monsters big and little" (PS, 234) against which revenge is as much a necessity as a desire, Kate suggests a way out of the dead end created by her myth of victim and victimizer. The sympathetic note on which the chapter closes shows that it is not simply the race that is diabolic. The universe itself victimizes man so that in "a soft, struggling thing" like the mud-chick he is capable of "seeing only another monster of the outer void" (PS, 235). As a result, he exchanges at every opportunity, no matter how trivial, his role of victim for that of victimizer. The way out of this impasse in which man oscillates between two destructive roles, the one physical and the other spiritual, is to reintegrate the pattern of scapegoat and assailant into the mythic cycle of the dying and reviving god. On the human level, this means the norm for character is a mediation of Kate's negative scepticism and Ramón's affirmative faith, of her passion and his detachment.

When, in Chapter XV, Kate goes of her own accord to the servants' quarters to hear the hymns of Quetzalcoatl sung, she is turning to the true, genuine myth that embodies the essence of life in Mexico. Instead of men oscillating between playing victim and victimizer, there are gods who alternately succeed each other in an ordered and inclusive round of living actions. The first two hymns narrate the myth of the aged Quetzalcoatl's meeting Jesus, his immolation and ascension, his death "beyond the blue outer wall of heaven. . . . At the heart of all the worlds" (*PS*, 242), his anointment, entombment, sleep, and finally his revival and preparation to succeed the exhausted Jesus.

With the third hymn the narrative moves away from its exclusive absorption in the timeless world of myth as Quetzalcoatl draws close to observe modern Mexico. Here the recurrent image defining its inhabitants is that of the stone of despair which, as both Jesus and Quetzalcoatl recognize, the Mexican people have swallowed. This stone symbolizes "their heaviness,/ Their lumpishness" (*PS*, 259), indeed just those things that inspired in Kate the greatest revulsion. And its removal is part of the purification rites Quetzalcoatl demands of his people under pain of a cosmic holocaust. His demands and aim are communicated, with the aid of the Stone of Change, an extinct falling star, to two men of Quetzalcoatl who in turn are to advise and warn the people. In this hymn the emphasis is upon purification and hope, though a warning note too is sounded. The conclusion mingles images of the Christian Resurrection and the myth of Cronus as Quetzalcoatl announces his goal: either the attainment of true manhood by his people or else "an end/ Of those ill-smelling tribes of men" (*PS*, 259).

The final hymn reiterates these alternatives, but the tone is much angrier, less hortatory and more peremptory. Quetzalcoatl views the mechanized world of his people and attacks them for having deserted their own essential capabilities. Then he introduces an eschatological dimension into the myth of cosmic disaster presented in the third hymn. Since "there are no dead dead" (*PS*, 276), one's fate after death is determined by one's behavior during life. The major alternatives are whether one had mastered the forces of the world or not. For "those that have mastered the forces of the world, die into the forces, they have homes in death" (*PS*, 277). On the other hand, "the dead of those who have mastered nothing, nothing at all,/ Crawl like masterless dogs in the back streets of the air,/ Creeping for the garbage of life, and biting with venomous mouths" (*PS*, 277). The afterlife of the former order, it is implied, can be achieved by obeying the behest of the god, the Morning Star: "Conquer. . . . Pass the dragons [of the cosmos], and pass on to me" (*PS*, 277). But if his people do not face and master the dragons of the elemental world, the result will be physical

pain and consignment to "the back streets of the air." It is significant
that this final hymn should inject a modified version of the dragon-
slaying ritual into Quetzalcoatl's myth. Its inclusion suggests that men
who enact it dramatically will be performing a magical ceremony that
will in effect create a cosmos, a unified world order of their own and
enable them to move from the winter of their discontent into the season of growth and fertility.[8] The effect of the last two hymns is to stress
the necessity of endeavor and transformation by the people if the announced coming of the god is to issue in their salvation rather than
destruction.

At this point in the novel, what we may call the myth and the antimyth of the dying and reviving god are juxtaposed. Both exist primarily in the individual's consciousness or in an essentially private or
secret world of which he is a member. In the next four chapters
(XVIII–XXI), however, they move into the public world where the reviving god and his Mexican assailant engage in a ritual combat that
results in the triumph of the former. This full-blown entry into the
world of human society occurs when Ramón and the men of Quetzalcoatl remove the symbols of the Roman Catholic faith from the church
at Sayula in a ritual which is simultaneously one of the expulsion of
evil and the funerary separation of the dying god. Lawrence prepares
for this dramatic event by having Ramón and Kate discuss their personal problems in the course of which Ramón interprets the existing
sexual relations between men and women as well as the political relations between men in terms of the myth of victim and victimizer.

The connection between this analysis of human depravity and the
ritual expulsion of Christ is the Church, which fails to help man coalesce his soul into the ruling power of his life. Instead, it "pushes
them more and more into a soft, emotional helplessness, with the un-
pleasant sensuous gratification of feeling themselves victims, victimised, victimised, but at the same time with the lurking sardonic
consciousness that in the end a victim is stronger than the victimiser" (PS, 295–96). As a result, the carrying out of the four different images of Christ—the dead Christ of Holy Week, the scourged

8. The modification which changes killing the dragon into simple mystery is re-
quired because of Lawrence's commitment to theosophical views concerning the beast's
divinity. See William Y. Tindall, *D. H. Lawrence and Susan His Cow* (New York,
1939), 155–59.

Christ, the Savior of the Sacred Heart, and the image of Jesus of Nazareth—is an expulsion of the evil that accrues to a deity when stifled by an alien and debased institution. The images dramatize the essential situation: in the world the god is indeed dead and so has become part of the antimyth. That is, he is simultaneously victim and victimizer of his worshippers. He is the former because his worship has encouraged "sensuous looseness" which has led to "the old, unfathomable hate" (PS, 296). And he is the latter because his priests with their cant about love and kindness lure his worshippers into "a soft, emotional helplessness" (PS, 295).

It is in the ritual attitude to this dead Christ, however, that the antimyth of scapegoat and assailant is first drawn into the larger pattern of the dying and reviving god. Christ's departure is molded into a form approximating the rites of Adonis combined with those of Hercules and Asiatic kings and heroes in general. The images of the dead god are accompanied by wailing women as they move in a slow procession to the water's edge, where they are committed to the waves by being placed on a ship that takes them to their funeral pyre. The whole impression created by this act is one of a mingled reverence, sorrow, and ecstasy. This bears out the hymns' suggestion that Christ and Quetzalcoatl are not antagonistic to one another but are friends and divine successors who respect the function of the other. The effect is to free Christ from his role as victim-victimizer and to assimilate him to the larger role of the dying god who is part of an unceasing cycle of existence.

Nowhere is this separation of the deity from his professional advocates more clearly shown than in Chapter XIX, which deals exclusively with the attack on Jamiltepec and Ramón planned by the priests and the Knights of Cortes. The action is neither a piece of bravura realism nor a lapse from the novel's total ritualistic pattern. It forms the traditional ritual combat that takes place when the reviving god appears. Significantly enough, the struggle lies between Ramón and professional assassins hired by the Church, not between Quetzalcoatl and Christ. It is the institution rather than the deity that is Ramón's antagonist. Anticlericalism rather than denial of Christ is the rallying point for the men of Quetzalcoatl. And the defeat of the traitors and sinister killers signals the permanent incarnation of Quetzalcoatl in Ramón. This is suggested not only by his triumph over his enemies and the return of his soul from its flickering sojourn in a world beyond life. It is also intimated by Kate's sudden feeling of being willing to die with him, by his appearing as if "some blind super-consciousness seemed to possess him" (PS, 315), by his remoteness of manner and inability to recognize her, as if he were another being, and by his "primitive, gleaming look of virginity" (PS, 317) which reminds us of her own transformation after contact with the heart of the cosmos and the living god. By her own secondary participation in the combat Kate dramatizes her commitment to the worship of Quetzalcoatl and at the same time her dying out of the world she had known for so long. Thus, in her own actions and reactions is encompassed the whole significance of the ritual combat—death for the evil and the exhausted, triumph for the life-giving and the resurrected.

With the triumph of Quetzalcoatl's representative, the novel turns to a celebration of this highly important and dramatic act. Thus, the succeeding chapters center on two mythically crucial observances, the sacred marriage and the inauguration of the god. In the first case, Kate slowly recovers from the shock of her participation in death, which in a way represents her abandonment of her civilized attitudes. Then in a dramatic scene, for the first time she fully senses the masculine power of Cipriano and what it means for her:

> She could see again the skies go dark, and the phallic mystery rearing itself like a whirling dark cloud, to the zenith, till it pierced the sombre, twilit zenith; the old, supreme phallic mystery. . . . Once you entered his mystery the scale of all things changed, and he became a living male power, undefined, and unconfined. The smallness, the limitations ceased to exist. In his black, glinting eyes the power was limitless, and it was as if, from him, from his body of blood could rise up that pillar of cloud which swayed and swung, like a rearing serpent or a rising tree, till it swept the zenith, and all the earth below was dark and prone, and consummated. . . . He was once more the old dominant male, shadowy, intangible, looming suddenly tall, and covering the sky, making a darkness that was himself and nothing but himself, the Pan male. And she swooned prone beneath, perfect in her proneness. (PS, 331–32)

In envisaging her marrying Cipriano, Kate is not so much acting under the impetus of the shock of exposure to violence as testifying to the subtle interrelation of death and sex enshrined in many primitive myths. The existence of the one signals the necessary presence of the other. And when she imagines this new sexual experience in the form of the myth of the earth and the sky, she indirectly presages her own inclusion in Quetzalcoatl's pantheon, for she identifies herself with a deity as well as with nature. A short journey to Jaramay serves as a transitional rite that mediates between her separation from the old and incorporation in the new life. After it she agrees to mime the sacred marriage of the gods by having Quetzalcoatl unite her and Cipriano. The ritual character of this ceremony is underscored by such acts as her ceremonial divestiture and assumption of fresh garments, her being led into a garden and standing barefoot in the rain, and her recitation of a vow that invokes the rain, earth, sky, and Morning Star. All of these aim at sealing the irrevocable nature of the wedding.

Following the marriage ceremony, which serves as Kate's declaration of her entry into the mythical world of Quetzalcoatl, the new religion announces the inauguration of its god who functions also as a temporal lord or king. Kate's appearance in the world of myth is paralleled by Quetzalcoatl's first appearance in the world of so-called reality. Chapter XXI is composed essentially of four scenes or nodes of significance: Kate's reactions to both worlds, the installation ceremony of the god, its interruption by Carlota, and Kate's flowering as a woman. Substantially, Kate's refusal to marry Cipriano in a civil ceremony and her shrinking from the importunities of peasants at her window show that she does not yet fully understand the nature and relations of the two worlds. For her the realm of religion or myth and that of reality must be kept separate. Reality still exists for her exclusively as a material phenomenon to which begging is an inevitable concomitant. Myth and religion are somehow held to be pure and uncontaminated by such sordid necessities as food and shelter or their monetary equivalents, to be, in short, humanitarian utopias for sensitive psyches.

To convince her of the erroneous nature of this view is the next stage in her education and character development or transformation. The first lesson is provided by the installation ceremony, for it gives her the opportunity to exhibit what is still her deepest feeling about the primitive character of this religion, namely, fear. At the same time, it reveals the true cause of human fear. The first drums announcing the ceremony, the facing of the audience with Cipriano, and the entry into the church, all send a tide of fright washing through her. The thematic centrality of this emotion is made clear when she views the ceremony in terms of the myth of the victim and wonders whether she herself is a sacrifice. Faced with the imminent appearance of the risen god, she is again tempted by the antimyth of the victim and assailant, tempted to see it as the core of reality.

When Ramón as Quetzalcoatl speaks, however, she finds something stronger than her fear—his will—and so enters the church to witness his enthronement. Here Lawrence devises his own symbols but at the same time has them conform to the archetypal pattern of primitive ritual. Thus, the various colored insignia Ramón wears testify to this being an enthronement ceremony. In turn the bowl of multicolored liquids together with Ramón's words show that this is also a sacrament of initiation. This last point is made in three ways by Lawrence. First, Kate is struck just before the ceremony begins by the way in which the church windows resemble "a strange maze" (*PS*, 361). The significance of this is that the labyrinth or maze traditionally emblemized the difficulties attendant upon reaching the center where the consecration or initiation was performed. Second, in observing Ramón after Carlota's interruption of the ceremony, Kate sees that "his old connections were broken" (*PS*, 367), even that most intimate one between husband and wife. In this way, his initiation into godlike power is seen negatively, as a necessary separation or disengagement from an earlier and different way of life. And third, the sacramental character of the ritual is dramatically attested to both by Carlota's protest against what she sees as a parody and profanation of the Christian Eucharist and by Cipriano's savage comparison of the two forms of sacrament.

The initiatory aspect of the scene operates on two levels, for while Ramón is clearly initiated into a new role, the people and Kate are also inducted into a new world. Though once again frightened by the prospects before her, she now is subject to a stronger power. This is her passionate desire for that sacrament which is mentioned in the Welcome Song to Quetzalcoatl and which, for her, can be acquired only through Cipriano. In reaching this conclusion, she has responded to the complex of the ceremony itself, her response to Carlota's interruption, and her reflections inspired by the dying woman and the religious drumming and dancing of the natives. In overcoming her fear, she ceases to wonder whether she is a sacrifice, and she does so because "the hardness of self-will" (*PS*, 376) has been dissolved.

Once the triumph of Quetzalcoatl is complete and Kate begins the unfolding of her own essential nature or character, the central focus of the novel swings around to the incarnation of Huitzilopochtli in Cipriano. Thus Ramón's efforts to change the world of his people are carried one step further. For in letting "'General Viedma be swallowed up in the red Huitzilopochtli'" (*PS*, 392), Cipriano is manifesting what he and Ramón urged on the natives, the divinization of the individual through contact with the deepest resources of his own being. Through the incarnation symbol of their own appearance and behavior, Ramón and Cipriano show their people the way to salvation. Social reform is to be achieved via theomorphic transformation, for though he does not say so explicitly, what Ramón aims at is the liberation of the god in each man. The method by which this is to be achieved in Cipriano's case once again shows the eclecticism and originality of Lawrence in his conforming to the large and therefore loose ritual pattern of primitive initiation. The blindfold which plunges him into darkness, the reiterant questions, the binding of his limbs, the handling of the genitalia, and the trancelike sleep, all reflect in greater or lesser measure initiatory ceremonies particularly those involving mimetic death and rebirth.

This ceremony, however, is but the private aspect of Cipriano's incarnation. He must not only become the god, he must also demonstrate publicly his acceptance of the role and all that it entails. This he does in the chapter entitled "Huitzilopochtli's Night," where amid darkness, fire, and song his divine function is both announced and enacted. He represents "the anger of the manhood of men" (*PS*, 400) and the "master of the dream" (*PS*, 402). In short, he is the guardian deity of the new community founded by Ramón or, as his song has it, "the watcher" (*PS*, 402). And in making the serpent his image, Lawrence reflects what he found in much of his reading about myth and ritual: the guardian spirit frequently took the form of a snake and the avenging spirit of the dead also appeared as a serpentlike creature.

Huitzilopochtli's first act is to oversee the execution of Ramón's treacherous attackers, who were but extensions of those Ramón sees responsible for the deathlike torpor of his people and country at large. Here in this sacrificial punishment the power of the god is exhibited as a warning to those who would be enemies and as an encouragement to those who are his followers. Shocking and depressing as these executions are, nevertheless, Lawrence takes some pains to fit them into a ritualistic context designed to soften the wantonness of the act. Perhaps the most striking technique here is the use of dramatic dialogue in exchanges between Cipriano and the guards and later Ramón. The aim of this is to underscore the fact that these men are all playing roles, either as gods or their worshippers. Hence their actions are removed to a ritualistic plane corresponding to the mythic level of the characters. A similar ritualistic amelioration is provided by the green leaf of Malintzi, the expiatory ceremony performed by Ramón, and the designation of the executions as a purificatory rite enabling the victims to be revivified as true human beings.

Despite these efforts to dramatize a justification of cold-blooded violence, Kate is still shocked and wary of Cipriano. Significantly enough, she is not most deeply troubled by the brutality of the acts. As the widow of an Irish revolutionary she can understand and so accept the rationale of their ideology. What she balks at is the fact that "they seemed nothing but men" (*PS*, 413). That is, to her their incarnation as Quetzalcoatl and Huitzilopochtli has not become a fact. The reason is one familiar to Lawrence's readers—revulsion against "the exertion of pure, awful will" (*PS*, 413). Ultimately her acquiescence to Cipriano as Huitzilopochtli and to her own nature as Malintzi occurs after her encounter with Cipriano in which he urges her incarnation. This, however, is not capitulation but transformation, for she now sees him as motivated by "not will at all" but instead by "the living, flickering, fiery *Wish*" (*PS*, 417) which is primary. In the wish for his "ultimate achievement" (*PS*, 415) to be the living Huitzilopochtli, he repeats in his own way Kate's earlier longing to achieve a wholeness of being. Her recognition that they are seeking the same thing and that its achievement lies through the realization of a new pantheon leads her to accept the incarnation of "the goddess bride, Malintzi of the green dress" (*PS*, 420) in her own person.

For Kate, however, the ritual appropriate to such divine beings, namely, the sacred marriage, is enacted more easily than its public equivalent. In substance, the last three chapters of the novel contain Kate's struggle to find and reveal herself publicly in the modern social world as the goddess-bride of a man-god. Her inability to "definitely commit herself, either to the old way of life, or to the new" (*PS*, 459), her envy and contempt for Teresa, her suspicion of the natives, even the intermittency of her contact with Cipriano, all testify to the difficulties of celebrating myth in an "amythical" world. Nor does Kate succeed in discovering a mode of behavior that reflects a single-minded acceptance of the myth. While this may be interpreted as a failure of belief, it may also, in a larger context, be regarded as an appropriate pattern of action. The ritual that best reflects the position of myth in the modern world is, Lawrence seems to suggest, one of advance and retreat, which mirrors Kate's psychological drama of hesitation and accession. Thus, Lawrence, like the twentieth century in general, finds his imaginative paradigm in the collocation of myth and irony and metaphor rather than in literal patterns of transcendence and immanence together with a sceptical delineation of their boundaries of relevance.

*

In the foregoing we have seen a number of the ramifications attendant upon Lawrence's postulation of ontological duality in character. A more common and more flexibly varied use of myth in conjunction with characterization emerges when we survey some of the major literary treatments of the scapegoat figure and his rituals. Modern writers have seized eagerly upon the paradoxical possibilities inherent in the scapegoat and exploited them with subtlety and originality. Cruelty, desire, self-preservation, witting and unwitting sacrifice, jealousy, hope, and fear, all help to shape the character of the scapegoat as he appears both in reality and in imagination. Yet the modern writer is far from unique, for the concept of the scapegoat and his narrative and characterological deployment in literature are found in many cultures and times. From earliest days it has traditionally been one of the chief means by which men have sought the preservation of society, the honoring of the gods, and their own psychic release. The paradox that a figure destined for punishment and sacrifice should also be honored and even worshipped is fraught, as we shall see, with tragic, ironic, and even comic possibilities.

Before, however, considering some of the specific ways in which writers throughout history have realized these possibilities, we would do well to look at some general features of the scapegoat if only to forestall our regarding the term in its limited, contemporary sense wherein it is synonymous with "sucker" or "fall guy." Our sources of information concerning this figure are essentially threefold. Even yet the most familiar tradition of the scapegoat is probably the Judeo-

Christian as presented in the Bible. Leviticus 16 recounts the gradually evolving customs in the ritual of atonement, but for our purposes it is enough to note that a live goat selected by lot had the sins, crimes, and general iniquities of Israel ritually transferred to it by the high priest and then was sent out into the wilderness as a religious presentation to Azazel, the demon of the desert. Apart from the fact that in postexilic times the general sacrificial system of the temple, including the scapegoat ritual, was abandoned, leaving remission of sins to be achieved solely through genuine repentance of the heart, the most interesting thing about the custom was the restricting of the sacrifice of a sin-receiver to an animal.

When we move to the classical world, we find that though animals still figure prominently in such rituals, the scapegoat may often also be human. As a number of scholars have shown, the festival of Thargelia, for instance, which celebrated the offering of first fruits at harvest time, was dominated by the ceremony of the *pharmakos* or scapegoat. Two individuals—sometimes two men, other times a man and a woman—one representing the men of the community, the other the women, were led out of the city, ceremonially beaten to the sound of music, and then either expelled or stoned to death. Versions of this human sacrifice were also performed at other times and places in Rome as well as Greece.

Finally, when we step even further back, into the world of primitive cultures via the richly detailed pages of *The Golden Bough* and related works, we encounter an even broader handling of the scapegoat. No longer is this role consigned solely to human beings or animals. Sticks, stones, trees, and images of all sorts are used to effect the transference of evils, sins, and misfortunes of every kind from the afflicted individual, family, or dwelling. However diverse and random or infrequent the occurrence, the operative factor is constant: the principle of vicarious suffering dictates the impulse and the action.

Out of the dense welter of instances before him, Frazer, for instance, draws four main conclusions, which however anthropologically contestable nevertheless have certain useful implications for the interpretation of scapegoat figures in literary texts.[9] First, he suggests that regardless of the nature of the evil afflicting the individual or the

9. See Frazer, *The Golden Bough*, IX, Chap. V.

community, whether intangible or material, the ritual intent is to achieve a complete removal and clearance of all the evils and ills besetting those involved. In short, the focus is upon what Jane Harrison termed riddance or rituals of aversion, upon purification through vicarious suffering. Second, the practice may be either occasional or periodic, with the latter increasingly common. It is usually on an annual basis that is correlated with a major seasonal change, which in turn is equated with the beginning of a new year. Here the aim is to effect a new lease on life for the individual and the community. Third, the scapegoat ritual itself is preceded or followed by a Saturnalian interval in which social hierarchies are inverted, carnival revelry and hedonistic feasts enjoyed, and sexual profligacy and promiscuity practiced. Depending on when it occurs in relation to the scapegoat sacrifice, the Saturnalian experience is either a final plunge into evil before purification or a brief and clearly delimited expression of relief at the removal of all those things afflicting and oppressing man's spirit. And fourth, the scapegoat includes among its candidates the divine man or king-god whose ritual death at the hands of his subjects originally formed a ritual separate and distinct from that of the scapegoat. The chief points involved in this elision are the increased probability of misinterpretation as a result of the loss of the sense of divinity and the replacement of it with a notion of mere, ordinary human victimhood.

For interpretation of the scapegoat and his rituals we are essentially indebted to the disciplines of anthropology and psychology. Classical representatives of the former, like Frazer, Jane Harrison, and others, suggest that the scapegoat is the community's religious attempt to free itself of everything that it takes to be maleficent, corrupting, and painful. This attempt is based on what Frazer calls a mistaken association of ideas and what Freud labels a species of magical thinking. Both agree that this mode of reasoning derives from an early, primitive, almost precivilized state of man's development. But both also make it quite clear that this method of thinking and responding to threats to survival does not disappear with the advent of civilization and rational approaches to human misfortune and error. It continues to lurk just below the surface of man's civilized veneer and to haunt the not so distant recesses of his mind as a result either of the residue of religious superstitions (Frazer) or of the propensity for regression (Freud).

One of the fullest attempts to interpret the personal and cultural significance of the scapegoat occurs, however, neither in Frazer nor in Freud but in Carl Jung and depth psychology. Briefly put, this view holds that in the process of ego development a part of the personality, called the shadow, is repressed for the sake of the ego ideal. The shadow is the negative part of the psyche, consisting of all those qualities, values, and attitudes which the persona finds most despicable, unbearable, and hateful. These elements generate a powerful, though largely unconscious, guilt feeling in the individual and the group. Freedom from the distress of this feeling, from this unconscious conflict, is achieved by the activity known as projection, whereby the negative qualities resident in the psyche are projected or transferred to the external world and experienced not as something within but as something outside and alien to one. So seen, this entity, individual, type, or group is blamed, attacked, punished, and otherwise eliminated, for it is literally the stranger, the enemy, the personification of evil. By instituting such a scapegoat and performing the ritual expulsion, the individual and the group discharge their own repressed negative drives and behavior impulses. In this way, the mind eliminates, at least for a time, those feelings of guilt, inadequacy, and insecurity that inevitably haunt the psyche which refuses to face its shadow. Such a psychological interpretation, as opposed to the anthropological description, fulfills two functions. It explains the perdurability of the scapegoat and it also suggests that adaptations of the ritual are constantly being made in order to conform to the prevailing values and norms of social structures, which are subject to the endless dynamics of nature as well as of history.

When we turn to literature, we find that the twin foci of anthropology and psychology, of the primitive and the civilized, of the ancient and the contemporary converge in a number of texts which both recapitulate and extrapolate from the forms of the scapegoat in their respective cultures and times. Indeed, one modern writer and critic, who began by examining the scapegoat role in a single author and then was impelled to consider a number of other authors, ultimately was led to a highly radical conclusion. Rayner Heppenstall remarked: "After a while it began to seem to me that all the key characters in fiction were scapegoats in one sense or another. Indeed, I began to wonder whether the whole of our narrative and dramatic literature were not a concerted effort to find and employ scapegoats."[10] Perhaps a speculation of such an inclusive order is ultimately indefensible as well as programmatically pointless, though obviously some would not agree. Nevertheless, it does at least serve to call attention to the wide variety of uses to which the scapegoat can be put by the resourceful creative imagination. It would be absurd to declare that all literary ways of handling the scapegoat have been classified, but it is certainly possible to identify some of the major forms that come readily to mind. And it is to these that we turn now, considering them in terms of two central categories: formal structures or strategies and types of scapegoat. Both obviously will bear on the question of myth and character, since whether as pattern or person these categories will reveal the additional dimensions provided the character as mimesis of the individual human being by this facet of metamyth. Just as obviously, since the concentration is taxonomic rather than analytic as it was in the case of *The Plumed Serpent*, much is deliberately left unsaid about the particular texts discussed.

The first category is in many ways the most difficult to assess and describe, for it involves authorial attitudes which determine the shape and design of the text and these are notoriously slippery things to pin down. Any sustained examination of the sort mentioned by Heppenstall quickly makes us aware that there is a significant difference in texture and structure among works whose authors are conscious of the scapegoat and his tradition and those who are not. Immediately, however, one recognizes that precisely what a writer has conscious knowledge of at a particular moment of creation is an extremely murky and problematic issue in the majority of instances. So it is better perhaps to couch the difference in formal terms and to say that some writers make an overt use of the traditions of the scapegoat, while others deploy a more covert strategy. Novelists like August Strindberg and Jocelyn Brooke and short story writers like V. S. Pritchett title certain of their works "The Scapegoat." From this it is obvious that they recognize the concept and they wish their readers' response to be structured by the awareness that the concept is being utilized to shape

10. Rayner Heppenstall, "Bernanos: The Priest as Scapegoat," *Partisan Review*, XIII (1946), 449. For a sustained and sophisticated advocacy of the scapegoat's centrality, see René Girard, *Violence and the Sacred*, trans. P. Gregory (Baltimore, 1977).

the text's design. In Strindberg's novella *The Scapegoat* the shaping force in the tale is largely the Christian notion of the titular figure wherein it is merged with the biblical image of the suffering servant. After enduring enormous vicissitudes at the hands of parents, teachers, his beloved, the courts, the police, and society generally, the attorney Libotz prepares to leave the remote Swedish town where the aged come to "prepare themselves for the final journey."[11] He hears two inhabitants jestingly refer to him as the scapegoat. Quietly he contemplates the image and finds in it his salvation:

> It seemed to him an innocent jest, yet it was true. And he recalled to his mind the Feast of the Atonement of the Old Testament, at which a goat, loaded down with the sins of all the people, was driven out into the desert, consecrated to Azazel, or in other words, the Evil One—who thereby regained what was his. This role was neither a grateful one nor an honorable one. But had not Christ carried the same burden of disgrace and dishonor? And did not this have a meaning beyond our understanding?
>
> The outcast, also, felt some of the sting of this, the onus of bearing the hatred of others, being laden with it, with their meanness and maliciousness, which they had grafted onto him.
>
> Could it be that he was the serum animal, who had within him the virus of poison and ills, which through him was to be transmuted, transubstantiated into the curing remedy? As long as he did not return hatred with hatred, he was out of reach of their power. But the moment he let himself be influenced and was roused to anger, he felt the poison. In order to keep his thoughts aloof from bitterness, he kept repeating to himself passages from the Bible that had impressed themselves most on his mind. And these passages had the accumulated effect of the truth of ageless centuries upon his childlike mind. (*S*, 169–70)

In Brooke's case, however, his novel is shaped not by a Christian perspective on the scapegoat but by a pagan and primitive one. The thirteen-year-old boy who ultimately assumes the scapegoat role is redheaded, presented with mistletoe by his uncle who finally performs the physical sacrificial act, psychologically compelled to become a

11. August Strindberg, *The Scapegoat*, trans. A. Paulson (New York, 1967), 4. Subsequent references to this edition are hereafter cited parenthetically in the text as *S*.

thief and criminal, indulged with festivities and fireworks, and finally slain on a stone altar that reminds him of Stonehenge. It is clear that Brooke means these details from primitive rites to open to us the awesome and psychologically disturbing prospect of the ancient ritual being performed in a modern, ostensibly civilized setting under a compulsion that is partly unconscious wish and partly tragic necessity spiritually ordained.

The conscious deployment of scapegoat images and actions in both cases is central to the narrative thrust and thematic design as well as to the delineation of character. Most obviously, the titles employed activate reader awareness of the mythic dimension long before that of the characters the great bulk of whom remain either ignorant of it or at best dimly and hesitantly sensitive to analogies and paradigms linking their situations to those of the metamyth. But the choice of quite different source materials and traditions markedly affects the results of the deployment of the mythic figure. For Strindberg, the scapegoat character is a paradigm of suffering who ultimately achieves a contemplative and compassionate perspective on his fate through the apprehension of his divine affiliations. As a result the novel ends on a note of transcendence and acceptance: "And Libotz trudged forward again, toward the highroad, and went to face new experiences—which he could not help but foresee, but no longer had any fear of" (S, 175). For Brooke, on the other hand, the scapegoat is a human victim created at the moment of his entry into a world which sees him as an alien and ethical inferior with pathological qualities. Consequently, Brooke's narrative and the psychic disintegration of his characters—both the scapegoat and his assailant—move inexorably toward the tragic finality in which the participants regress in trancelike acquiescence to primal emotions acted upon but scarcely understood. In the final pages pity and terror converge in a vision of human waste and failure constrained by a necessity beyond the bounds of comprehension:

> Wearily, he stooped over the prostrate body, and shifted it into a more decent position. Bending lower, he gently kissed the pale, dawn-chilled face; then, unhurriedly, laid his hand on the smooth flesh above the heart: knowing, before he did so, that it had already ceased to beat.
>
> From far away, at the barracks over toward Glamber, came the

faint nostalgic note of a bugle, sounding reveille. Gerald turned away, seeing everything clearly at last: knowing that the long initiation was over; the rites observed, the cycle completed.[12]

When literary texts employ a more covert use of the scapegoat, not only is there a subtle alteration in the reader's response but the central characters too deepen into the mysteries and enigmas of human personality rather than limning the problematic, puzzling, or awesome nature of the theme of ritual sacrifice. This can be seen in a work such as Nathaniel Hawthorne's "My Kinsman, Major Molineux," where the scapegoat proper appears only in the final pages of the story, utters no words, and disappears as part of a local tar-and-feathering. Daniel Hoffman has shown beyond question that Robin's kinsman is an American colonial scapegoat-king. But this fact is revealed only at the end of the story so that the scapegoat motif is not part of the conscious shaping forces in the work. The reading experience instead revolves primarily around the central character's involvement with issues of quest or search, mystery or puzzle, and transformation. In such a work the function of the scapegoat is not so much actively structural as it is revelatory of character. Robin's confrontation with his uncle occurs precisely at the point when he is ready to perceive the infantile inadequacy and stultifying consequences of his original dependency on the sustaining support of another person. The "overwhelming humiliation" and "foul disgrace" he sees visited upon his kinsman are prophetic of the fate which awaits his own humorless obsession with social and economic advancement and cultural dependency.[13] Thus, his joining in the Saturnalian laughter of the community signals his emancipation from and the demise of an inadequate because external authority figure. The two coalesce in Robin's objectively realized perception that with the end of a sentimental and selfish attachment to familial authority there comes also a genuine feeling and regard for the ultimate paternal force or factor in one's existence: "On they went, like fiends that throng in mockery around some dead potentate, mighty no more, but majestic still in his agony. On they went, in

---

12. Jocelyn Brooke, *The Scapegoat* (New York, 1949), 209.

13. Daniel Hoffman, *Form and Fable in American Fiction* (New York, 1961), 113–25; George Parsons Lathrop (ed.), *The Complete Works of Nathaniel Hawthorne* (Cambridge, Mass., 1883), III, 639. Subsequent references to this edition are hereafter cited parenthetically in the text as *CW*.

counterfeited pomp, in senseless uproar, in frenzied merriment, trampling all on an old man's heart" (*CW*, 640). In short, the scapegoat is the dramatic means by which the youth's initiation into maturity is effected. It is a beneficent trauma which catalytically alters and deepens the mystery of human personality development rather than being, as in the case of Jocelyn Brooke's novel, a ritual paradigm forecasting the novel's action and enriching its theme.

Hawthorne's story suggests another pair of formal strategies that condition the use of the scapegoat in literature. When one studies the anthropological material dealing with the communal reliance on the scapegoat and his rituals, one is struck by the necessary discrepancy between the purpose and the possible achievement. That is to say, one may taunt, revile, and humiliate selected individuals, and one may expel or sacrifice them in order to purge a community of plague, pollution, and evil as energetically as one can manage, without effecting the desired result. And yet this does not seem to have altered the enthusiasm with which societies have pursued the goal of, as Frazer says, "a fresh start in life, happy and innocent." In a remarkable way, the scapegoat ritual, like many primitive rituals, resembles the belief in apocalypse, which, as Frank Kermode has observed, "can be disconfirmed without being discredited."[14] In actual societies, in other words, the lack of social, agricultural, medical, and military efficacy in no way invalidates the ritual in the mind of its adherents. In short, anthropologically and sociologically, the scapegoat ritual is necessarily efficient and perpetually successful.

When one turns, however, to its literary expressions, it is a far different matter. Most works concentrate upon inefficient or unsuccessful instances of the ritual, and when they do dramatize successful rites, as in William Golding's *Lord of the Flies* or James Baldwin's "Going to Meet the Man," they do so with such an ironic inflection that the efficacy itself is called into question. One might, of course, attribute this to the fact that literature is a relatively recent human mode and so may have a more sceptical view of the practicality of ancient rituals. Yet even when one goes back to classical times, a tragedian such as Euripides in a play like *The Bacchae* reveals a profoundly ironic per-

14. Frazer, *The Golden Bough*, IX, 73; Frank Kermode, *The Sense of an Ending* (New York, 1967), 8.

spective on the scapegoat. As William Arrowsmith has remarked, "there . . . the god and his victim meet." [15]

Though Euripides' scepticism and irony concerning the scapegoat are fully as profound as those of modern writers like William Faulkner and James Baldwin, he also shows us one of the central mysteries that may surround the figure, and he does so by choosing the king as his ritual antagonist. From the available anthropological material it is clear that there have been three main types of scapegoat: the hero or king, the criminal or knave or slave, and the fool or clown. As *The Golden Bough*, for example, makes clear, the use of the hero or king as the scapegoat is the result of fusing the periodic ritual slaying of the king as a representative of the dying and reviving god with the sacrifice of a scapegoat for the benefit of society at large. Frazer rationally but implausibly suggests that this fusion is the result of forgetfulness as to the meaning of the king's sacrifice coupled with an impulse to economy of ritual and manpower. Literature provides both more varied and subtle answers, though all seem to devolve into a watchful tentativeness before the awesome contradiction inherent in sacrificing one's touchstone against death and guardian of fertility in order to escape material and spiritual evils. Thus, Euripides makes Pentheus, the king and linchpin of communal order and stability, suffer the fate of the scapegoat, but this exercise of divine justice concludes with the community bereft of its traditional source of authority and exposed to the terrors of potentially radical change. The authentication of Dionysus' divinity is achieved but at a cost which might well seem to presage spiritual, moral, and political bankruptcy, a cost which reflectively considered throws not inconsiderable doubt on the viability of religious observance.

If Euripides is concerned with the terrible power of the god and the loss of the city's central symbol of order, centuries later D. H. Lawrence limns a portrait of an individual who driven by his own personal anguish and demoniac autonomy grows into something like heroic stature. His assumption of the scapegoat's role becomes a savagely ironic acquiescence in the nullity of modern society and his participation in world combat the chief emblem of psychic fissures. In "En-

---

15. William Arrowsmith, Introduction to *The Bacchae*, in *The Complete Greek Tragedies*, ed. D. Grene and R. Lattimore (4 vols.; Chicago, 1958), IV, 534.

gland, My England" Egbert begins as a rather ineffectual esthete and "epicurean hermit" (*T*, 208) redeemed only by "a delightful spontaneous passion" (*T*, 205). With his firstborn daughter's maiming and his own exclusion from his family, he contracts into "the triumphant loneliness, the Ishmael quality" (*T*, 223) in which nevertheless he is "an erect, supple symbol of life," one dedicated to "the mystery of blood-sacrifices, all the lost, intense sensations of the primeval people of the place" (*T*, 222). And with the advent of war he emerges as the soldier who grimly accepts "his own degradation" (*T*, 226) at the hands of his spiritual inferiors in the army. By exercising his belatedly discovered capacity for tragic choice, he becomes enough of a hero to endure all the rites of the scapegoat. Through these he achieves a feeling of participation in an inescapable experience that sustains him through even his death agonies. Yet the culminating irony is that the experience is one of dissolution and total forgetfulness eagerly sought in preference to a life of will and memory and communion with others.

In general, the hero cast as a scapegoat seems to have to be something of a *manqué* figure, something less than the full-blown tragic or epic hero. Even Dr. Stockmann in Henrik Ibsen's *An Enemy of the People* is marked by an ingenuousness that encourages his impulsiveness. He becomes a scapegoat not so much as a result of making tragic choices quite deliberately but by following out in doggedly determined fashion the increasingly sinister consequences of purely rational decisions and responses. It is this fact, realized in the course of the play with impressively cumulative power, which makes his final discovery that "the strongest man in the world is he who stands most alone" such a profoundly ironic and poignantly pitying epitaph for the hero as scapegoat.[16]

This mystery of the sensitive, perceptive, powerful individual plunging relentlessly forward to assume the mantle of the unaware, helpless victim makes of those works which contain it haunting forays into the depths of individual emotional disquietude. When, however, the scapegoat is not the hero-king but the criminal or slave, the nature of the work and the characters in it take a quite different turn. Those two brilliant companion stories, William Faulkner's "Dry September" and James Baldwin's "Going to Meet the Man," take a more program-

---

16. Henrik Ibsen, *Six Plays*, trans. E. Le Gallienne (New York, 1957), 255.

matic and unequivocal stance concerning the scapegoat, one in which dramatic refutation and frustration replace contemplative awe. Both are lynch tales with a helpless black man as scapegoat and both are dedicated to showing the irrationality and psychological abnormality of the ritual. Faulkner concentrates on presenting the arbitrariness of the selection of Will Mayes as scapegoat through the eyes of Hawkshaw, the barber and epitome of the ordinary rational mind investigating the mares' nests of rumor and violent impulse. Baldwin, on the other hand, shows the subtle and far-reaching personal and social consequences of an impressionable child's having witnessed the brutal burning, mutilation, and slaying of a nameless, silent, black stranger. Jesse's vague perception of his parents' sexual excitement at the emasculation of the victim, his own desire to be identified with the emasculator, and his sense of supreme joy as "he watched the hanging, gleaming body, the most beautiful and terrible object he had ever seen till then," all combine to make him feel that he had survived a fundamental initiation experience which "had revealed to him a great secret which would be the key to his life forever." This acceptance of a world and life that create scapegoats is, Baldwin shows, absolutely fatal to Jesse. Later in life, as deputy sheriff, his casual, dehumanized miscegenation, his brutality toward local civil rights leaders, his impotence with his wife, and his secret terror of being involved in an incipient and incomprehensible race war, all follow from that initial experience. The terrible irony resident in man's passionate acquiescence to bloodlust wherein sexuality and death feed upon and demean one another is that it affords man a parody of revelation, a mock integration of selfhood. The "key" to Jesse's life is not the means to enter into a larger, richer, more meaningful region of existence. Instead it forever locks him into a constricted, blind round of callous insensitivity which he slowly and dimly realizes to be a genuine hell, a place rooted in and ringed by hatred. It is as if Baldwin has taken Eliot's image of *Dayadhvam* and pulled it inside out so that cultural solipsism effectively debars forever the rejuvenation of the wasteland. In "Going to Meet the Man" Baldwin's injunction is not "Sympathize" but "Recognize" even as the spiritual and psychological setting mirrors Eliot's Dantesque inferno:

> I have heard the key
> Turn in the door once and turn once only

We think of the key, each in his prison
Thinking of the key, each confirms a prison.[17]

Faulkner and Baldwin focus on the means and consequences of society's criminalization of an ordinary individual as a way of rationalizing the ritual of the scapegoat. For them, the criminal, like the hero, is *manqué*, a pseudo or institutional criminal whose chief lack is that of inherent or actual criminality. In so doing, they raise as a central issue of character the true locus of criminality by shifting the term's reference from a legal to a moral context. The ostensible scapegoat-victim becomes a cipher whose structural function is to reveal the ironic process by which the representative of society who assumes the role of ritual instigator and purifier becomes the corrupted victim of his community's ills. But for others, from Fyodor Dostoyevsky to Jean Genet, from the amoral rogue of the picaresque to the deformed sadistic killers in Graham Greene, the genuine criminal is a much more primitive, less displaced form of the scapegoat. In some cases the criminal's role is explained in naturalistic sociological terms, as when Popeye in Faulkner's *Sanctuary* has his sadism and impotent sterility attributed to heredity. Yet in the majority of instances the criminal-scapegoat in modern literature serves to dramatize religious motifs and themes. Thus, Dostoyevsky grapples with the antithetical notions which Konstantin Mochulsky calls the "idea of Rastignac" and the "idea of Napoleon," the image of the altruistic murderer who is essentially a Christian humanist and that of the demoniac atheistic superman beyond redemption.[18] Out of his struggles emerges the central contention of *Crime and Punishment*, namely, that Raskolnikov ultimately stands forth as a religious scapegoat. He carries into the Siberian wastes the infinite spiritual freedom of the irreligious which blights man's personal and communal life by subjecting him to the blind forces of an imperturbable and relentless fate.

Almost a century later Jean Genet in works like *Our Lady of the Flowers* and *Miracle of the Rose* evokes the criminal as a scapegoat for almost diametrically opposite purposes. For him, crime is a potential source of spiritual wonderment and worship, as Richard Coe has ob-

17. James Baldwin, *Going to Meet the Man* (New York, 1958), 247; T. S. Eliot, *Collected Poems, 1909–50* (New York, 1952), 49.
18. Konstantin Mochulsky, *Dostoevsky: His Life and Work*, trans. M. A. Minihan (Princeton, 1967), 280 ff.

served.[19] To come into contact with the sacred through transgression is necessarily to suffer the scapegoat's punishment, isolation, and death ordained by a society and religion striving for a rational existence. By having his characters violate virtually all of man's multifarious taboos, Genet simultaneously invests them with the roles of criminal and scapegoat in a radical transformation of society's judgment and the prevailing anthropological pattern. Instead of receiving the multiple sins of others and suffering death in order to ensure the perpetuation of the world of others, Genet's characters perform the violations and evils repressed by most people precisely in order to become scapegoats. For Genet, that is the route into isolation, solitude, and the realm of the sacred which embraces the infinitude of mystery and the suprarational. In short, Genet becomes a criminal in order to become a scapegoat, for that is the point of contact with the sacred and the moment of escape from the profane. Where Dostoyevsky celebrates the scapegoat ritual as an exercise in spiritual transcendence on the part of his characters, Genet ceaselessly performs, both actually and imaginatively, that ritual as a declaration of divine immanence on the part of his characters and himself.

The final major form of the scapegoat is the fool or clown who is allowed to play the absolute monarch as a temporary substitute for the actual ruler. Anthropologically and existentially, the fool's lot is scarcely more palatable than that of other types of scapegoat. Yet in literature a broader range of associations and significance accrues around the figure of the fool. He is not only the knockabout burlesque figure of Roman comedy and the astringent wit and honest touchstone of reality and truth associated with the Shakespearean clown; he is also the harmless dunce, the gentle prey of retardation, and the guileless possessor of ultimate good fortune and luck. In virtually all of the subforms, however, there is a basic incapacity for the simple habits and quotidian rituals of ordinary existence. When this riddle is associated with the Christian tradition, as in Dostoyevsky's *The Idiot* and Strindberg's *The Scapegoat*, the scapegoat assumes in greater or lesser measure a kind of helpless sacrificial sanctity. Prince Myshkin is in virtually every conceivable aspect resident in a world he is not part of, does not comprehend or even recognize. Yet what Aglaya intuitively

19. Richard Coe, *The Vision of Jean Genet* (New York, 1969), 186–89.

calls his "essential mind" grasps the spiritual purpose and achievement of the scapegoat: the stranger and outcast to everything by his very alienation's impact on others effects the novel's vision of paradise in which sin and evil vanish. The smiles, the rueful shakes of the head at Prince Myshkin's aberrations, confusions, and faux pas are replaced in Strindberg by incredulity, mockery, and hatred issuing from Libotz's incapacity to function effectively without eliciting the shadow qualities of others.

So long as the individual's incapacity is rooted in congenital mental limitations of one sort or another, modern writers are inclined to treat him more as a victim and less as a scapegoat unless, as in Dostoyevsky's case, he can also be invested with some sort of supernatural or sacred associations. Thus, Faulkner's Benjy in *The Sound and the Fury* or Darl in *As I Lay Dying* or Ike in *The Hamlet* and John Steinbeck's Lennie in *Of Mice and Men* are basically moral victims of an individual or group self-regard which leads to callous and dehumanized indifference. Whatever aspects of the scapegoat may envelop them are a function more of psychological dynamics than of anthropological ritual and symbolism. More fully developed scapegoat figures appear with characters whose foollike nature is the result of a pompous and self-important inexperience—as with Hawthorne's Robin—or of a suspicious and fearful lack of familiarity with another race, as with Bernard Malamud's Yakov Bok in *The Fixer*. In the former case, the scapegoat is cast in his role partly by his own smug bumpkin nature and partly by society's efforts to teach him the secret truth about himself and so to redeem him.

Malamud's novel takes the opposite course. Yakov, all too aware of his ignorance before the mysteries of the Gentile world, apprehensively struggles to conform to the mores of its inhabitants. Yet unerringly he always does or says precisely that which leads him to become a national scapegoat to czarist anti-Semitism. Harrowing though *The Fixer* is in its slow-motion enactment of authoritarian and judicial ritual, Yakov transforms the scapegoat role from one of helpless sacrificial victim to that of legally accused prisoner whose crimes, sins, and guilt must be proven. Despite appalling physical and mental torture, threats, temptations, and appeals from guards, judicial officials, fellow prisoners, friends, and relatives including his wife, Yakov continues to make the apparent blunder or mistake that threatens his very exis-

tence. Yet by doing so, he makes his scapegoathood into both a
weapon for his liberation and a refutation of the rationale for the use
of scapegoats. His apparent folly in insisting on a thorough legal disposition and conclusion of his case is a brilliant comic transcendence
of the tragic necessities ordained by the invoking of the scapegoat ritual. We are simultaneously appalled and convulsed by the dogged
effrontery with which Yakov thwarts society's ritual as he responds to
his visitor's good news that the czar planned to include him in a general amnesty:

> Then he asked, Pardoned as a criminal or pardoned as innocent?
> The former jurist testily said what difference did it make so long
> as he was let out of prison. . . . Yakov said he wanted a fair trial,
> not a pardon. If they ordered him to leave the prison without a
> trial they would have to shoot him first.[20]

The scapegoat as fool finds in his own folly the only certain means
of assuring his release from his role; by insisting on a trial, Yakov
destroys the ritual as a viable communal response. William Blake
once observed that if a fool will persist in his folly, he will become
wise. Yakov Bok persists relentlessly in the folly of his innocence and
emerges with a deeply integrated conviction born of experience which
explodes the underlying premise of the scapegoat and his ritual. At the
end of the novel he has a hallucinatory conversation with Nicholas II
in the course of which he totally undercuts the attitudes which insistently generate scapegoats:

> Excuse me, Your Majesty, but what suffering has taught me is the
> uselessness of suffering, if you don't mind me saying so. Anyway,
> there's enough of that to live with naturally without piling a
> mountain of injustice on top. . . . In other words, you've made
> out of this country a valley of bones. You had your chances and
> pissed them away. . . . You say you are kind and prove it with
> pogroms. (*F*, 333–34)

The principle of vicarious suffering that Frazer finds animating the
concept of the scapegoat is denied by its moral and psychological an-

---

20. Bernard Malamud, *The Fixer* (New York, 1966), 294. Subsequent references to
this edition are hereafter cited parenthetically in the text as *F*.

tithesis, the principle of individual human responsibility whose ultimate form rests in Yakov's final recognition that "you can't sit still and see yourself destroyed" (F, 335).

With this we see that for the scapegoat and his rituals the only admissible place in the human economy is in the imaginative world of literature where the destruction is solely linguistic. This fact is brilliantly and uniquely dramatized in *Finnegans Wake*, where the scapegoat ritual is celebrated in song and in fact while itself being comically mutilated in a verbal reenactment of man's immemorial penchant for irresponsibility. Thus, Joyce has the scapegoat ballad accompanied by "the flute, that onecrooned king of inscrewments" (FW, 43:31−32). And the victim's death is reported in accents that merge the archetypal and the comic in a linguistic displacement that affords a responsible place for irresponsibility in the human economy: "As hollyday in his house so was he priest and king to that: ulvy came, envy saw, ivy conquered. Lou! Lou! They have waved his green boughs o'er him as they have torn him limb from lamb. For his muertification and uxpiration and dumnation and annuhulation" (FW, 58:5−9). Out of the multiple and complex interrelations of myth and character, then, emerges finally a firmly delineated sense of both the limitations inherent in the linguistic mimesis of man as object and the inexhaustibility of the mimesis of man as subject of which literature alone is capable. The active agency of myth reveals character as a fiction, while character's absorptive embrace of myth testifies to the latter's inexpungible role as existent.

For walk wherever we will, we tread upon some story.

CICERO

FIVE · Myth and Narrative: The Nature of the Tale and the Name of the Teller

ANY ATTEMPT, such as has just been made, to explore the inter-actions of character and mythic beings or metamythic typologies inevitably involves us in the notion of narrative. Whether man or god, hero or devil, what is central in myth as in the literary tale or story are the actions performed by the character and the events that befall him. While these are rendered in drama through the immediacy of the character's voice, in fiction they are represented mediately by the narrative voice. Significant though this difference is, no attempt will be made here to tease out its consequences for the interrelation of myth and literature. More accessible yet equally rich in implications is a consideration of specific interactions between particular myths and certain narrative strategies in literature. Several general, but nonetheless important, observations quickly emerge from even a preliminary glance at this interaction. One is that there are a number of ways in which mythic and fictional narratives may coexist and interpenetrate in the same literary work. These ways not only have specific and meaningful functions for the individual work but carry a number of rich implications for larger issues such as the relation of fantasy or imagination and reality. A second thing to appear is the continuity obtaining between what we may call symbolist-ironist and comic-ludic deployments of myth in modern literature. Yet another striking feature is the centrality of the notion of story to myth and fiction alike. In effect, these suggest that the underlying and perhaps ultimate issues here are those of the nature of the tale and tale-telling activity together with the problematic and even enigmatic question of the name of the teller, that is to say, the conceptual identity of the narrator.

Two contemporary American novelists who have shown a very clear interest in both the nature of myth and the problems of narrative

are John Updike and John Barth. From them we shall find ample reasons for the creative artist's continuing to find myth of crucial and central importance to his fictions. Primary among these is the fact that
myth by regularly dealing with impossibilities in a narrative form constitutes a formal and conceptual matrix which gives rise to the stories
of literature, that is, to the tales whose form as well as their content is
fictional. Narrative, as historical writing shows us, need not be—
perhaps should not be—fictional. Story, on the other hand, always is
and must be and the reason is that it is genetically coterminous with
myth (and legend and folktale) insofar as it deals with impossibilities
whether ontological, epistemological, or historical. Even the story that
is most relentlessly realistic and veridical remains something imag-
ined, invented, fictional and so existentially impossible even as predic-
tion. In short, no story known to man has ever historically occurred
with the requisite degree of accuracy so that it could be labeled an
event and thus possible. What is not possible is impossible, and it is in
this tautology that both myth and the narrative of story reside. Because each is a serial or successive fictional presentation, each serves to
drive the identity of the teller, the speaker as ultimate narrator, into
the anonymity of the human voice engaged in imaginative articulation. Myth because of its communal nature and its prototypical or
primitive role does so unconsciously and naturally. Story or fiction,
however, in the history of literature does so consciously and deliberately as a result of being driven to utilize the narrator as a character or
figure and then to query his identity successively until he dissolves into
the tale itself where there is only the story, a written record of the human voice narrating what is not the case so that by the very act it becomes so.

*

Like so many literary works, John Updike's *The Centaur* has elicited a
variety of critical responses. Yet despite the growing acceptance of the
book as an important, carefully structured, highly wrought gauge of
the contemporary sensibility, critics in the main are still uncertain,
therefore distressed, and thus ultimately dismissive concerning the
presence of mythic materials in the narrative mix. The most emphatic
statement of this view is Tony Tanner's: "The more elaborate network
of allusions to the Chiron myth, in my experience of reading the book,
does nothing to or for the foreground reality which Updike puts be-

fore us with his customary meticulous annotations."[1] Whether other readers' experience of *The Centaur* corroborates Tanner's judgment is doubtful, particularly if it has been formed less by casual impression and more by conscious questioning of the nature, function, and motive of the mythic element in the novel. A sustained consideration of this last aspect will produce, it is hoped, a clearer sense of the informing thrust of *The Centaur*'s narrative as a whole.

There are three chief sources of illumination concerning the part played by myth in the novel: the 1968 *Paris Review* interview with Updike, the novel's epigraph, and the text itself. In the interview the author explains the impetus for the use of mythic material as follows:

> I was moved, first, by the Chiron variant of the Hercules myth— one of the few classic instances of self-sacrifice, and the name oddly close to Christ. The book began as an attempt to publicize this myth. The mythology operated in a number of ways: a correlative of the enlarging effect of Peter's nostalgia, a dramatization of Caldwell's sense of exclusion and mysteriousness around him, a counterpoint of ideality to the drab real level, an excuse for a number of jokes, a serious expression of my sensation that the people we meet are *guises*, do conceal something mythic, perhaps prototypes or longings in our minds.

From this it is apparent that the initial attraction of the myth lay in its thematic dimension. It is as a narrative of self-sacrifice, a story of an individual's undeserved misfortune and willingness to release a hero from mortality that the Chiron myth first grips Updike's imagination. In his telling the tale, however, he introduces both biographical and religious preoccupations, with the result that some have been led to regard the novel as "basically another Olinger story" dominated by the Kierkegaardian struggle against the sickness unto death.[2] Clearly these elements, as well as a number of others, are important aspects of the work, but to suggest that they are basic and the mythological ancillary or contributory only is to misconstrue the relations of myth and history in Updike's work and to ignore his own assessment of the primacy of the mythic in *The Centaur*.

1. Tony Tanner, *The City of Words* (New York, 1971), 287.
2. C. T. Samuels, "The Art of Fiction XLII: John Updike," in *Writers at Work*, ed. George Plimpton (New York, 1977), 442; Alice and Kenneth Hamilton, *The Elements of John Updike* (Grand Rapids, Mich., 1970), 156.

In the same interview Updike also counters the suggestion that history is normally absent from his work. He claims, among other things, that "*The Centaur* is distinctly a Truman book" and that "the atmosphere of fright permeating [it] is to an indicated extent early cold-war nerves." More generally, he observes that most of his characters "all talk about history, and the quotidian is littered with newspaper headlines, striking the consciousness of the characters obliquely and subliminally but firmly enough" and concludes with the emphatic declaration that "my fiction about the daily doings of ordinary people has more history in it than history books, just as there is more breathing history in archaeology than in a list of declared wars and changes of government." Of particular interest in these remarks is the way in which Updike aligns his penchant for "density of specification," for, as Tanner remarks, "things . . . observed in minute detail—brands, prices, foods, cars, household appliances and furniture," with history, the shaping force and record of man's endless temporal and cultural transformation.[3] The loving, bittersweet recollection and creation, effected through the meditative interplay of memory and imagination, that have characterized Updike from his earliest prose work are to him a kind of history in which the living, breathing impact of a realized but changing identity far outweighs the serial itemization of factual events. This distinction between history as lived and history as recorded is not a new one among American novelists—Faulkner for one employed it with consummate skill and conviction—but in Updike's case it has certain distinctive implications that bear directly on *The Centaur*.

At first glance, it appears that the overt insistence not only on the presence of mythic elements but on the variety of their structural and functional deployment which characterizes *The Centaur* has little connection with Updike's stress upon the historicity of the quotidian permeating his fiction. And what connection it might have seems to be essentially dialectical, opposing mirror images polarized in irresolvably antagonistic premises and modes of realization. Yet there is a connection in Updike's mind that is more organic than logical and subsumptive than contrastive. And the clue lies in his remarks about narrative and storytelling. In elaborating on his reasons for incorporating mythic parallels in *The Centaur*, he admits to a general attraction

3. Samuels, "The Art of Fiction," 444; Tanner, *City of Words*, 280.

for the "old stories" of Greek mythology and then goes on to reveal the scope of his involvement with the challenge of narrative forms:

> I have read old sagas—*Beowulf*, the *Mabinogion*—trying to find the story in its most rudimentary form, searching for what a story *is*— Why did these people enjoy hearing them? Are they a kind of disguised history? Or, more likely I guess, are they ways of relieving anxiety, of transferring it outwards upon an invented tale and purging it through catharsis? In any case, I feel the need for this kind of recourse to the springs of narrative, and maybe my little buried allusions are admissions of it.

Later in the interview Updike makes two other remarks that bear on this matter. Discussing his notion of the primary goals of fiction, he observes:

> Narratives should not be *primarily* packages for psychological insights, though they can contain them, like raisins in buns. But the substance is the dough, which feeds the storytelling appetite, the appetite for motion, for suspense, for resolution. The author's deepest pride, as I have experienced it, is not in his incidental wisdom but in his ability to keep an organized mass of images moving forward, to feel life engendering itself under his hands. . . . No wisdom will substitute for an instinct for action and pattern, and a perhaps savage wish to hold, through your voice, another soul in thrall.

And in his final comment Updike declares that he thinks of his books as possessing "the mysteriousness of anything that exists" and aligns this quality with his earliest and most basic conception of the artist and art: "My first thought about art, as a child, was that the artist brings something into the world that didn't exist before, and that he does it without destroying something else. A kind of refutation of the conservation of matter. That still seems to me its central magic, its core of joy." [4]

From these comments it is clear that Updike finds both his greatest challenge and his ultimate satisfaction as fiction writer in the problems of narrative, in the recounting of patterned action in a voice enthrall-

4. Samuels, "The Art of Fiction," 443, 453, 454.

ing to the listener. Because of this passion for telling stories, he is driven to seek the essence of the story, its original form, in which it satisfied some profound need of the human psyche for that pleasure which is found in the relief of anxiety through immersion in past event. But in following this movement backward into origins and essence, Updike encounters—as the examples of *Beowulf*, the *Mabinogion*, and Greek tales indicate—myth. In doing so, he finds, however, not a bloodless abstraction, an eternal thematic pattern of wisdom, but what the audience of Homer and Herodotus had found before him, namely, a traditional story about the past of the human race, a story originally identified by the interchangeable terms *mythos* and *logos*.[5] In such stories the mythic and historical elements are not antagonistic forces vying for supremacy and ultimate authenticity but coordinate aspects of a narrative that unflinchingly encompasses the spectrum of conceivability. Thus, in *The Centaur* the quotidian details of a Trumanesque, cold war America and the limpid vision of an immemorial Chiron and his pupils interact in a cooperative effort to render in a viable form the story of the nature of narrative in the twentieth century.

The novel's story in its most inclusive form is not so much a narrative about George Caldwell, his putative artist son Peter, Chiron, Prometheus, Zeus, or Ceres as it is a tale about the modern writer's drive, efforts, and need "to keep an organized mass of images moving forward." Because, as the interview makes clear, Updike is uncertain about the viability of the authorial presence in contemporary fiction, *The Centaur* does not overtly introduce the writer as character or as voice into the narrative. The novel does, however, utilize several narrative styles and points of view whose effect is to increase our consciousness of the fictiveness of the narrative, of the presence behind the narrative masks of a shaping, manipulative voice speaking in several idioms. The end result of this technique is to create through the action and narrative of the novel the shadowy, spectral, but dominant figure of the storyteller himself (not, as Updike insists in the interview, to be identified with John Updike the man) bringing something into the world that did not exist before without destroying something else. In so doing, Updike seeks to fulfill in his own diffident, controlled fashion

5. See J. A. K. Thomson, *The Art of the Logos* (London, 1935), 19.

that aspect of his craft to which he referred in saying that "there is, in fiction, an image-making fiction, above image-retailing." With the making of the image of the storyteller as myth recounter, Updike provides *The Centaur*'s "secret," the "bonus for the sensitive reader," the "kind of subliminal quavering" that he feels books should possess. And if the image he has made is less immediate and stark than that of "a coarse universal figure like Tarzan" it is nonetheless powerful and compelling.[6] The story of man's storytelling propensity is one in which, as *The Centaur* subtly and luminously demonstrates, myth and history, the archetypal and the quotidian are inextricably intertwined.

Perhaps the central quality of the storyteller is suggested by the novel's epigraph from Karl Barth: "Heaven is the creation inconceivable to man, earth the creation conceivable to him. He himself is the creature on the boundary between heaven and earth." Since Updike has avowed himself predisposed theologically to Barth, critics have related the epigraph to the prevailing religious dilemma of twentieth-century man as emblematically rendered by the twy-form of Chiron. This doubtless is a relevant dimension of the novel's theme, but the epigraph has additional, even more significant connections with myth and the storyteller. The crucially operative terms for *The Centaur* are not the religiously flavored "heaven" and "hell" but the imaginatively oriented "conceivable" and "inconceivable." The inconceivability of heaven is an index of creative, imaginative limitation, whereas the conceivability of earth circumscribes the ordinary scope of the human imagination. But since a variety of religious perspectives have rendered something of the nature of heaven, there is clearly a sense in which the inconceivable is expressible. Man's ultimate and basic position on the boundary between the conceivable and the inconceivable is identical with his power to narrate what Aristotle called probable impossibilities, to tell stories that breach the constrictions of what mankind conceives to be the case. And the individual who regularly encompasses the ordinary and the extraordinary, the conceivable and the inconceivable, is the maker of fictions, the teller of stories, whom today we call the writer.

While Barth and Updike as Christians stress the creatureliness and finiteness of man, *The Centaur* reveals a secular variant of the later

6. Samuels, "The Art of Fiction," 453, 443, 453.

Barth's stress upon the sacred narrative and God's entrance into man's world through the Word. As the central figure described in the novel, Chiron's centauric nature represents Barth's boundary creature struggling to reconcile the conceivable and the inconceivable but destined to find them forever antinomies, however variable and shifting their content. On the other hand, the narrative developed through nine chapters and an epilogue and cast in a variety of styles and points of view is a made thing that includes not only inconceivable mythic monsters, gods, goddesses, and events but also all too conceivable ordinary fathers, sons, mothers, sweethearts, and actions. Its maker is the teller of the story, and it is he who through the narrative word provides the means by which the more-than-human impinges directly on ordinary mankind, who in this case is identified with the reader of the novel.

Seen from this perspective, *The Centaur* appears less a piece of tricksy ingenuity, stylistic bravura, and leg-pulling pastiche than a daring, tautly economical exploration of the meaning and scope of narrative and the potentialities of the storyteller as a figure at the very heart of human achievement. At the core of the storyteller's art, as we have seen, is myth, "what is said." Looking at the twentieth century from its last quarter, we can see clearly enough the enormous frequency with which its major authors have been drawn to the resources of myth. Even more significant, of course, is the variety of ways in which these resources have been mined by writers like Joyce, Lawrence, Thomas Mann, André Gide, Faulkner, and others. Updike himself specifies five distinct ways the Chiron myth functions in *The Centaur*. Given this, it is not perhaps too much to suggest that he is not only utilizing many of the major modalities of myth but also striving to structure them into a single narrative form.

The obvious starting point for such an endeavor is the tale as originally told or, lacking that, some redaction that imitates both the content and stylistic antiquity of the story. Such a point of departure occurs in *The Centaur* with the passage prefixed to it from Josephine Preston Peabody's *Old Greek Folk Stories Told Anew*, a work that stood in relation to its generation as Edith Hamilton's *Mythology* does to ours. Obviously one cannot say for sure why Updike fastened on a late-nineteenth-century redaction rather than one of the classical versions by a mythographer like Apollodorus or Ovid. But part of the answer appears to be that the ancient accounts of Chiron's myth were so

tersely phlegmatic as to generate virtually none of the stylistic resonance Updike associates with the writer's craft. Another part of the
answer may be that accounts such as Peabody's represent the late-
nineteenth-century narrative norm from which the modern novelist
must depart if he is to tell his stories in his own idiom. In short, the
Peabody redaction functions as both model and anathema for Updike
in his quest to reunite myth and narrative in the twentieth century. As
the former, it is the narrative paradigm of what Updike calls "the en-
larging effect of Peter's nostalgia" and the stylistic adumbration of the
pastoral motif which receives its most extended development in Chapter III. At the same time, Peabody's genteel conventions of language—
"still needful," "wandering the world," "strange mischance," "blame-
less as he was"—and crude superimpositions of Christian perspectives
on the classical narrative—"expiate that ancient sin," "accepted as
atonement," "heard his prayer"—illustrate the moribund verbal and
functional attitudes toward myth held by late-nineteenth-century writers. What T. S. Eliot said of Gilbert Murray almost fifty years before,
Updike repeats implicitly twenty years ago: a serious writer or translator cannot use the assumptions and practices of a defunct literary
movement and still have, as Eliot put it, "the slightest vitalizing effect"
upon the genre and language in which he works.

Updike himself employs a number of tactics and techniques in his
effort to produce a vitalizing effect on the novel, which as a narrative
form he sees demanding an involvement with the original impulse to
myth. The most daring of these occurs in the very first sentence of the
novel and implicitly sets the tone and establishes the mode for virtually everything that follows. The novel begins:

> Caldwell turned and as he turned his ankle received an arrow.
> The class burst into laughter. The pain scaled the slender core of
> his shin, whirled in the complexities of his knee, and, swollen
> broader, more thunderous, mounted into his bowels. His eyes
> were forced upward to the blackboard, where he had chalked the
> number 5,000,000,000, the probable age in years of the universe.[7]

In terms of the original Chiron myth, the first sentence establishes the
Caldwell-Centaur equation clearly enough, but it also does something

7. John Updike, *The Centaur* (New York, 1963), 3. Subsequent references to this
edition are hereafter cited parenthetically in the text as C.

even more important. It introduces the axiom of the conceivability of the inconceivable as both central to *The Centaur* and to the narrative activity of the storyteller. Most critics have treated Caldwell's wounding by an arrow and his hobbling out of the school, across the parking lot, and into Hummel's garage to have it removed as an actual event sanctioned with verisimilitude by analogues ranging from the likes of *Blackboard Jungle* to contemporary news stories. To treat this initial event as a "cruel joke" played by small-town adolescent sadists, none of whom appear as such in the remainder of the novel, is to impose on the story a heavy burden of misunderstanding of the nature of myth and its centrality to narrative.

Actually what Updike is doing here is demonstrating powerfully and dramatically that narrative involves the inconceivable fully as much as the conceivable and that when the inconceivable is narrated, it is myth. His point is precisely that the storyteller *says* Caldwell was wounded by an arrow and that the authenticity of the claim lies not in its empirical possibility or its verisimilitude but in the teller's "ability to keep a mass of images moving forward." This ability emerges immediately in the subsequent sentences. The mythic event is absorbed in the narrative which flows into the predictable response of the class and then on (in the third sentence) into the characteristically extravagant self-absorption of Caldwell before in the next sentence bringing him to confront the origin of life, itself a temporal equivalent of the inconceivability of the wounding. Had Updike wished to, he could easily have adapted the original myth to narrative plausibility by the use of metaphor (as when he makes Argus "the trophy case with its hundred silver eyes" [C, 5]), historical rationalization (as when Hephaestus-Hummel's limp is said to be due to "a childhood fall" [C, 8]), or contemporary substitution (as when the chariot of the dead provided by the gods becomes a black prewar Buick with a shattered grille). That he didn't is further evidence of his concern to point up the radically fictive nature of the narrative enterprise and hence its reliance on the inconceivable and myth.

At the same time, narrative art is not simply a matter of the inconceivable; it also recounts the mundanely and prosaically conceivable, history as lived. Both are part of a continuum of imaginative and verbal possibility so that the richly detailed accounts of Caldwell's and Peter's experiences driving to and from home in the old Buick or of living conditions in the Caldwell home are essential to Updike's story of story itself. To focus on the inconceivable exclusively not only blunts and minimizes the inconceivability but renders the scene infinitely more remote. As if to show us both the charm and the danger of such a narrative limitation, Updike gives us a full-fledged example in Chapter III. There the narrative is cast exclusively in terms of the ancient Chiron and his role as teacher of the children of Olympus:

> Chiron hurried, a little late, down the corridors of tamarisk, yew, bay, and kermes oak. Beneath the cedars and silver firs, whose hushed heads were shadows permeated with Olympian blue, a vigorous underwood of arbutus, wild pear, cornel, box, and andrachne filled with scents of flower and sap and new twig the middle air of the forest. (C, 93)

No contemporary references or allusions intrude so that the narrative deals with the conceivable elements of an old teacher and his pupils who worship and study together in a distant past rather than with the inconceivable features of a half-horse half-man who instructs the children of immortal gods and goddesses in fantastic tales presented as natural science. The romance quality of the narrative follows inevitably from a concentration on the past and the conceivable. The plangent nostalgia for a golden age of pastoral simplicity, beauty, and wisdom that dominates the chapter is the narrative and mythic equivalent to Peter's nostalgia for the earlier world he had known when his parents were huge, remote, and godlike. And just as Chapter III carries the self-indulgence of the artist toward himself, his present achievement, and his past origins, coupled with an underlying doubt as to his authenticity, so it embodies both the narrator's indulgence in his having rendered the remote conceivable and moving and also his haunted sense that it is insufficient and its perfection already threatened. The very brevity of the chapter and the fact that it ends in mid-sentence are testimony to its incompleteness as a narrative mode for myth.

It is in the first two chapters that Updike presents the two major modes of mythic narratives he envisages for the modern novel. Chapter I actually utilizes two techniques to this end, one of which might be called Joycean and the other post-Joycean. The first can be described as the method of ascription by contemporary symbol, for it consists in identifying automobile mechanics as Cyclopes, their boss as Hephaestus, and a fellow teacher as Pholos. This is exactly what Joyce did when he re-created Aeolus as the journalist Crawford or Eumaeus as Skin the Goat or Circe as Bella the brothel keeper. Many of these equations have been identified by critics, and there is no need to rehearse or add to them here. As in Joyce's case, many of the equations are either shifting, in accord with specific contexts, or uncertain because of conflict between the ascription and the ancient myth the result of which is to afford Updike "an excuse for a number of jokes" the most extended of which is the Mythological Index itself.

More generally, this Joycean technique operates to provide what he calls "a counterpoint of ideality to the drab real level." The fullest instance is obviously Caldwell himself, whose debilitating efforts to teach indifferent students receive a more heroic, noble cast when viewed as part of Chiron's perennial civilizing role among mankind. The fact, however, that so many of the characters seem less to celebrate than denigrate their mythic counterparts pulls against an overly simple interpretation of ideality. Here, like Joyce, Updike is not concerned to juxtapose a noble ideal of perfection against the ignoble, the tawdry, and the flawed. Rather he aspires to subtle interplaying patterns of the significant and the archetypal with the trivial and the commonplace. Thus, Zimmerman like Zeus becomes more than an incisively drawn academic bureaucrat tyrannizing over his domain. He also assumes something of the incalculability of action, behavior, and wisdom of the ruler of Olympus.

A reversal of this technique and a further complicating of the concept of ideality appears with Vera Hummel. As Al's wife and the gym teacher at Caldwell's high school, she is the object of adolescent sexual fantasies (many of which are couched in rumor form), exerts her feminine nature by flirting mildly with the Reverend March at the basketball game, and feels affection for George Caldwell. Nothing that occurs or that is known for certain in the novel connects her with the passionate indiscretions Aphrodite shared with Ares. Though Caldwell claims to know that she has done something unexpected to hurt her husband, its precise nature is never stated. Consequently, all the rumors, hints, casual gestures, and unspecified knowledge become a matrix creating the regional myth of her as the local Venus. The narrative arc described by her life in the context of the novel dramatically recapitulates Updike's major thesis of the connection between myth and narrative, for the myth of her as Aphrodite is coordinate with the tales and stories traditionally told about her in the student underworld. In short, on the historical ordinary plane of narrative she is the focus for hearsay and gossip. Yet on the ancient level of narrative, inspired by Caldwell's memory of Vera in the first chapter, she appears as a "taunting small-faced goddess" (C, 23) who can describe herself as "a compulsive nymphomaniac" and "a born whore" (C, 27) inviting Chiron to perform a stallion's role and who blasphemes the gods as "a prating bluestocking, a filthy crone smelling of corn, a thieving tramp, a drunken queer, a despicable, sad, grimy, grizzled, crippled, cuckolded tinker" (C, 26).

Clearly the ideality of this form of myth is far from that bestowed on Chiron in Chapter III; it is the ideality of pure accuracy, of quintessential character and nature unallowed by social circumspection or moral inhibition. As such, it serves to bring down the subjects of ancient worship from their remote Olympian heights but only in order to give them greater primacy as dominant human drives, needs, and values. The wanton Venus of Chapter I enshrines for Updike an ideality and value rooted in the incalculable mystery of life as a matter of unpredictable action and unpremeditated experience. This is underlined at the very end of the episode when Caldwell musing on his earlier glimpse of a Vera naked from the shower reflects: "Love has its own ethics, which the deliberating will irrevocably offend" (C, 31). Driving home the specific relevance of this observation to Caldwell and his insistent pursuit of knowledge verbally formulated, Updike concludes: "Then as now, Caldwell stood on that spot of cement alone and puzzled, and now, as then, climbed the stairs with a painful, confused sense of having displeased, through ways he could not follow, the God who never rested from watching him" (C, 31).

The second major mode of mythic narrative, the one labeled post-Joycean, operates throughout the scene immediately following the meeting of Chiron and Aphrodite. It utilizes not so much a method of ascription as one of elision in which characters, events, and conversation slide back and forth from ancient to contemporary referents. When Caldwell returns to his classroom after his visit to Hummel's garage, he is apprehensive that the principal, Zimmerman, may have taken charge of the class. On entering the room, he finds that this is true, but the truth proves, in Updike's narrative, to be as complex as the ideality of Aphrodite, for principal and teacher segue narratively into god and victim:

> Zimmerman's lopsided face hung like a gigantic emblem of authority, stretching from rim to rim of Caldwell's appalled vision. With a malevolent pulse, it seemed to widen still further. An implacable bolt, springing from the center of the forehead above the two disparately magnifying lenses of the principal's spectacles, leaped space and transfixed the paralyzed victim. The silence as the two men stared at one another was louder than thunder. (C, 31)

What starts as a metaphor of anxiety expands in the course of the narrative into a complete fusion of ancient event and contemporary character, of conceivable persons and inconceivable actions, of scientific fact and mythic tale.

Zimmerman begins as the principal making his monthly visit to the teacher's class, but as the lesson proceeds he acts out Zeus's lecherous penchant for seducing unwary mortal females. To Caldwell he appears as an old bull (a typical Zeus disguise) caressing Iris Osgood's arm, then hugging her, and finally removing her blouse and bra so that "her breasts showed above her desk like two calm edible moons rising side by side" (C, 45). The class itself—Mark Youngerman with his cup ears and acne, Becky Davis with her purple lipstick, Iris Osgood with her plump bovine beauty, and Betty Jean Schilling with her bubble gum—is composed of thoroughly conceivable and recognizable because typical individuals. But as the science class proceeds with Caldwell furiously struggling to teach them about the origins of the universe and life, they become party to actions of an inconceivable surreality. When Youngerman jumped up from his seat, "his acne leaped to the wall; the paint began to burn, blistering in slowly spreading blotches above the side blackboard. Fists, claws, cocked elbows blurred in patch-colored panic above the scarred and varnished desk tops" (C, 42).

This is a signal for the classroom to take on the lineaments of the science lesson itself and ultimately for the narrative to assume the most radical features of myth. Two ordinary pranksters dump on the floor from a paper bag very extraordinary contents—a mass of trilobites whose importance in the development of existence Caldwell has just been expatiating upon. The result is an account of an inconceivable universe:

> Most were just an inch or two long; a few were over a foot in length. They looked like magnified wood lice, only they were reddish. The bigger ones wore on their ruddy cephalic shields partially unrolled condoms, like rubber party hats. As they scuttered among the scrolling iron desk-legs, their brainless heads and swishing glabellae brushed the ankles of girls who squealed and kicked up their feet so high that white thighs and gray underpants flashed. In terror some of the trilobites curled into segmented balls. As a sport the boys began to drop their heavy textbooks on these primitive anthropods; one of the girls, a huge purple parrot feathered with mud, swiftly ducked her head and plucked a small one up. Its little biramous legs fluttered in upside-down protest. She crunched it in her painted beak and methodically chewed.
> (C, 43)

For the surrealist using such a technique, the goal is the dislocation of existence and the universe and the derangement of the senses in order to make either a metaphysical statement or a philosophical statement about the impossibility of metaphysics. But for Updike the design is to show how characters, scene, setting, and action—all the analyzable elements of fiction—are resolvable into and dependent upon the narrative act itself.

Caldwell's science lesson about nature and man's origins is Chiron's creation myth in a contemporary context. The former's talk about the lepothrix, the volvox, the trilobite, and the Tyrannosaurus rex and the latter's tale of Night impregnated by the wind laying a silver egg in Darkness' womb from which emerged Eros, a double-sexed, four-headed, golden-winged creature, who set the universe in motion and gave birth to all existent things are both equally inconceivable as facts. They become conceivable, however, when narrated as traditional stories about the past of the human race, when, in short, they are presented as myths. The information and figures about the size and age of the universe mean nothing to Deifendorf and the others. It is only when Caldwell tries "to reduce five billion years to our size" (C, 38) by making the creation of the universe begin last Monday at noon with "the greatest explosion there ever was" (C, 38) and then narrating the story of the consequences until "one minute ago, flint-chipping, fire-kindling, death-foreseeing, a tragic animal appeared . . . called Man" (C, 46) that a measure of interest and meaningfulness is generated. The partial nature of Caldwell's success with his creation myth as compared to the complete attentiveness of Chiron's students is deliberate on Updike's part. Caldwell in halting and improvised fashion endeavors through narrative to connect knowledge with its roots in myth, but he lacks both the tradition and the audience expectation. The success of Chiron two chapters later in producing a story that is both meaningful and satisfying is less a dream romance about a pedagogical golden age than an index of the necessity of the modern narrator's consciously acknowledging and incorporating into his tales myth's capacity for relieving anxiety through an enthralling and satisfying inconceivability.

What Caldwell struggles to do futilely but with brilliant abandon in the first chapter Updike achieves in the course of the novel as a whole. Even while we are conscious of the teacher's failure ultimately to teach the nature of creation, we are aware of the narrator's success in shaping an engrossing and moving tale of man's origins which utilizes for normative focus a persona who is both sardonic and compassionate about the inconceivable, about human limitations, and about the need for storytelling. This awareness at the outset provides the explanatory clue to Updike's shifting points of view in the course of the novel. The protean elision of characters and the surrealistic metamorphosis of settings and events in the first chapter breach the surface of objectivity provided by the third-person narration. They call attention to the narrative act itself and hence to the first-level narrator being a conscious and deliberate fiction created by the second-level or existential narrator. This breach is widened into a full-scale awareness of the fictive reality and inconceivable conceivability of the narration by the deliberately abrupt and startling shifts in point of view in the subsequent chapters which simultaneously maintain the other major techniques of mythic narrative already mentioned. Thus, Chapter II catapults us into the historical immediacy of 1947 and the exacerbations of Peter's adolescent world just as we have become accustomed to the problematic condition of the older Caldwell. From the situation and concerns of the father to those of the son and from third-person to first-person narration, all is different in emphasis and focus. The continuity that obtains is afforded by the context of the family, the presence of myth, and the fact of narrative. The quotidian and familiar issues of family life anchor us in the conceivable, whereas Prometheus and Hermes show forth in the shapes of Peter and the scruffy hitchhiker to consolidate the presence of the inconceivable. The two—the conceivable and the inconceivable, history as experienced and myth as narrated—come together at the very end of the chapter when Peter perceives his father in a new light: "for the first time his death seemed, even at its immense stellar remove of impossibility, a grave and dreadful threat" (C, 93).

Subsequent chapters project us variously into the third-person world of unadulterated ancient myth, the first-person spectatorial passage of Peter through his father's peripatetic movements on behalf of knowledge, and the third-person neutrality of an obituary notice in which the presence of the narrator is implicitly denied in order to confirm it the more subtly. The result of these shifts, together with the other techniques employed, is to make our awareness that we are being told a story an essential part of the story itself. In a variety of ways the inconceivable is made conceivable by the second-level narrator, and with this the ineradicability of myth in narrative is affirmed even as its recovery is demonstrated. Such is the burden of achievement carried by the final chapter in which Chiron the centaur narratively merges with George Caldwell recalling his father, worrying about his son, seeing his old Buick as a mythic object, and psychologically and spiritually accepting his sacrificial fate to go on living. The narrative transition, so casual as to be all but invisible, from Chiron to Caldwell is represented as an alteration in "the chemistry of his thought" in the course of which it is discovered that a life of self-sacrifice opens up "a total freedom" (C, 296) to one. What Chiron and Caldwell perceive, the existential narrator achieves. Ultimately it is the chemistry of *his* thought that elides the centaur into the contemporary man. By the sacrifice of his own verbal identity (Updike remarked that "we sit down at the desk and become nothing but the excuse for these husks we cast off"[8]) the narrator gains the total freedom of the storyteller to whom narrative aware of its mythic origins is the conceivability of the inconceivable. The freedom to narrate is demonstrably attainable, but as the

8. Samuels, "The Art of Fiction," 434.

Epilogue indicates, it is rarely sought since few choose to attend to the remote but concrete objectivity of phenomena which alone can teach us how to take the immense human step into storytelling.

*

As we have seen, Updike harks back in some of his narrative techniques to ones developed by James Joyce while at the same time using others that form a bridge with post-Joycean treatments of myth. This duality of technical focus suggests a related historical point of more than passing significance. That is the general relationship between the so-called modernist and postmodernist writers on the issue of myth and literature.

One thing appears clear from even the most cursory glance at the major exemplars of modernism such as James Joyce, Thomas Mann, D. H. Lawrence, William Faulkner, William Butler Yeats, and T. S. Eliot. And that is a willingness, indeed perhaps even a compulsion, to utilize the patterns, themes, images, and figures of ancient myth in their creative efforts. The mere iteration of titles such as *Ulysses*, *Finnegans Wake*, *Joseph and His Brothers*, *The Plumed Serpent*, and *The Waste Land* suggests the truistic character of this observation. More recently, however, at least in America, writers, particularly of imaginative prose, are regarded as having turned their attention away from what has existed or already does exist in order to imagine worlds which do not yet exist or may never exist. Myth is said to have given way to fantasy. The ideal of an autonomous, self-contained work of art has been replaced by the notion of a self-reflexive act of consciousness whose verbal manifestation is an open-ended form in which language itself is the central theme.

Contemporary American fiction has become, in Tony Tanner's titular phrase, a "city of words," a protracted concentration on the very idea of "fiction" as an informing concept that dictates the character and implications of all human endeavors. In this connection, Tanner observes:

> The notion that what we think of as peculiarly human life, particularly social life, is a fiction, an invented superstructure which man the engineer has erected on "natural" reality, is not a new one. But it is one which seems to have been entertained by American novelists of the past two decades to an extent that makes it

begin to look like an obsession. . . . Where another civilization
might celebrate man's powers of fabrication and his ability to sup-
plement the given world with his own creations, there is a traditional line of American thought which suspects that these powers
and abilities might be cutting man off from "reality"—reality
being whatever was there before man started heaping up his fictions on it.

Yet when Tanner comes to deal specifically with a writer such as John
Barth, he shows pretty clearly that Barth at any rate is *not* erecting his
fictional fictions on a postulated "natural" reality and that Barth is *not*
at all suspicious of this activity's cutting man off from reality. Indeed,
it is precisely Barth's exuberantly radical and sustainedly conscious
generation of fictions in his work that leads Tanner to fear that Barth
is unable to be serious about any literary or imaginative or intellectual
form whatever, that he has, as Tanner puts it, exposed himself to "the
hazards of mental play uncorrected by the limitations of the world."[9]

Our purpose here, however, is not to quarrel with Tanner so much
as to suggest an explanation of the problems he has called attention to.
Put most simply, the present contention is that an informed historical
analysis will reveal not so much a shift of interest away from myth on
the part of modern literature as a modulation of its concept and role.
In short, the contemporary involvement with the concept of fictions
stems in large part from modernism's interest in myth. As a result of
the latter's substantive questions, such as "What is myth?" and "Of
what elements does it consist?" and "What are its origins?," artists, as
well as others, have gradually come to recognize that a myth is a fiction of a particular order, that it is a narrative, and that it originates in
the storytelling and -hearing propensity of the human mind and society.

Nowhere is this modulation and interpretation of myth in literature more clearly and emphatically developed than in the work of John
Barth. Virtually all of his creative efforts—novels, stories, tapes—
involve mythic materials whether in the form of characters (as in *Lost
in the Funhouse* and *Chimera*), structural patterns (as in *The Sot-Weed
Factor*), themes (as in *Giles Goat-Boy*), or concepts (as in *The End of
the Road*). To work out the various roles of these facets and to trace
their development fully would demand more space than is available

9. Tanner, *City of Words*, 29–30, 241.

here. Nevertheless, a sketch of the ways in which Barth joins myth and narrative, ways central to the novelist, will enable us to apprehend more concretely both the modulated continuity and the chameleonic persistence of myth in literature. Such a sketch may most usefully culminate with a consideration of *Chimera*, which brings together in particularly forceful manner the issues Barth has joined with regard to myths, fictions, and the act of narration.

Barth began his career with the publication of *The Floating Opera*, a work which he has characterized as "a philosophical minstrel show" and one of a series of three (the other two being *The End of the Road* and *The Sot-Weed Factor*) "nihilistic amusing novels." Its central thematic preoccupation is the nature and place of value in the human economy viewed largely from a sceptical stance. His hero, Todd Andrews, embarks on a quasi-philosophical *Inquiry* into the causes of his father's suicide, an exploration which he finally comes to realize is hopelessly incomplete because, as he remarks, "I'd been studying only myself." [10] This concern with the self, its nature and definition, is Barth's first locus for an explanatory grounding of the concept of value. In *The Floating Opera* he sees the self nonpejoratively as a series of masks designed to solve a problem or master a fact of overwhelming importance to the individual. Unlike some of his critics, Barth does not view this series as a problem, for he sees the self not as an entity but as a process.

His second novel, *The End of the Road*, amplifies this perception by considering more closely the nature of that process. Here Todd's more or less unconscious and instinctual choice of masks assumes a greater measure of awareness in the concept of Mythotherapy. This is introduced by Jacob Horner's black doctor as a means of treating his intellectual and emotional paralysis. In this notion Barth begins to draw together his interest in the mind's capacity for a plurality of possible interpretations of events and characters and his fascination with the complex act of narration. As the doctor makes clear, human beings are characters and their lives are stories of which they are the authors. Assigning roles to ourselves and others, he says, is "myth-

10. J. J. Enck, "Interview with John Barth," in *The Contemporary Writer*, ed. L. S. Dembo and C. N. Pondrom (Madison, 1972), 22, 26; John Barth, *The Floating Opera* (Rev. ed.; New York, 1967), 222. Subsequent references to this edition are hereafter cited parenthetically in the text as *FO*.

making, and when it's done consciously or unconsciously for the purpose of aggrandizing or protecting your ego—and it's probably done
for this purpose all the time—it becomes Mythotherapy." [11] Now the
interesting thing for our purposes is not myth's participation in the
defense mechanisms of the ego, but its alignment with the human propensity for casting existence in the narrative form of a story. Jacob
Horner, the novel's protagonist, is driven by his accumulated experience with role playing and role players to recognize their inadequacy
so that he concludes:

> Mythotherapy, in short, becomes increasingly harder to apply, be-
> cause one is compelled to recognize the inadequacy of any role
> one assigns. Existence not only precedes essence: in the case of
> human beings it rather defies essence. And as soon as one knows
> a person well enough to hold contradictory opinions about him,
> Mythotherapy goes out the window, except at times when one is
> no more than half awake. (*ER*, 122)

The End of the Road itself does not, it is true, actively demonstrate
Barth's development of the problems and techniques of narrative in relation to actual or a particular myth as an explicit theme. But it does
foreshadow that development in two ways: one explanatory and the
other iconic. The former is introduced by the doctor. He observes that
because most people's lives are more than one story, that is, lack a co-
herent plot, they usually spend a great deal of time reconceiving their
roles as heroes and those of other persons as minor characters. Consistency of character, he goes on, is due to one of two factors:

> It's either because he has no imagination, like an actor who can
> play only one role, or because he has an imagination so compre-
> hensive that he sees each particular situation of his life as an epi-
> sode in some grand over-all plot, and can so distort the situations
> that the same type of hero can deal with them all. (*ER*, 83)

As the novel makes clear, Jacob Horner essentially belongs to the class
of those deficient in imagination. His efforts at role playing are fum-
bling and abortive and he is insufficiently imaginative to place himself
in the active role of hero. Actually, despite the doctor's diagnosis of his

11. John Barth, *The End of the Road* (New York, 1969), 83. Subsequent references
to this edition are hereafter cited parenthetically in the text as *ER*.

being too unstable to play one part all the time, Horner does virtually that. His role is that of the imaginative as well as the physical and psychological paralytic. He finds himself frozen into immobility, at least of a moral and intellectual order, by his ability to entertain two conflicting opinions simultaneously. It is this ability that links him to Todd Andrews and to Barth's subsequent narrator-characters who not only entertain but recount multiple versions of the same myth or story.

Yet if Horner is incapable of assuming the hero's role, he is not unperceptive about the significance of myth for the story of human life, which is man's response to existence. At the beginning of the novel, he finds in his rented room a "heroic plaster head of Laocoön" which annoys him "with his blank-eyed grimace" (ER, 9). As the toils of his adulterous relationship with Rennie Morgan, his strained and fruitless interrogations by her husband, and his final harrowing efforts to effect her abortion wind increasingly tighter around him, the mythic image of Laocoön recurs. At the end of the novel, he faces it again in a scene that speaks powerfully though obliquely both of Horner's fate and the future direction of Barth's fiction. With Rennie dead, her husband dismissed from his teaching position, and Horner's own reputation incredibly still intact, Jacob is so overwhelmed by what he calls significantly enough the "incompleteness" of the events and his inability to decide his feelings, his moral responsibility, or his future actions that he identifies with Laocoön: "The terrific incompleteness made me volatile; my muscles screamed to act; but my limbs were bound like Laocoön's—by the serpents Knowledge and Imagination, which, grown great in the fullness of time, no longer tempt but annihilate" (ER, 187). By this time the legendary figure is no longer a grotesquely ugly icon of inscrutability; it is a friend with whom he can share "a silent colloquy":

> "We've come too far," I said to Laocoön. "Who can live any longer in the world?"
> There was no reply. (ER, 187)

And yet there is an answer, as Horner's subsequent actions make clear. His admission that "I don't know what to do" and his final directive to the taxi driver, "'Terminal'" (ER, 188), together with his leaving the bust of Laocoön on the mantelpiece, all speak eloquently of his fate and its fictive significance. The impossibility of decision brings him as a character quite literally to the end of the road so that what is cast as a directive functions as a declaration. Whether he proceeds to the Greyhound bus terminal and the health farm in accordance with the doctor's instructions or whether he lapses into the same paralysis he experienced in Pennsylvania Station at the beginning of the novel is all one so far as his viable functioning in the world is concerned: he at any rate can no longer live in the world of opinion, decision, and action. Like Laocoön, who exposed lies and spoke the truth but was guilty of grave sexual improprieties, Jacob Horner is strangled by those chthonic forces of myth resident in the self's process of interaction with the world of others.

For Barth's fiction, however, the situation is not so final or fatal. Over against Horner's anguished renunciation of a world whose reality is jagged, incomplete, and absurd, there is Barth's comic dismissal of the genre or form in which he had been working. Admitting in an interview that after *The End of the Road* he had lost interest in writing realistic fiction, he went on to remark in characteristically only semi-facetious fashion:

> One ought to know a lot about Reality before one writes realistic novels. Since I don't know much about Reality, it will have to be abolished. What the hell, reality is a nice place to visit but you wouldn't want to live there and literature never did, very long. . . . Reality is a drag.[12]

In short, where Horner's position is that if one can no longer live in the world, then one must cease to exist, Barth's as a writer is that if the world appears untenable, then one is misconstruing it and must detect the category mistake and formulate a better model.

What these models may be he suggests in his subsequent fiction even as he produces mythic alternatives to the figure of the prophetic and suffering victim, Laocoön. Thus, in *The Sot-Weed Factor* he grounds life in past history and organizes it around the figure of the wandering hero. *Giles Goat-Boy*, on the other hand, has affinities with the futurity of science fiction even as it traces out the multiple possibilities of irony and humor in the figure of the scapegoat, whose central presence is perhaps one reason Barth has suggested the novel

12. Enck, "Interview with John Barth," 26.

can be viewed as "a comic Old Testament . . . a souped-up Bible."[13]
And finally, *Chimera* places "elsewhere" in the mythic present of fictions in which storytellers are heroes (or heroines) and heroes such as
Perseus and Bellerophon are storytellers. The progression in these last
three works is steadily toward an increased concern with the theme of
narrative itself. In seeing this motif as crucially bound up with the phenomenon of myth, he stands with writers such as John Updike and
John Fowles in making of his novels the story of contemporary narrative and in doing so he, like them, reveals, as we have already said, that
narrative involves the inconceivable fully as much as the conceivable
and that when the inconceivable is narrated, it is myth. Thus, though
the particular techniques and preoccupations of *Chimera* differ significantly from those of, say, *The Centaur*, its informing thrust to see the
genetic and functional interpenetration of myth and narrative is of the
same order.

However much the two works differ, they and their authors nevertheless have at least one thing in common, and that is a concern with
the nature and origins of story. Where Updike speaks of his interest in
the old sagas such as *Beowulf* and the *Mabinogion*, Barth goes even
further afield to testify to his fascination with "the element of story—
just sheer extraordinary, marvellous story." Speaking of the young
writer, he suggests that "*The Arabian Nights* may be a better mentor
for many than, say, J. D. Salinger."[14] He also goes on to declare how
delighted he would be to have written a work called *The Ocean of
Story*, which happens to be the title of C. H. Tawney's translation of
Somadeva's *Kathā Sarit Sāgara*. Its ten volumes may well occupy the
four feet of library shelf space that so entrances Barth. This engross-
ment with story, with learning its very techniques, and with telling
about it and them lies at the very heart of *Chimera*, making up as it
does both its subject and its form. The novel is composed of three
main stories—*Dunyazadiad*, *Perseid*, and *Bellerophoniad*—each of
which contains subordinate stories that conspire separately and in
concert to raise issues concerning narrative inspiration, methods, origins, and values. As these subtitles make clear, the first story is Barth's
rendering of Scheherazade's narrative efforts to avoid death at King

13. Enck, "Interview with John Barth," 23.
14. Enck, "Interview with John Barth," 19.

Shahyrar's hands; the second and third his variants on the exploits, recorded and unrecorded, of the Greek mythic heroes Perseus and Bellerophon.

At first glance, there seem to be no very clear connections between these three major units in themselves. The gap between Oriental popular tales and classical myths seems too wide to bridge, and while Perseus and Bellerophon are both heroes, there is no immediately compelling linkage discernible there either. Yet a closer scrutiny reveals that Barth is working very deliberately by bringing these three tales together under the thematic and conceptual title of *Chimera*. All three deal with nonexistent but real, that is, fictitious monsters which ultimately stand revealed as the opposite of terrifying. Similarly, all three are concerned on the level of plot and character with the maintenance or prolongation of life. From this it is possible to infer that Barth is suggesting that myth is a fiction which presents the incredible in order to support or sustain human existence. His straining of the bounds of the believable is his way of underscoring the fact that though myth may lack rational or logical justification as such a support system, it nevertheless has the inescapable empirical justification provided by its own efficacy as such a system. Thus, *Dunyazadiad* is Scheherazade's sister's account of how their tales originated, how they served to ward off death at Shahyrar's hands, and how they are ultimately revealed as fictions that not only celebrate life and the redemption of the individual but demonstrate how these are achieved within the confines of mortality. *Perseid* recounts its hero's early conquest of Medusa the Gorgon as well as his later passionate absorption in the achieving of "immortality—by petrifaction" through being transformed into a star.[15] And finally, *Bellerophoniad* narrates the protagonist's fulfillment of the pattern of the mythic hero, his paradoxical discontentment that issues in his failed effort to gain immortality through entrance into Olympus, and his final achievement of that goal through what might be called a process of narrative incorporation.

In the course of the three tales, we move from the function of story in and of a mortal world to the dynamics of storytelling wherein the first-person protagonist-teller becomes immortal through becoming the tale itself. For in the first tale, the brief last section suggests that

15. John Barth, *Chimera* (New York, 1972), 132. Subsequent references to this edition are hereafter cited parenthetically in the text as *Ch*.

what is learned from *The Arabian Nights* is that every story "must end in the night that all good mornings come to," that is, in death and destruction, and that to accept this joyously is "to possess a treasure, the key to which is the understanding that Key and Treasure are the same" (*Ch*, 55–56). While in the other two tales, the very activity of telling their own life stories dramatically renders the tellers' dialectic of immortality in which contentment and dissatisfaction are poised as the inevitable lot of all who experience and articulate that experience in language.

Once, Barth seems to be saying, the author, whom earlier we called the second-level or existential narrator, entertains the related notions of a protagonist as teller and the teller as character, he is inevitably committed to a dual movement toward, on the one hand, perfection, completion, and self-realization and, on the other, toward the flawed, the incomplete, and self-criticism. Thus, this novel with its triple beginnings and triple endings, which themselves structurally both call into question such notions as "beginnings" and "endings" and demonstrate the necessity of their persistence, concludes on this dual note. Perseus replies to Medusa's final question as to whether he is happy with the way the story ends:

> I'm content. So with this issue, our net estate: to have become, like the noted music of our tongue, these silent, visible signs; to *be* the tale I tell to those with eyes to see and understanding to interpret; to raise you up forever and know that our story will never be cut off, but nightly rehearsed as long as men and women read the stars . . . I'm content. (*Ch*, 133–34)

Bellerophon, who ends by being transformed into his own tale through the medium of Polyeidus, his magelike tutor, is, on the other hand, far from content with the story he has been telling. His final words to the world at large before moving from character and teller to tale are: "I hate this, World! It's not at all what I had in mind for Bellerophon. It's a beastly fiction, ill-proportioned, full of longeurs, lumps, lacunae, a kind of monstrous mixed metaphor—" (*Ch*, 308).

The net effect of this dialectic thrust so far as the genre of the novel and the activity of storytelling are concerned is that both emerge as endless. The latter coils back on itself ceaselessly driven to articulating a narrative other than the ones it has already generated since each inherently poses the possibility of saying otherwise. Similarly, the novel as a form expands yet further and further in its effort to be inclusive, to render all points of view, all possible intricacies of plotting, and all varieties of character (including all within a single character) in order to protract its own end, which Barth suggests can be likened to the reader's own end. Small wonder that while working on the ever-enlarging *Giles Goat-Boy*, he should envision having to write *The Ocean of Story*. For never to reach the end of a story is never to die, while at the same time the very persistence of human beings and the race, with their inveterate and unavoidable capacity for storytelling, means that their story has not come to an end.

Indeed, this sense of the endlessness of storytelling is represented in *Chimera* in at least two ways. In the final part of *Dunyazadiad* Sche-herazade envisages writing Dunyazade's story but admits to not being able to conclude it because she is in the middle of her own. Since Barth ends the tale on the very next page, there is clearly a very real sense in which her tale does not end in *Dunyazadiad*. In storytelling there is always one more twist of the plot, one more incident to be recounted. And if *Dunyazadiad* is principally about the impetus to narrative and storytelling, then the other two are proto-novels, tales about heroic protagonists who move relentlessly toward a denouement that is also their ultimate fate. This fact introduces the second way of emphasizing the implicit endlessness of fiction, for each successive attempt here by Barth to tell a tale is longer than its predecessor. Thus, *Perseid* is approximately half as long again as *Dunyazadiad*, while *Bellerophoniad* is over twice as long as *Perseid* and three times as long as *Dun-yazadiad*. The same point is made even more graphically by Barth's total canon to date; to divide the length of *The Floating Opera* into that of *Letters*, for instance, is to demonstrate through quantification the incremental character inherent in fictionalizing and storytelling.

That this growth of story is representative only is testified to by an important section of *Bellerophoniad* in which Bellerophon incredibly enough comes upon a letter in a bottle. It tells him about a contempo-rary American novelist named Jerome Bonaparte Bray who applies to the hero of Barth's first novel for financial assistance in producing a truly revolutionary novel entitled *Notes* (since published as *Letters*) which will dispense with plot, character, subject, and meaning in or-der "to transcend the limitations of particularity" (*Ch*, 256). Even more striking is the fact that this projected novel plans to have at its *Phi*-point ("point six one eight et cetera of the total length") "a single anecdote, a perfect model of a text-within-the-text, a microcosm or paradigm of the work as a whole" (*Ch*, 256) which will be none other than *Bellerophoniad*. In short, the last section of *Chimera*, which represents a growth of substantial measure over the first two parts, will in turn form but an anecdote in *Notes*. The process of storytelling, as distinct from novelistic invention, clearly is endless and cumulative even as it is repetitive. What is is continually being drawn into what will be; reality is enveloped by possibility when man perceives himself as a process not an entity and story as an activity not an event. And what makes this perspective of such paramount importance is precisely Barth's recognition of the multiform fashions in which story informs human endeavors and activities.

It would, however, be a mistake to regard Barth's position as a denigration of the value and reality of story. For him the very elaborateness of the lie testifies to its myth-producing and reality-reflecting character. Both stem from its roots in language where the supreme distinction of the human creature is located. As Jacob Horner remarks in *The End of the Road*:

> To turn experience into speech—that is, to classify, to categorize, to conceptualize, to grammarize, to syntactify it—is always a betrayal of experience, a falsification of it; but only so betrayed can it be dealt with at all, and only in so dealing with it did I ever feel a man, alive and kicking. It is therefore that, when I had cause to think about it at all, I responded to this precise falsification, this adroit, careful myth-making, with all the upsetting exhilaration of any artist at his work. (*ER*, 112–13)

And what this fictional character declares, the fictional author in *Chimera* underscores. J. B. Bray describes his *Bellerophoniad* as being "'the crucial flaw which perfects my imitation of that imperfect genre the novel, as the artful Schizura unicornis larva mimes not the flawless hickory leaf (never found in fact), but, flawlessly, the flawed and insect-bitten truth of real hickory leaves'" (*Ch*, 257). In short, the value of story, for Barth, is precisely that through distortion and falsification it mirrors the flawed imperfection of reality not the static perfection of ideality, which is a conceptualized pattern of the mortal experience within which we all dwell. And however plausible and compelling the pattern, it can never be other than one among a plurality of possibilities. Thus, to speak, and perhaps even to think, about experience is in some sense, for Barth, to tell a succession of stories that ceases only with the teller's death. The mark of the supreme storyteller is to produce stories that are connected and related without being mere repetitions. As a result, the ultimate, though unrealizable, goal is to tell a single story that subsumes or includes all others, even those not yet in existence as well as those lost in the past.

Such an ambition may be not only a desired ideal but a practical narrative necessity when one follows out to their logical conclusions all the implications of the activity of storytelling. At any rate, something rather like this notion seems to inform much of the later work of Barth and *Chimera* in particular. Indeed, when one stands back from that book and attempts to identify its major features, one finds that they appear to accord, surprisingly enough, with ones that have dominated various of his previous works. The two most obvious components of *Chimera* are sex and myth, and not far behind them we can identify the factors of value and fiction. Sex is treated neither as erotic transcendence (as in Lawrence) nor as physical acrobatics (as in Henry Miller) but as comic puzzle so that it functions as a kind of paradigm of human relations, especially those between men and women. While recognizable and significant in *The Floating Opera* and *The End of the Road*, sex assumes its characteristic Barthian comic form only in *The Sot-Weed Factor*. Similarly, though myth (as we have seen) is relevant to *The End of the Road*, it becomes fully explicit only in the arabesques woven on the scapegoat figure in *Giles Goat-Boy*. The issue of the nature and possibility of value, on the other hand, is a crucial concern as early as *The Floating Opera*. There the two-edged character of the proposition "Nothing has intrinsic value" is explored in such an open-ended way that the novel concludes with a fresh speculation on the subject and the observation "But that's another inquiry, and another story" (*FO*, 252). Whether, as Todd Andrews muses, "values less than absolute mightn't be regarded as in no way inferior and even be lived by" (*FO*, 252) is an issue Barth has raised in all his subsequent stories. Actually, his preoccupation with the value of value has led in a very real sense to his work issuing in its current concentration on the concept and role of fictions.

It would be possible to treat all four of these elements—sex, myth, value, and fiction—as simply thematic modulations. This, however, would in the long run simplify and distort Barth's very complex and highly self-conscious notion of the activity of storytelling. Some sense of what this entails emerges from the fictive Barth-as-Bellerophon's proposed esthetics lecture. It is, he says, to deal with "*the Principle of Metaphoric Means, by which I intend the investiture by the writer of as many of the elements and aspects of his fiction as possible with emblematic as well as dramatic value: not only the 'form' of the story, the narrative viewpoint, the tone, and such, but, where manageable, the particular genre, the mode and medium, the very process of narration—even the fact of the artifact itself*" (*Ch*, 203). What Barth has done is to invest sex, myth, value, and fiction with the "emblematic" values of narrative or storytelling itself, that is, with the values of character, narration, point of view, and theme. Put another way, his focusing on the sexual games and exploits of legendary and mythic figures is a kind of skeletal rendering of the motivations, compulsions, and relations obtaining among human characters. What sex is to character, myth is to narrative structure, the rationale for actions occurring in a sequence determined by the author. It is the recounting of this sequence of actions taken by characters that is the role of the narrator or narrators, thus establishing the point of view element in story. But precisely by this recounting, what is underscored is the story's nature as a fiction; characters, events, sequence, narrators, all are fictions, inventions either whole or in part of the author. Hence, it is no accident that Barth should begin with the fictional Scheherazade's suggesting to her sister that they imagine their pseudo-actual situation as a plot of a story. Explicit claims to reality, explicit assertions of the fictional nature of other stories, and explicit charges of the fictiveness of characters' lives—such as we find being made by Scheherazade, Anteia, and J. B. Bray—all conspire to enhance the fictive, illusory nature of the claims and in so doing call attention remorselessly to point of view and narrative being thoroughgoing fictions.

Barth's technique for developing these four elements as the essentials of the constitutive story of story is a compound of repetition, variation, and contradiction so that what emerges as the dominant narrative movement is a combination of arbitrariness and improvisation or transformation. Character, for instance, as the locus in sexuality would suggest, is rendered flatly though not statically. Scheherazade, for example, is the traditional vizier's daughter determined to save virgins from a savage and insatiable monarch, but she is also in turn a wily and equally savage feminist, a brilliant scholar and student, and an unwitting magician of language capable of conjuring up a genie whose Maryland origins and admiration for *The Thousand and One Nights* make him suspiciously like John Barth. Both Perseus and Bellerophon are heroes who have performed the incredible feats attributed to them by the traditional myths. At the same time, Perseus is a middle-aged, henpecked husband seeking to retrace his youth in an endeavor to regain something he has lost. He is both the model hero whom Bellerophon is concerned to emulate and also the discontented man who must reverse the style of his youthful exploits if he is to regain his heroic stature and recognition. Similarly, Bellerophon experiences, at least to his satisfaction, the adventures with Pegasus, Chimera, and the rest, but his whole story embraces his revelation that he is really his twin brother Deliades and the transformation of this figure into an immortal voice "always ultimately addressing the reader from pages floating in the marshes of what has become Dorchester County, Maryland, U.S.A." (*Ch*, 143).

This movement from the arbitrary to the transformational is rendered most graphically in the sexual exploits of the characters in the three tales. The arbitrariness of their sexuality and of their character is brought out by the uninflected perfunctoriness of its narrative rendering. Thus, Dunyazade recounts her lovemaking with her sister in a tone that parodies implicitly the exotic refinement of literary Oriental eroticism: "'When we'd had enough of each other's tongues and fingers, we called in the eunuchs, maidservants, mamelukes, pet dogs and monkeys; then we finished off with Sherry's Bag of Tricks; little weighted balls from Baghdad, dildoes from Ebony Isles and the City of Brass, et cetera'" (*Ch*, 4–5). Or later in the tale, her bridegroom-to-be, in attempting to explain his single-minded devotion to his first wife, declares that though he kept a harem of concubines, it was for the sake of his "'public image'" and that they were "'reserved for state visitors'" (*Ch*, 42). Such punctiliousness and solicitude for his beloved is weakened in its credibility when a moment later he observes: "'The harem girls, when I used them, only reminded me of how much I preferred my wife; often as not I'd dismiss them in mid-clip and call her in for the finish'" (*Ch*, 43).

Yet offsetting or qualifying this arbitrariness is the transformation of character such as occurs in Shah Zaman when he hears of how Scheherazade has through her stories brought his brother "'back to the ways of life'" (Ch, 52). He resolves to find out if she has a sister and declares:

> If she does, I'll make no inquiries, demand no stories, set no conditions, but humbly put my life in her hands, tell her the whole tale of the two thousand and two nights that led me to her, and bid her end that story as she will—whether with the last goodnight of all or (what I can just dimly envision, like dawn in another world) some clear and fine and fresh good morning.
> (Ch, 52)

The same use of repetition, variation, and contradiction is also deployed throughout the mythic structure of *Chimera*. In the opening tale, Dunyazade and Shah Zaman are relational and experiential repetitions of Scheherazade and Shahyrar in respect to their sibling roles and their involvement in marital betrayal and its behavioral and narrative consequences. But the tale is also a variation on the original story, for while in both Scheherazade is cast as the storyteller, it is actually, at least through the long first part, Dunyazade who narrates the events. Part II works a further variation by employing an anonymous omniscient narrator who presents Shah Zaman's story as part of the culmination of Dunyazade's tale while through the medium of dramatic immediacy nullifying our awareness of the narrator's presence.

With even greater clarity, the two Greek tales develop this tripartite pattern. Both Perseus and Bellerophon provide redactions of their traditional heroic exploits, though by manner of dialogue and matter of actual event they also create variations of the ancient tales. Perseus does sever Medusa's head and Bellerophon does annihilate Chimera with his lance. But in the Barthian account, which is presented as the first-person narrative of both heroes, Athene reconstitutes Medusa to provide Perseus with the revelatory romantic conclusion to his life and tale, while Polyeidus, Bellerophon's tutor, supplies the hero with the traditional spear and lump of lead with which to slay the monster, only now the weapon is a larger version of a primitive writing tool and the lead its point which has placed upon it "several sheets of paper from the prophet's briefcase impregnated with a magical calorific" (Ch, 226). In both cases, then, the monster proves to be fictional, and so a contradiction of the original story. Medusa is not a monster but a beautiful woman ill-treated by fate and the gods. She brings to Perseus his own self-recognition through a "blinding love, which transfigured everything in view" and with this his true immortality, which he has sought so long in vain and which consists in their both being "where we talk together" (*Ch*, 133).

Even more pointedly fictional is Chimera, whom even at the moment of *agon* Bellerophon does not see but "only, on the rock-face, a blurred silhouette in soot of what I took to be the beast herself" (*Ch*, 227). And at the tale's conclusion Bellerophon sees the chimerical nature of his entire life when he comes to perceive the actual value of Chimera as a paradigm of his conscious effort to be a mythic hero:

> What I saw was that it's *not* a great invention: there's nothing original in it; it neither hurt nor helped anyone; it's preposterous, not monstrous, and compared to Medusa or the Sphinx, for example, even its metaphoric power is slight. That's why, up there in the crater, it cooperated in its own destruction by melting the lead on my lance-point: its death was the only mythopoeic thing about it. Needless to say, the moment I understood *that* was the moment I really killed Chimera. (*Ch*, 304–305)

From even these all too few examples, it is clear that both Barth's characters and the structure of their actions and tales underscore the primacy of point of view and narration. The nature of a character and of the events involving him is determined by who the teller is and by the degree of self-consciousness he brings to the act. It is Barth's own highly aware recognition of this that leads him to focus directly on *The Thousand and One Nights* and classical myth, for both are part of the origins of storytelling and so in some sense constitutive of its basic nature. Each model, in Barth's hands, reveals the fictive quality of the storytelling enterprise. The former does so by its concentration on issues of technique, form, and pattern; the latter by its reliance upon impossible and improbable events and characters. Taken together as subject-models, legend and myth move toward each other's emphasis, as *Chimera* demonstrates, so that what results is a fictive parody of their fictional nature.

In *Dunyazadiad* the two sisters, appalled by the king's deflowering and slaughter of the nation's virgins, search for a solution first in political science and then in psychology and finally as a last resort in mythology and folklore. There miracle and magic are conjoined and found to reside in words. So long as Scheherazade conceives the issue as "'the trick is to learn the trick'" (*Ch*, 7), they are frustrated and helpless. But when she sees the matter as storylike and coming "'down to particular words in the story we're reading,'" the problem is construed in terms of key and treasure and the answer in the formula "'the key to the treasure *is* the treasure!'" (*Ch*, 8). And with these words, the Genie, who though not identified, sounds remarkably like J. B. Bray, the fictive author of *Notes* (itself once only fictive but now real, though still fictive) who in turn reminds us of the author of *Giles Goat-Boy*, suddenly appears. Incredibly enough he comes out of the twentieth century with that knowledge of the tales in *The Thousand and One Nights* not possessed by Scheherazade because she has not yet recounted them and does not know them. And with this discovery of the magical power of words, Scheherazade and the Genie embark on a complex and engrossing discussion of the techniques and possibilities of storytelling. These include tales-within-tales, meshing tales in which the resolution of one is also that of the other, plot-function tales which play a role in the narrator's own life, and framed and framing tales that are artlessly and arbitrarily related. Strikingly enough, all of these narrative strategies occur in *The Thousand and One Nights* itself, a fact which further complicates both specifically and generally the question of the ultimate identity of the narrator.[16] Both agree that while stories take more than technique, "'it's only the technique that we can *talk* about!'" (*Ch*, 24). Both also agree there are a multitude of relations between narrative and sexual art not only between conventional dramatic structure and the rhythm of sexual intercourse but between teller and listener or reader. That this is more than an ingenious metaphor and comic exuberance appears near the end of the story when Shah Zaman admits that love is ephemeral but concludes that "life itself was scarcely less so, and both were sweet for just that reason—sweeter yet when enjoyed as if they might endure" (*Ch*, 39). Here, story (a verbal fiction) is love (a behavioral or emotional fiction) is life (a limited, because mortal, reality when value consists in its fictive possibility).

16. On the strategies, see M. I. Gerhardt, *The Art of Story-Telling* (Leiden, 1963), esp. Chap. V.

The crucial point dramatically developed and recapitulated in *Perseid* and *Bellerophoniad* contains Barth's implicit answer to Tanner's fear that he ignored "the limitations of the world." It also answers other critics who suspect that he himself has become lost in the fun house of solipsism and ever-receding and -multiplying narrators. His mythic characters talk in a slangy contemporary colloquial fashion; some such as Polyeidus and Calyxa do not appear in the ancient mythographers; others such as Megapenthes and Anteia are given novel traits like homosexuality and radical feminism; still others, such as Polyeidus and Bellerophon, want either to get out of their lives and into their tales or myths or else to get out of myth and into another personage whether fictional or historical. In this way, variation is seen to be indigenous to myth even as are repetition—evidenced by such things as recurrent tales of heroes questing for immortality, sibling rivalry, and impossible, that is, unreal monsters—and contradiction as when two classical variants are encompassed in the same tale so that Medusa is both a literally petrifying monster and a beautiful woman or as when Anteia rejects the traditional myth of Perseus and Megapenthes in order to advance Robert Graves's theory of mythic matriarchy while Bellerophon clings to the reality and legitimacy of the story he has read, which proves to be Barth's *Perseid.*

All three aspects of Barth's technique are, in short, facets of the nature of fiction and myth which themselves are narrative mirrors of those concepts, forever changing, recurring, and reconstituting, by which man distances self from others and objects in order to think all of them. In his letter concerning his "quintessential fiction," *Notes,* which he says is designed to redeem mankind by the restoration of a new golden age, J. B. Bray observes:

> *Inasmuch as concepts, including the concepts* fiction *and* necessity, *are more or less necessary fictions, fiction is more or less necessary.* Butterflies *exist in our imaginations, along with* existence, imagination, *and the rest. Archimideses, we lever reality by conceiving ourselves apart from its other things, them from one another, the whole from unreality. Thus Art is as natural an artifice as Nature; the truth of fiction is that Fact is fantasy; the made-up story is a model of the world.* (*Ch,* 246)

The propensities of tale-telling for involved intricacies and exaggerated impossibilities, so amply demonstrated in *Chimera,* call attention to its fictionality, but they do more. When carried to their nearly logical conclusion, they culminate in what earlier was called a fictive parody of their fictional nature and so of the conceptual fictions like fiction and myth we generate in order to understand man's experiences. It is for this reason that Barth, J. B. Bray, and Bellerophon move steadily toward the diagrammatic as being the codification of the linguistic tales each is engaged with. Thus, the intricacies of narrative and plot are reduced to Bray's diagrams of the "Right-Triangular Freitag" and the "Golden-Triangular Freitag." These, it is purported, "prescribed exactly the relative proportions of exposition, rising action, and denouement, the precise location, and pitch of complications and climaxes, the relation of internal to framing narratives, et cetera" (*Ch*, 251–52). And similarly, the improbabilities and impossibilities of characters and actions most obvious in myth are phrasally codified in the elaborate diagram of the Pattern of Mythic Heroism by which Bellerophon has been trying to structure his life in order to become like Perseus. Parody, then, for Barth is the end point toward which myth and narrative, fiction and concept inevitably move as they endeavor to remind us of the nature of reality. And in a world populated by infinitely expanding universes as well as more recent ones that threaten to collapse on themselves, black holes in space, lasers, quasars, antiprotons, and quarks, who is to say that the parodic is not the real.

Creatures of all kind
Are porous, breathe, fuse with their media;
  Closures but seem.
    Given a mind,
    Much more so . . .

ELIZABETH SEWALL

SIX · Myth and Point of View: The Triadic Self

TRADITIONALLY the concept of point of view has come to refer, in the main, to the perspective from which the novel or tale is being told or the scenes, actions, and characters being observed. But as the previous essay and the work of Updike and Barth not to mention that of Borges, Nabokov, Pynchon, Fowles, and others has made clear, the nature or identity of the tale-teller becomes ultimately a much more speculative issue once the fact and nature of tale-telling are taken into account. The complication of point of view and the multiplication of narrators that have occurred in twentieth-century fiction and even some poetry have inevitably led writers and critics to puzzle over what it is that they do when they tell a story. This, in turn, generates a curiosity as to precisely who is telling the story. Characters as narrators yield to authors inside and outside the tale as narrators and then to mysterious voices speaking from a region that is ultimately, as Barth suggests, coterminous with the tale itself. As we have seen, this development brings with it an intensified recognition of the ineluctably fictive character of the narrative enterprise, a recognition that comes to be incorporated in specific versions of the enterprise so that what results is, in a sense, fictions about fictions. And when one realizes that most human accounts of experience and reality, however conceptualized, observe at least a quasi-narrative structure as part of their explanatory function, then fictionality with the attendant threats of arbitrariness, provisionality, and even falsehood appears on the verge of engulfing all of man's capacities and modes for objective knowledge and with them the epistemological security that enables a thinking and therefore active life to exist. It is at this point that novelists like Barth and Nabokov find their mimetic mode of narrative producing parody as the most accurate rendering of reality. By making what is the case not the case and vice versa, the parodist demonstrates both the full inclusiveness of reality and also its capacity for endless transformation.

Clearly these and other implications inherent in narrative have profound ramifications for myth itself and for point of view as both a literary and an existential concept. Insofar as myth is narrative, it is fictive and so implicitly parodic and therefore mediatory of reality. On the other hand, the fictive insofar as it employs a narrative mode is mythic, that is, encompassing the inconceivable. Such developments, like those of the character of *écriture* and the creative nature of criticism, postulate new relationships between literature and other forms of human activity and consciousness.

Literature's loss of a privileged position logically entails, at least for some, a similar deprivation for criticism or commentary. Similarly, language's indeterminacy of meaning, rigorously insisted upon, leads to literature's enfoldment into the ultimate silence of the material object and criticism's paralysis in the face of an infinite progress of attribution. Such a situation implies a bleak fate for the notion of point of view and an even more threatening prospect for the cultural role of literature. As a literary concept, that is, as an element embodied in a literary text, point of view becomes a mimesis not of desire but of inescapable avoidance. Through the rendering of a certain character's or persona's perspective or perspectives, point of view, as a facet of a text, as a critical concept, becomes a demystification of itself. By stressing what it is, a particular value-saturated interpretive set, it calls itself into question as a limited—because singular—but accurate and therefore authentic view of anything. It becomes, in short, a view with no point. Parody and the inconceivable come together to make the point that no view is possible. And as an existential concept, as a notion referring to the prevailing stance, thrust, or attitude of the author revealed by the esthetic object, point of view faces a similar extra- or supratextual dilemma. It becomes either a cultural straitjacket made up of historically possible *topoi* or endless reflexivity in search of a ceaselessly retreating and metamorphosing self. The end result is to conceive of literature as but a mere sociohistoric mirror, a medium devoid of original messages, concepts, or insights. Or else it is simply a verbal manifestation of the human mind's limitless capacity for proliferating fictions lacking referentiality and therefore relevance.

The notion of literature as either a plaster cast of reality or an idle lucubration relativized into insignificance by its awareness of itself is clearly one of some moment. Certainly it suggests to anyone puzzling over the relationships between myth and literature that he might better explore issues of function and significance rather than matters originary or substantival. Instead of searching for the meaning of myth in its origins whether social, religious, or psychological and instead of regarding a myth's literary nature as being an irreducible matter or substance which, like Locke, we can neither identify nor define but which is nevertheless subject to protean manifestations, we may be able through a radically different strategy to see myth more nearly in an immediate, not mediate, relation to reality as approached through literature. Some answers may then appear that bear on the dissolution of the self threatened by the nature of the tale or narrative and the attendant perplexities surrounding the identity of the teller, perplexities of such ultimate starkness as to call the nature and reality of the self into question.

Elsewhere we have mapped some of the ways in which modern writers "have deployed myth to create verbal structures of an essentially contextual nature, to make diagnostic cultural analyses, to dramatize and to participate in psychological dynamics, and to achieve philosophical positions of existential detachment."[1] Here, however, the problematic of point of view and self impels us to probe the nature of the voice or voices heard in the language of a literary work. Instead of the reader or critic taking myth to be the interpreter of literature— as is the case when the focus is upon the metonymic organization of a work's structure—he here finds literature itself to be a process of metaphoric substitution. It is this which reverses the relationship, making literature the interpreter of myth insofar as it, explicitly or implicitly, establishes an attitude, a point of view toward specific myths. How the author uses them stipulates their meaning for him. This point of view, however, is less a matter of technique than, as we shall see, a matter of

1. John B. Vickery, "Mythopoesis and Modern Literature," in *The Shaken Realist*, ed. Melvin J. Friedman and John B. Vickery (Baton Rouge, 1970), 223.

the self's functional differentiations, of its voices, engaging the myth's thematic, structural, and affective potentialities.

Though these differentiations doubtless operate in fiction—Barth, as we have seen, is a seminal figure in this regard—the sheer physical and linguistic bulk of its texts makes it an unwieldy mode for exploratory and illustrative purposes. The modern lyric is of a more manageable order and even here a further restriction of attention is desirable. Thus, limiting present consideration to selected lyrics that engage the myth of either Orpheus or Persephone (a choice that though intuitive is not wholly fortuitous) reveals several things. One has to do with the various poetic intersections of the self and the myth. Another has to do with the relationships of self and myth as embodied in poetry and the twentieth-century realities of both. Though these realities are perhaps radically different from those of the ancient classical world, nevertheless they testify to the perdurability of the mythic schemata informing present and past. And however multiform the realities of the present, it seems clear that they will include the factors of loss, communication, and survival that so powerfully and hauntingly inform Persephone and Orpheus.

As one begins to read those modern poets who have engaged the myths of Orpheus and Persephone—poets like Rainer Maria Rilke, Paul Valéry, Robert Lowell, and Edwin Muir—one is immediately struck by the variability and complexity of consciousness informing the poems. This is the direct consequence of the subject-object relation obtaining between poem as utterance and myth as story or report. When pondered further, the works in question yield, in various relationships and degrees of primacy, three orders of self: the "historical" or personal, the mythic or metapersonal, and the creative or metamorphic. However protean their manifestations and however multiform their relations, they are all grounded in and composed of the voices uttering the language of the poetic text. As a result, their definitions and existence are a function of the fact of language not of its nature. In short, the self's existence is rescued from the uncertain realms of metaphysics or psychology by being identified with the voices inhering in language use and presence.

The first order of self is called the historical or personal in order to suggest that it postulates a temporal and singular identity for its voice which may be either actual or hypothetical. It identifies the "I" of the poetic persona as, say, the voice of Anne Kavanaugh in Lowell's "The Mills of the Kavanaughs." Alternatively, this locution may refer to the poet as an existent person, that is, the voice in the poem as that of an unspecified person who yet at some level is the poet, if only by the very fact that the poem is his poem. This is the voice, for instance, who in Valéry's poem declares: "In the mind's eye, under the myrtles, I create/ Orpheus, Man of Wonders!"[2]

The mythic or metapersonal self is the "I" of the mythic *figura* represented in the poem, and, as we shall see, may exist in either an affirmative or a negative relation to the personal self. Perhaps the most unmediated instance of the mythic self is that occurring in Kathleen Raine's "Kore in Hades," in which there is complete grammatical congruence of personal and mythic. Yet the deliberate referentiality of the mythic self is not contingent on the use of the first person. This we see most clearly in poems as tonally different as Rilke's "Orpheus. Eurydice. Hermes" and David Gascoyne's "Orpheus in the Underworld." There the *figurae* are developed in the third person but as real entities whose contextual being is of the same quasi-historical order as the personal self.

And finally, by the creative or metamorphic self is meant the reflexively aware intersection point of the actual and the potential, the determined and the anticipated, and the known and the unknown, which taken together make up the three dimensions of the thinking world of consciousness. Because of its protean nature, generalization about the creative self is difficult. One thing we can say perhaps is that it is that quality of linguistic intentionality envisaging both symmetrical and asymmetrical relations between the personal and mythic terms of the self. It is the deliberate consideration of the nature, presence, and role of this creative self that Lawrence Durrell takes up in his poem "Orpheus." There he first defines our knowledge of Orpheus as "intimations from the dead" and then raises the metaphysical question of existence when he asks: "Do you contend in us, though now/ A memory only?"[3] Ultimately Durrell answers this question in the affirmative

2. Paul Valéry, *Collected Works*, ed. J. Matthews, trans. J. Lawler (Princeton, 1971), I, 9. All quotations from this poem are from this edition.
3. Lawrence Durrell, *Collected Poems* (London, 1960), 17. All quotations from this poem are from this edition.

and in a manner which sees the artist (painter as well as poet) as Orpheus defined as the perdurable celebrator of love and loss, terms whose reference is infinitely broader than the erotic, the personal, and the material.

The second and in many ways more interesting and significant point to emerge from a consideration of these and other poems is the manner in which the dynamic character of the multiform self as subject and object forces us to a recognition that its actions generate a series of poetic (that is, linguistic *and* ontological) modes. These modes range along an attitudinal spectrum from negation or annihilation of one or more of the orders of self through definition of the self to affirmation of it and the subject reality of its object, myth.

The attitudinal mode of negation or annihilation expresses itself in three different inflections, though these, of course, are representative only. In many ways, the most dramatic of these is William Plomer's poem "Persephone." It, in effect, annihilates the mythic self by having the personal self enact a relentlessly rational or intellectual role. It distances itself from the mythic self by a temporal transformation from what Samuel Beckett calls "the mythological present" to the historical past. The entire context is that of the late eighteenth century so that Pluto appears "Busbied and in Hessian boots," riding "in a black barouche," and carrying "a small cloisonné box" of snuff.[4] The focus of this rake's interest is, predictably enough, a young lady whose sole contact with myth is her name, for

> Proserpine was in a bonnet
> And a yellow grenadine
> With a high Directoire waist
> And silver spangles on it,
> Muslined and beribboned, shod with sandals criss-cross
>   laced—
> Merveilleuse or muscadine?

The effect of this perspective is to deny the reality of the myth by making of it a literary or possibly even operatic fiction, a dramatic illusion that deliberately and radically calls attention either to the Teufelsdröckhian reality substrate or to the arbitrary assigning of ob-

4. William Plomer, *The Family Tree* (London, 1929), 63. All quotations from this poem are from this edition.

viously fictive values to the mythic schemata. In short, the tale is either that of an eighteenth-century maid betrayed, for whom the nominative designation invokes in the manner of a Restoration comedy a pretty and witty arabesque on the ugly fact of seduction and rape, or else it is a translation of the classical story into a historical period and literary mode that call attention to the disparity between the two forms and to the diminution of what one critic has called the "indeterminability of its significance." Either way, the mythic *figura* is presented as an otherness of itself, which in the context of the lyric's reality statement emerges as the negation and hence annihilation of the mythic self.

A less categorical but still largely unequivocal attitude of negation emerges in the course of Stephen Spender's "No Orpheus No Eurydice." The central difference in strategy from Plomer is that Spender does not so much annihilate as avoid the mythic self. He does so through concentrating on the personal self construed as a historically contemporary but anonymous persona who occupies not an affirmative but a negative relation to the mythic self. This relationship, however, is not so much asserted as discovered in the course of a carefully controlled ambiguity of identity and syntactic prolongation of the conditional. The first two stanzas carefully polarize the affirmative and negative relational possibilities for the personal and mythic selves. Identity is apparently denied by the entertaining of death via "bullets, precipices,/ Ropes, knives," but it is quickly affirmed—at least ostensibly—when the personal self's thoughts

> paint his pale darling
> In a piteous attitude standing
> Amongst blowing winds of space,
> Dead, and waiting in sweet grace
> For him to follow, when she calls.[5]

Similarly, the second half of the poem extends the conditional formulation of the mythic schemata first enunciated in "if he started/ Upon that long journey/ Of the newly departed" through two stanzas before concluding, "He would never find there/ Her cold, starry, wondering face," thereby preparing for the stark declaration of "he is no Orpheus,/ She no Eurydice" of the conclusion.

5. Stephen Spender, *Ruins and Visions* (London, 1942), 21. All quotations from this poem are from this edition. The version in *Collected Poems* has some significant changes from this earlier version.

What happens here, then, is that the personal self surmounts the other onto which the mythic self has been projected through the deployment of both irony and fact. The personal self articulating the poem creates an *imago* for itself through the third-person pronominal use, which in turn allows for an ironic deflation of the *imago*. Thus, the second stanza develops the self's image as Orpheus, the sustainer of Eurydice, prepared to answer her call, but this rather magniloquent pose is evaporated at the opening of the third stanza, which reveals that his image of her waiting for him is justified on the grounds that "how can he believe/ Her loss less than his?" This irony not only matches the last stanza's flat facticity in denying that either figure is mythic; it also compounds by the stanza's subsequent explanation of why the personal and mythic selves do not meet:

> She has truly packed and gone
> To live with someone
> Else, in pleasures of the sun,
> Far from his kingdoms of despair
> Here, there, or anywhere.

The juxtaposition of "pleasures of the sun" and "kingdoms of despair" finally completes the avoidance of the personal self's alignment with the mythic self of Orpheus by glancingly hinting that the persona lies closer, if anything, to Pluto, whose kingdom is compounded of darkness and despair for those who come to it. The significance of this is that it shows the creative self entertaining the intersection of personal actuality and mythic potentiality, but ultimately denying it. The reason it does so is that the personal self (here the poet as existent person) wants the identification for itself while at the same time it is aware of its own incapacities for such an act as seen through its projection of both actualities and potentialities onto the other of the third-person-pronominal identities. In this way, the personal self does not so much annihilate the mythic self as skirt it by refusing to confront the possibility directly. The result is a poem in which irony's distancing into self-superiority ultimately stands forth as a tacit admission of anxious self-inferiority.

The third and final instance of negation of the self occurs in Denis Devlin's "A Dream of Orpheus." Strikingly enough, it effects the negation (via absorption) of the personal self by the creative self's mediation of the mythic self as a substantival reality. That is to say, the poem's reality statement simultaneously presents the mythic self in a negative relation to the personal self and in an affirmative relation to the creative self. Devlin is able to do this because he begins with the personal self in its formal immediacy as a first-person-pronominal entity: "Low and knelt on my heels . . ./ I stroke and stroke the sheets murmuring the old endearments."[6] But then memory, spurred by the ghostly nature of the beloved, acts to bear in upon the personal self its ineffectuality. Not it but the other as nature, embodied in the images of lark, earth, and diurnal time, possesses the power to effect movement and action. The result is to cast the figure of the personal self as static, immobilized by the greater synergic power of nature which lies beyond the self. But since time is a repetitive continuum, the stasis of self is quickly supplanted by the separation and then obliteration of the personal self as it declares, "Orpheus I am not whose grief sang so melodious." At this juncture the self is absorbed in memory of the mythic schemata as it defines the relations of Orpheus to the world of nature and animals, to the hellish void that is the underworld, and to song. With death's warning that it is "only life's limpness," the lyric statement of the poem becomes that of the creative self meditating on Eurydice, whose death is seen as a murder that violates the natural order of the pastoral world in which "all lie"—even enemies—"blandly sailing to death/ . . . remotely harmonious/ In the god's lazy eyes." The incredibility of this violation is measured by its having "denatured" (the word is Devlin's) both human reality and the forms in which it is known. With this the creative self both senses the imminent dissolution of the mythic self and the need for its reconstitution.

Significantly, the meditative focus shifts from Eurydice and reality to Orpheus and language. Through his power of both words and things, a universal silence ensues in the world. In the midst of this silence the mythic self attains an affirmative relation with the creative self through scenic specificity of details and the near ritualistic sequence of actions. Both culminate with Orpheus' musical and linguistic assertion of "the mortal sympathy linking plant, beast and man." In so doing, the mythic self *asserts* that reconstitution of the unity of living things which the creative self *enacts* in entertaining the actualization of the potential meaning of the mythic schemata. The effect of

6. Denis Devlin, *Collected Poems*, ed. B. Coffey (Dublin, 1964), 87. All quotations from this poem are from this edition.

this meeting of actual and potential is profound for the personal self. It gains a crucial solace in the face of its grief and metaphysical disorientation brought on by the fact that of the beloved it is "a ghost's hand only I hold." Thus, the personal self is able to enjoin itself finally to "Rise, turn away" but does not lose sight of the fact that the natural world it inhabits is helpless to reverse death or to make its subjects "perfect before death." This acceptance is made possible through its positive relationship with the creative self in which the personal self is submerged or swallowed up as the creative self locates both the eternity of grief and the perdurability of love and beauty made mutual between the living and the dead in the only place where it can exist in actuality while not precluding its potentiality elsewhere, namely, in myth itself:

> But Orpheus
> Grieves for her still; in the shell and web of her body, beauty
> Dreamt the forms his love made substance of and that she
>   dreams in him.

When we turn from the poetic mode that annihilates, denies, or avoids the self to that which seeks to define it, we find ourselves in an even more uncertain region the amplitude of whose pitfalls are testified to by minds as diverse as G. W. F. Hegel, Edmund Husserl, William James, and Carl Jung. How, we wonder, can poets hope to define the self when psychologists are reduced to metaphor, image, and analogy and when philosophers find themselves alternately multiplying kinds of definition and thrashing about amid the problematics of defining definition? A tantalizing and, in many ways, an attractive question, but one that like Francis Bacon's Pontius Pilate we will not stay to answer here. Instead, let us concentrate on the ways in which some representative modern poets have sought, both directly and obliquely, to define the self even as they are engaged in celebrating and drawing on it.

The submode which perhaps most attends to the inherent difficulties of the matter is that which approaches it by a method of temporal interrogation. Thus, Lawrence Durrell begins his Orpheus poem by tacitly admitting that the conventional approach to the *figura* is through its past manifestations. Orpheus is "known to us in a dark congeries/ Of intimations from the dead"—conflation, as it were, of

the Orphic tablets and poems, testimony of ancient authors, and subsequent deceased mythographers and scholars. Implicit dissatisfaction
with this approach is registered immediately when the pressing issue is
seen to be not the past reality but the present existence of Orpheus:

> Encamping among our verses—
> Harp-beats of a sea-bird's wings—
> Do you contend in us, though now
> A memory only?

This interrogation is that of the poet as existent person probing the
genesis and significance of his art and nature. The response, however,
is that of the creative self whose dynamic character enables it to perceive the already determined paradoxical mythic self (imaged in the
singing head of the dead *figura*) merging with, perpetually advancing
out of the past to fuse with, the personal self of the generic artist in the
perennial present of creative choice and decision. In, says Durrell, "the
poet's wrestling/ With choice you [*i.e.*, Orpheus] steer like/ A great albatross" to function as "Mentor of all these paper ships/ Cockled
from fancy on a tide/ Made navigable only by your skill." Here, then,
the definition of self proves both circular and circumspect. For self
proves to be consciousness' query concerning its own metapersonal reality coupled with its affirmative reply as to its reflexive tutelary autonomy in linguistically re-creating past personal objects and events and
experiences. And as the last lines reveal, the need and the rationale for
the definition lie in the justification and effectuating of poetry, for the
mythic self is but the "beloved famulus" to the creative self. It is these
two together who provide the personal self of the poet with that skill
"which in some few approves/ A paper recreation of lost loves."

Though Durrell ends on a note of encouragement for the practice
of poetry, it is clear—from the opening interrogative, the albatross image inextricable from Coleridgean foreboding of disaster, and the deliberate diminishment of poetry to the child's amusement over paper
boats spurred not by imagination but by "fancy"—that the self's definition is tentative and uneasy. The opposite is true of Paul Valéry's
"Orpheus," which energetically defines the creative self by the actions
with which it animates the mythic self. Here the portion of the mythic
schemata drawn upon is not the severed head of the singing Orpheus
but the resplendent full-bodied magical power of a divine being sum-

moned up by the personal self in a deliberate act of consciousness: "In the mind's eye, under the myrtles, I create/ Orpheus, Man of Wonders!" In what follows it becomes clear that the creative self is being defined as a series of actions participated in by the mythic self and its object or objects, a series which encompasses destruction or dissolution, transformation, and reconstitution. If the god sings, "he rends the all-powerful site"; the mountain's "bald peak" is transformed "into a trophy of majesty"; stones are not static but "moving" entities and find themselves magically transformed into things of awareness subject to antigravitational forces; "a rock walks, and staggers" like a man; and a partially stripped temple miraculously "soars/ And spontaneously assembles, taking shape in the gold light" of sunset. All of these acts occur in obedience to "the giant soul of the great hymn on the lyre!" These narrative actions occasioned by the mythic self are also a dramatic definition of the creative self as consciousness' actions of dissolution, transformation, and reconstitution. These actions not only separate the actual and the potential, the determined and the anticipated, and the known and the unknown but are themselves as much incipient as occurrent. As a result, the poem is both the quintessential act of consciousness and a representative description of the mythic *figura* rendered dynamic by the operations of the metamorphic self.

It is ironic in some ways that Valéry should at once see himself as evoking human perfection and yet concentrate on the transformational so heavily. When, however, we consider this fact in relation to Robert Lowell's use of the Persephone myth in "The Mills of the Kavanaughs," the alignment is more revealing. For through the *figura* of Persephone, Lowell struggles to define the self as a process of appearance and disappearance of its component forms or manifestations. In contradistinction to Valéry, Lowell sees all aspects of the self, not just the creative, as transformational. He further sees these changes as radically ontological rather than continuously epistemological. That is, while the self manifests itself in the three forms mentioned, it does so neither uniformly nor continuously. Historical, mythic, and creative embodiments of the self appear and disappear in a discontinuous passage through time that is the gradient of consciousness consequent upon the anguish of human imperfection. This ontological discontinuity necessarily thwarts any and all critical efforts to reconcile Anne Kavanaugh's relations to Persephone, Daphne, and Eve into a thematic and conceptual unity. The poem's lyric statement recalcitrantly asserts the asymmetrical nature of these relations and stubbornly insists upon the gaps rather than the connections between the *figurae*. Indeed, it is perhaps just here in the poem's lyrical character that the nub of the problem may reside. At first glance we may consider it dramatic (and hence mimetic in Käte Hamburger's terms) since it possesses personae who engage in dialogue or at least quasi-antiphonal monologues and who participate at varying levels in the actions of what may best be called a proto-plot. Given also the stress laid by Lowell on the poem's being a revery, it is clear that, on one level, the historical self is the fictional Anne Kavanaugh. But at the same time, the epigraphs from Matthew Arnold and William Carlos Williams, which lie outside the dramatized revery of Anne, alert us to a deeper and more encompassing personal self, that of the poet as existential being whose voice—so fraught with anguish over the recognition of and recoil from the ontology of deprivation—is his reality. The dramatic form is the poet's technique for distancing his involvement so as to render it articulable, while the revery mode testifies to the poem's being a lyric statement of the poet's sense of the totality of self-discontinuity.

This plurality of historical or personal self is repeated on the meta-personal level in the *figurae* from classical and Christian myth and on the metamorphic level by the intermixture of revery, dream, and speech. It is Lowell's perception that the self as he knows it shifts in accord with an unknown dynamic from the personal to the mythic and the creative in permutations and combinations that are as unpredictable as they are inevitable. What, however, principally distinguishes Lowell's rendering of the incommensurability of the self as discontinuous is his refusal to despair of the fact. The apparent preoccupation with the terrors of the fragmented self is in reality the recognition of the undesired but unavoidable discontinuity of focal consciousness occasioned by the nature of man and the human condition. And that this is far from a hopeless state is testified to by the major action of the creative self in the course of the poem. For it is reflexively aware not only that a series of selves appears and disappears but that the initial inclination of the self is toward its own fascination and love and that this is what makes its dissolution a threat. The Douay Bible (a powerful symbol for Lowell at the time of writing), Harry Kavanaugh, and Anne herself, all in their different ways bear out this fact.

The Bible, acting as Anne's dummy in a game of solitaire, tells her that "her gambling with herself/ Is love of self."[7] Harry, by the waterfall that is "Jehovah's beard," declares "I am married to myself." And Anne herself, called Cinderella by her bridesmaids, replies "Prince Charming is my shadow in the glass." Such self-love necessarily seeks the perpetuation and continuity of the personal self. That the self should actually prove to be discontinuous testifies surprisingly enough, in the last analysis, to the ultimate beneficence (perhaps divinely conferred) of existence. Crucial here are the fact and form of the underlying manifestations of the self's discontinuity. This manifestation first confronts death as the extremity of otherness to the self and then discovers that death is not a polar opposite to but a version of the self. It is the creative self, that awareness of her voice and of its differing qualia ("she whispers," "she wonders," "she thinks," "she marvels"), which recognizes that the personal self's narcissistic introversion is also the mythic self's reaching out to the ultimate other of death:

> they have found
> Me their Persephone, gone underground
> Into myself to supplicate the throne
> And horn of Hades to restore that stone.

And it is this perception that the historical self of Anne Kavanaugh comes also to articulate at the end of the poem as the basic separation of her husband from herself. He, like she in the beginning, saw death as "Nothing but ruin." She, however, realizes that there is no reason why we must "mistrust/ Ourselves with Death who takes the world on trust." Pluto's seduction of Persephone is not a taking of life by death but a giving of life to death. And in this action of the self is embodied the final acceptance of the appearance and disappearance of the self as the existentially recurring norm.

If the myths of Orpheus and Persephone are schema by which Lowell and Valéry define the self as forms of transformation and dialectical action, just the opposite is true of poets such as Rilke and David Gascoyne. They concentrate their attention on the multidimen-

7. Robert Lowell, *The Mills of the Kavanaughs* (New York, 1951), 4. All quotations from this poem are from this edition.

sioned "givenness," on the ontological solidity of the self. While this is bodied forth in a variety of ways, their definition stands out in almost Aristotelian simplicity as the being of beings. Both poets generate this formulation through a quiddity of detail in the physical world which in surrounding also defines the self's existence. In his early "Orpheus. Eurydice. Hermes," Rilke takes care that both scene and characters are invested with a specificity of fact that anchors the self in the stasis of unalterable being. Thus, though the underworld's association with the remote depths of the self is rendered by its description as "the strange unfathomed mine of souls," it is also concretized as a region of "rocks/ and ghostly forests. Bridges over voidness/ . . . meadows" through which runs "the pale strip of the single pathway" to the world of the living.[8] Animating the whole is the blood which ultimately becomes man's but here lies "like blocks of heavy porphyry in the darkness." Similarly, Orpheus appears as "the slender man in the blue mantle" whose hands lie "hanging,/ heavy and clenched, out of the falling folds," while Hermes moves along the single pathway

> the travelling-hood over his shining eyes,
> the slender wand held out before his body,
> the wings around his ankles lightly beating,
> and in his left hand, as entrusted, *her*.

By this physicality together with a deliberately measured narrative progression, Rilke gradually concentrates the reader's attention on Eurydice, whose solidity of being is precisely *not* physical but what can perhaps only be called an ontological condition of postmortality that is indistinguishable from the self's totality as natural organism:

> Wrapt in herself she wandered. And her deadness
> was filling her like fullness.
> Full as a fruit with sweetness and with darkness
> was she with her great death.
>
> . . . .
>
> She was already root.

This settling of the mythic self into a uniquely personal state of autonomy and independence ("nor yonder man's possession any longer")

---

8. Rainer Maria Rilke, *Selected Works*, trans. J. B. Leishman (2 vols.; London, 1960), II, 188. All quotations from this poem are from this edition.

crystallizes, for Rilke, in Eurydice's loss of consciousness of Orpheus and the mythic schemata. When Hermes reports Orpheus' backward look, "she took in nothing, and said softly: Who?" This response not so ironically but no less conclusively than that in Spender's poem annihilates the erotic egotism of Orpheus. In so doing, it embodies the creative self's awareness of three things: of the known backward glance of Orpheus and the hitherto unknown reaction of Eurydice; of the mythic schemata of figural actions; and of the attribution of unique and personal values to the figural variable.

Even more starkly rooted in the stasis of the quintessential autonomy of the self is David Gascoyne's "Orpheus in the Underworld." For here not only the self but the body in which it lodges is motionless as is the setting framing both:

> Curtains of rock
> And tears of stone,
> Wet leaves in a high crevice of the sky:
> From side to side the draperies
> Drawn back by rigid hands[9]

The effect of this immobilized nature is, as in Rilke, to focus the reader's act of attention on the mythic *figura*, only in this instance it is Orpheus not Eurydice who is attended. An even more crucial difference is the fact that the mythic self exists not as an independent self-sufficient entity but as a convulsion of paralyzed trauma on the *figura*'s part:

> And he came carrying the shattered lyre,
> And wearing the blue robes of a king,
> And looking through eyes like holes torn in a screen;
> And the distant sea was faintly heard,
> From time to time, in the suddenly rising wind,
> Like broken song.

So profound is this condition that even the self's capacity for articulation, that is, for consciousness, is fragmented by death, loss, and descent so that "from between half-open lips,/ Escaped the bewildered words" of nothing more than "broken song."

9. David Gascoyne, *Collected Poems* (London, 1965), 37. All quotations from this poem are from this edition.

The creative self here apprehends the way in which its anticipations of variables of signification, that is, the possibilities of Orpheus' responses being other than they are, are restricted by the determinations actually made. The broken bewilderment of the mythic singer-poet precludes the suasive meliorations developed in, say, Devlin's poem or the ironic diminutions of the personal self effected by Spender. There is a pressure inward on the mythic self by the poetic interpretational values which shape it into determinacy at the same time as the potentialities of the mythic schemata struggle to maintain viability and, in the final analysis, indeterminability. As a result, the personal self stands awestruck at the fate contingent upon man's exceeding the human condition, awestruck and reflectively elegiac before the enormities implicit in the impossible experience, which for Gascoyne's Orpheus is that of

> his bright night
> And his wing-shadowed day
> The soaring flights of thought beneath the sun
> Above the islands of the seas
> And all the deserts, all the pastures, all the plains
> Of the distracting foreign land.

These two inflections of the self's definition as the being of beings, the ironical and the elegiac, both point unmistakably to the poetic mode of the affirmation of the self. It would be as idle as it would be erroneous to suggest that the senses of affirmation are either neatly or completely classified. Yet on the basis of the texts under consideration here, it is possible to say that three chief senses of affirmation emerge: a "having" (of, say, dream and memory) as in the cases of Edwin Muir and Kathleen Raine; a "doing" (of a ritual) as in Lawrence; and a "saying" such as appears in the dithyramb-dominated consciousness of Hart Crane. In all three, what differentiates them, and the very notion of affirmation, from the other poetic modes of the self is the fact that affirmation entails not only ontological assertion but axiological imputation. The self, for these poets, not only is; it is valuable and a value in itself, because of its quintessentially human capacities of receiving, performing, and articulating.

The first of these senses of affirmation is exemplified in Edwin Muir's "Orpheus's Dream" and Kathleen Raine's "Kore in Hades."

The first, as its title indicates, is concerned with the mythic self's having of a dream, while the latter poem enacts the self's having of a memory whose finality is consequent on the annihilation of the present. The Muir poem opens with a radical displacement of the Orpheus schemata which mirrors the dreaming condition of the mythic self:

> And she was there. The little boat
> Coasting the perilous isles of sleep,
> Zones of oblivion and despair,
> Stopped, for Eurydice was there.
> The foundering skiff could scarcely keep
> All that felicity afloat.[10]

The self's consciousness is projected onto the image of the vessel so that the *figura*'s intertwining of awareness and unconscious response to self-occasioned loss may be symbolized (that is, tacitly and obliquely recognized) and the mechanism of its therapeutic release established. The dream vision of Eurydice as simultaneously present and alive generates not only the unconscious' unalloyed happiness at the full realization of its deepest wish but also the sense that the recovered feminine presence is "the lost original of the soul." The dream's recovery of the beloved is also the recovery of the animating power of the self which is its basic function.

If the first stanza focuses on the recognition of Eurydice's image, the second registers that creative movement of the mythic self outward to the personal self seen as the triumphant questing action of human beings in general. The winning of "the lost original of the soul" is achieved not by the singular mythic *figura* but by the "we" of the vessel, by all who have gone beyond the protective confines of "earth's frontier wood" and embarked on the sea of sleep, dream, and danger. Orpheus implicitly emerges as the mythic prototype of all men standing in need of "forgiveness, truth, atonement, all/ Our love at once." And what the dream-encapsulated moment of wish fulfillment does is to give "us pure and whole/ Each back to each." The separation of self from self and of self from itself that follows upon the twin disasters of loss and survival is assuaged by the dream, which is the creative self's

---

10. Edwin Muir, *Collected Poems* (2nd ed.; London, 1965), 216. All quotations from this poem are from this edition.

sense of the intersection of the determined (Eurydice's loss) and the desired (her presence).

For Muir the phenomenon of the dream is if not the entirety at least a substantial part of the creative self. Only through the dream fulfillment of the wish, which is a compound of conscious apprehension of the terrible truth about the personal self and its mythic avatar, the desire for forgiveness, and the willingness to atone, can guilty, stricken lovers confront directly the reality of their past act and its immutable, timeless consequences. Only after the dream and its integrative activity working in and through the creative self can the personal and mythic selves

> dare
> At last to turn our heads and see
> The poor ghost of Eurydice
> Still sitting in her silver chair,
> Alone in Hades' empty hall.

Muir finds the affirmation of the self in its capacity to counter the liabilities and vicissitudes of existence with the restorative and integrative dream that is capable of dialectically balancing the epistemological reality of "Eurydice was there" against the historical or temporal actuality of "The poor ghost of Eurydice." For Kathleen Raine there is no such succor developed in "Kore in Hades," though there is abundant evidence that her view of the dream's importance to the self is remarkably close to that of Muir. The reason for her stark rendering of the self's affirmation in this poem resides primarily in its focus on memory. In a word, her sense of the nature and role of memory is less Proustian than Rilkean. She too concentrates on the carefully detailed registering of past scenes and experiences in their full immediacy while underlining the irremediability of their pastness rather than their potentiality for creative metamorphosis into the present.

Informing all facets of Persephone's memory is the daughter's devoted bond to the mother, so intense and all-encompassing as to have seemingly originated in the prenatal state:

> I came, yes, dear, dear
> Mother for you I came, so I remember,
> To lie in your warm

Bed, to watch the wonder flame:
Burning, golden gentle and bright the light of the living.[11]

In the course of recollecting her girlhood, the maiden uses the key words "living" and "world," the multiplicity of the former establishing the unity and value of the latter. Not only the human female form but all living things stem from and are coterminous with "the one mother": "we are yours,/ We are you." The relational perceptions of the Persephone figure, crystallizing as they do in the notion of an ontological manifold of almost limitless dimensions, serve to fuse the mythic self of the Kore and the personal self of the poet. At the same time, these perceptions remind us that the mythic schemata is not merely a paradigm for human behavior but for divine actions as well. Demeter, "the one mother," has a human image, but she is also the original nurturing principle in the universe who wove her natural progeny into a "garden world without end." As a result, the mythic *figura* of the mother is reinvested in the middle sections of the poem with a more than human stature.

This gradual expansion of the personal self into the metapersonal and of the human individual into the universe creates both the almost unbearable joy of recollection—saved from the indulgence of nostalgia only by the subtle balancing of past and present verb tenses—and the anticipatory apprehension of the loss of paradise and the descent from Eden. In the penultimate stanza, everything builds to the remembered vision of a "garden world without end" only to be obliterated by the terse, uninflected statement of the final line: "Bright those faces closed and were over." Indeed, here the schemata's rape is seen as the annihilation of nature, life, time, and human relationships and its consequence or aftermath as an eternity of nullity:

Here and now is over, the garden
Lost from time, its sun its moon
Mother, daughter, daughter, mother, never
Is now: there is nothing, nothing for ever.

The power of this final stanza derives not only from its flat, bleak tone of finality underlined by the rhyme of "over," "never," and "ever" but

11. Kathleen Raine, *The Hollow Hill* (London, 1965), 6. All quotations from this poem are from this edition.

from the abruptness with which we are catapulted out of the won-
drous fulfillment of the pastoral world of parent and child and into a
realm characterizable only in terms of ontological and epistemological negation.

And yet this poem is not ultimately in the annihilatory mode of
those by Plomer, Spender, and Devlin. Actually it stands much closer
to the weighted gravity of Rilke and Gascoyne in seizing upon the creative self's affirmation of the self's limits. For what the last stanza renders is precisely the creative self's recognition that the mythic self of
the Kore is affirmed as fully known only when it is impinged on by the
unknown and so engulfed by "nothing, nothing for ever." At this juncture it is metamorphosed into the Persephone figure, who is preeminently the chthonic goddess of death and the dark underworld that lies
beyond or below man's ken. This transformation, however, is not the
denial but the affirmation of the self construed as the human awareness of the intersection of the known and the unknown. The fact that
the last line articulates the culminating denial that "there is nothing,
nothing for ever" implicitly asserts that there is a conscious something
other than existential and linguistic negation, which is the self. In
short, the articulation of the lyric statement quite literally is the affirmation of the self.

"Kore in Hades" carries us to the brink of Hades where all is
murky obliteration and definitional negation. In his "Bavarian Gentians," D. H. Lawrence goes one step further by plotting the self's ritual descent into the blank void of the not-self which is both antagonist
and temptation. The flowers of the poem's title become a talismanic
guide for the poet's personal self as it descends into the underworld of
death. There, as we have seen earlier, the myth of the rape of Persephone by the god of darkness and death brings the creative self to a
felt awareness and immediate knowledge of that which it is not. To the
living being, both sex and death entail another and a condition of un-
likeness so profound as to make it simultaneously unknown and fascinating. To risk, as "The Ship of Death" says, "the longest journey, to
oblivion" is precisely what Lawrence here shows the creative self ven-
turing upon in order to enact ritualistically and consciously what it
has been engaged in doing intuitively or instinctively throughout its
existence, namely, extending its awareness of myth into a sense, perhaps only postulated, of mystery, of matter into nothingness, and of

speech into silence. The risk of envelopment in endless darkness, nescience, and silence is one that Lawrence finds the creative self must
ultimately confront even though emergence from such an underworld,
as the myths of Persephone and Orpheus alike testify, may entail par-
tiality, incompleteness, and perpetual longing.

While Lawrence describes a ritual process for bringing myth and
language into contact with the mystery and silence from which they
originally emerged, Hart Crane struggles to make a verbal actuality or
event out of their impingement on one another. Though both adopt a
hortatory note, it is significant that the former stresses the futurity of
the melding while Crane, in the last section of *The Bridge*, concentrates on the presentness of the creative self's reflexive awareness of the
simultaneity of sound and silence that is the human articulation of
language. For Lawrence, the experience is still to happen and his paramount effort is bent on constructing a ritual to ensure the self's resolution in the face of its trial. But for Crane the articulation, the language
of the poem, is itself the action of the self's contact with the unknown,
which is both Cathay and the questioning of its reality or identity.
Here the mythic self is not the bereft lover but the "floating singer" [12]
who defies life's otherness, death, both unsuccessfully (Orpheus' head
is dead as it floats downstream) and successfully (Orpheus' song continues to be heard even after his death), thereby capturing on the existential level the dialectic of sound and silence that lies at the heart of
language. The mythic self's taking this form is a clue both to the
greater weight that falls on the creative self and to the negative relation
in which the mythic self stands to the personal self. Though the entire
section, and indeed the whole poem, grapples with the metamorphic
awareness of the multiform movements of consciousness between the
"is" and the "is not," nowhere is it more clearly rendered than in the
rapt invocation:

> O Choir, translating time
> Into what multitudinous Verb the suns
> And synergy of waters ever fuse, recast
> In myriad syllables,—Psalm of Cathay!
> O Love, thy white, pervasive Paradigm . . . !

12. Hart Crane, *Collected Poems*, ed. W. Frank (New York, 1946), 58. All quotations from this poem are from this edition.

Brooklyn Bridge apprehended as a perceptual metaphor in the act of occurrence here possesses "sibylline voices" whose "myriad syllables" conspire to utter "one song" only whose notes emanate "from deathless strings." All of these together are the self's awareness that poetry, whose rhythms are the interplay of sound and silence, speech and music, is the bridge between itself, the known, and the mysterious enchanting realms of Cathay, the unknown "Everpresence" that is "Answerer of all." It is the fabulous, remote, unknown dimension of existence toward which "the orphic strings" of poetry "leap and converge" to make it the object of desire and devotion ("O Love") even as they are acknowledged to be "Unspeakable." In the same way, the mythic self, the dismembered singer, defines the personal self of the poet negatively insofar as it maintains a referential silence only to have it sound forth, under the impress of the creative self's ongoing energy of imagining and entertaining possibilities, as the "One Song, one Bridge of Fire" that is the articulated language of the poem itself. For Crane, the personal self is the poem; the mythic self the recognition of heroic failure in endeavoring to forge a bridge of language devoid of silence, and the creative self the awareness of the inevitability of the effort despite its necessary doom. Because of this complex and ultimately tragic affirmation of the self we are left with the awesome susurrus of "Whispers antiphonal in azure swing," which catches up the love that is "saying" and the death that comes with silence as man persists in bridging world and other with those words, intricate and simple alike, that make up literature's labyrinthine yet open-ended answer to that most challenging of Rilke's questions: "If we are continually inadequate in love, uncertain in decision, and impotent in the face of death, how is it possible to exist?"[13]

13. Rainer Maria Rilke, *Letters*, trans. J. B. Greene and M. D. Herter Norton (2 vols.; New York, 1948), II, 146.

SELECTED BIBLIOGRAPHY OF
MYTH AND LITERATURE

Albouy, P. *Mythes et mythologies dans la littérature française*. Paris, 1969.

Aler, J., ed. *De Mythe in de Litteratuur*. The Hague, 1964.

Arvin, N. *Herman Melville*. New York, 1950.

Awad, L. *The Theme of Prometheus in English and French Literature: A Study in Literary Influence*. Cairo, 1963.

Barber, C. L. *Shakespeare's Festive Comedy*. Princeton, 1959.

Barksdale, E. C. *The Dacha and the Duchess*. New York, 1974.

Barthes, R. *Mythologies*. Paris, 1957.

Belli, A. *Ancient Greek Myths and Modern Drama*. New York, 1969.

Bianquis, G. *Faust à travers quatre siècles*. Paris, 1935.

Bloom, H. *Shelley's Mythmaking*. New Haven, 1959.

Bodkin, M. *Archetypal Patterns in Poetry*. London, 1934.

Bowra, C. M. *Primitive Song*. Cleveland, 1962.

Brylowski, W. *Faulkner's Olympian Laugh*. Detroit, 1968.

Budick, S. *The Poetry of Civilization*. New Haven, 1974.

Buenel, P. *Le Mythe de la métamorphose*. Paris, 1975.

Buhr, G. *Hölderlins Mythenbegriff*. Frankfurt, 1972.

Bush, D. *Mythology and the Renaissance Tradition in English Poetry*. Minneapolis, 1932.

Butler, E. M. *The Myth of the Magus*. Cambridge, 1948.

Campbell, J. *The Hero with a Thousand Faces*. New York, 1949.

———. *The Flight of the Wild Gander*. New York, 1969.

———. *The Masks of God*. 4 vols. New York, 1959.

Cassirer, E. *Language and Myth*. Translated by S. Langer. New York, 1946.

———. *The Philosophy of Symbolic Forms*. 3 vols. Translated by R. Manheim. New Haven, 1955.

Chase, R. *Quest for Myth*. Baton Rouge, 1949.

Cook, A. S. *Myth and Language*. Bloomington, 1980.

Cunningham, A., ed. *The Theory of Myth*. London, 1973.

Dabezies, A. *Visages de Faust au XXe siècle*. Paris, 1967.

Dalziel, M., ed. *Myth and the Modern Imagination*. Dunedin, 1967.

Derche, R. *Quatre mythes poétiques*. Paris, 1962.

Dickinson, H. *Myth on the Modern Stage*. Urbana, 1969.

Diez del Corral, L. *La Función del mito clásico en la literatura contemporánea*. Madrid, 1957.

Dorfles, G. *L'Estetica del mito*. Milan, 1967.

Dumezil, G. *Mythe et épopée.* 2 vols. Paris, 1968, 1971.

Durand, G. *Le Décor mythique de "La Chartreuse de Parme."* Paris, 1961.

———. *Les structures anthropologiques de l'imaginaire.* 2nd ed. Paris, 1963.

Elliott, R. C. *The Power of Satire.* Princeton, 1960.

Feder, L. *Ancient Myth in Modern Poetry.* Princeton, 1971.

Fergusson, F. *The Idea of a Theater.* Princeton, 1949.

Fiedler, L. *NO! in Thunder.* Boston, 1960.

Fontenrose, J. *The Ritual Theory of Myth.* Berkeley, 1966.

Franklin, H. Bruce. *The Wake of the Gods: Melville's Mythology.* Palo Alto, 1963.

Frye, H. N. *Fables of Identity: Studies in Poetic Mythology.* New York, 1963.

Galinsky, G. K. *The Heracles Theme.* Oxford, 1972.

Girard, R. *"To double business bound."* Baltimore, 1978.

Gould, E. *Mythical Intentions in Modern Literature.* Princeton, 1981.

Gusdorf, G. *Mythe et métaphysique.* Paris, 1963.

Hamburger, K. *Von Sophokles zu Sartre: Griechische Dramenfiguren antik und modern.* Stuttgart, 1962.

Hays, P. *The Limping Hero.* New York, 1971.

Herskovits, M. and F. S. *Dahomean Narrative.* Evanston, 1958.

Highet, G. *The Classical Tradition: Greek and Roman Influences on Western Literature.* Oxford, 1949.

Hoffman, D. G. *Barbarous Knowledge.* New York, 1967.

———. *Form and Fable in American Fiction.* New York, 1961.

Holtan, O. I. *Mythic Patterns in Ibsen's Last Plays.* Minneapolis, 1970.

Hunger, H. *Lexikon der griechischen und römischen Mythologie mit Hinweisen auf das Fortwirken antiker Stoffe und Motive in der bildenden Kunst, Literatur und Musik des Abendlandes bis zur Gegenwart.* Vienna, 1953.

Hungerford, E. *Shores of Darkness.* New York, 1941.

Jesi, F. *Letteratura e mito.* Turin, 1968.

Jones, J. *Adam's Dream: Mythic Consciousness in Keats and Yeats.* Athens, Ga., 1975.

Jung, C. G., and K. Kerenyi. *Essays on a Science of Mythology.* Translated by R. F. C. Hull. New York, 1949.

Kirk, G. S. *Myth: Its Meaning and Functions in Ancient and Other Cultures.* Berkeley, 1970.

Koppe, F. *Literarische Versachlichung.* Munich, 1977.

Kroll, J. *Chapters in a Mythology: The Poetry of Sylvia Plath.* New York, 1976.

Kushner, E. *Le Mythe d'Orphée dans la littérature française contemporaine.* Paris, 1961.

Langer, F. *Intellektualmythologie: Betrachtungen über das Wesen des Mythus und die mythologische Methode.* Leipzig, 1916.

Langer, S. *Philosophy in a New Key.* New York, 1948.

Lehnert, H. *Thomas Mann: Fiktion, Mythos, Religion.* Stuttgart, 1965.

Lessmann, H. *Aufgaben und Ziele der Vergleichenden Mythenforschungen.* Leipzig, 1908.

Lévi-Strauss, C. *Mythologiques.* 4 vols. Paris, 1964, 1966, 1968, 1971.

Levy, G. R. *The Sword from the Rock.* London, 1953.

Lucente, G. L. *The Narrative of Realism and Myth.* Baltimore, 1981.

MacCaffrey, I. G. *Paradise Lost as "Myth."* Cambridge, Mass., 1959.

McCune, M. W., *et al.*, eds. *The Binding of Proteus.* Lewisburg, Pa., 1980.

Malinowski, B. *Myth in Primitive Psychology.* London, 1926.

Maranda, P. *Mythology.* Harmondsworth, 1972.

Matthews, H. *The Hard Journey: The Myth of Man's Rebirth.* New York, 1968.

Matzig, R. *Odysseus: Studien zu antiken Stoffen in der modernen Literatur.* St. Gall, 1949.

Mauron, C. *Des métaphores obsédantes au mythe personnel.* Paris, 1963.

Merivale, P. *Pan the Goat-God: His Myth in Modern Times.* Cambridge, Mass., 1969.

Muhler, R. *Dichtung und Krise: Mythos und Psychologie in der Dichtung des 19. und 20. Jahrhunderts.* Vienna, 1951.

Munz, P. *When the golden bough breaks: structuralism or typology?* London, 1973.

Murray, H. A., ed. *Myth and Myth-making.* New York, 1960.

Neumann, E. *The Origins of the History of Consciousness.* Translated by R. F. C. Hull. New York, 1954.

Olson, C. *Call Me Ishmael.* New York, 1947.

Otto, W. F. *Gesetz, Urbild und Mythos.* Stuttgart, 1951.

Perrot, J. *Mythe et littérature.* Paris, 1976.

Petty, A. C. *One Ring to Bind Them All.* University, Ala., 1979.

Peyre, H. *L'Influence des littératures antiques sur la littérature française moderne.* New Haven, 1941.

Plumpe, G. *Alfred Schuler.* Berlin, 1978.

Porter, T. E. *Myth and Modern American Drama.* Detroit, 1969.

Prescott, F. C. *Poetry and Myth.* New York, 1927.

Raglan, Lord. *The Hero.* London, 1936.

Richardson, R. D., Jr. *Myth and Literature in the American Renaissance.* Bloomington, 1978.

Ridgeway, W. *The Dramas and Dramatic Dances of the Non-European Races.* Cambridge, 1910.

Riede, D. G. *Swinburne: A Study of Romantic Mythmaking.* Charlottesville, Va., 1978.

Righter, W. *Myth and Literature.* London, 1975.

Rosenfield, C. *Paradise of Snakes: An Archetypal Analysis of Conrad's Political Novels.* Chicago, 1967.

Rothschild, J. *Kain und Abel in der deutschen Dichtung.* Würzburg, 1933.

Rougemont, D. de. *Love in the Western World.* Translated by M. Belgion. New York, 1956.

Ruthven, K. *Myth*. London, 1976.

Schmidt-Henkel, G. *Mythos und Dichtung: Zur Begriff- und Stilgeschichte der deutschen Literatur im 19. und 20. Jahrhunderts*. Homburg, 1967.

Sebeok, T. A., ed. *Myth: A Symposium*. Bloomington, 1958.

Seiden, M. I. *William Butler Yeats: The Poet as Mythmaker*. East Lansing, Mich., 1962.

Seznec, J. *The Survival of the Pagan Gods*. New York, 1953.

Shumaker, W. *Literature and the Irrational*. Englewood Cliffs, N.J., 1960.

Sicard, M. I. *Don Juan mythe et réalité*. Paris, 1967.

Slochower, H. *Mythopoesis: Mythic Patterns in Literary Classics*. Detroit, 1970.

Slote, B., ed. *Myth and Symbol*. Lincoln, Neb., 1963.

Slotkin, R. *Regeneration Through Violence*. Middletown, Conn., 1973.

Smith, H. N. *Virgin Land: The American West as Symbol and Myth*. Cambridge, Mass., 1950.

Soyinka, W. *Myth, Literature and the African World*. Cambridge, 1976.

Speirs, J. *Medieval English Poetry*. London, 1957.

Stanford, W. B. *The Ulysses Theme: A Study in the Adaptability of a Traditional Hero*. Oxford, 1954.

Still, C. *The Timeless Theme*. London, 1936.

Strich, F. *Die Mythologie in der deutschen Dichtung: Von Klopstock bis Wagner*. 2 vols. Halle, 1910.

Trousson, R. *Le Theme de Prométhée dans la littérature européene*. 2 vols. Geneva, 1964.

Vickery, J. B., ed. *Myth and Literature*. Lincoln, Neb., 1966.

Vinge, L. *The Narcissus Theme in Western European Literature up to the Early Nineteenth Century*. Lund, 1967.

Vries, J. De. *Heroic Song and Heroic Legend*. London, 1963.

Watson-Williams, H. *André Gide and the Greek Myth: A Critical Study*. Oxford, 1967.

Watts, A. *Myth and Ritual in Christianity*. New York, 1953.

Watts, H. H. *Hound and Quarry*. London, 1953.

Weinstein, L. *The Metamorphosis of Don Juan*. Stanford, 1959.

Weisinger, H. *The Agony and the Triumph: Papers on the Use and Abuse of Myth*. East Lansing, Mich., 1964.

Wetzels, W. D., ed. *Myth and Reason: A Symposium*. Austin, 1973.

Wheelwright, P. *The Burning Fountain*. Bloomington, 1954.

White, J. J. *Mythology in the Modern Novel*. Princeton, 1971.

Zimmer, H. *The King and the Corpse*. Edited by J. Campbell. New York, 1948.

INDEX